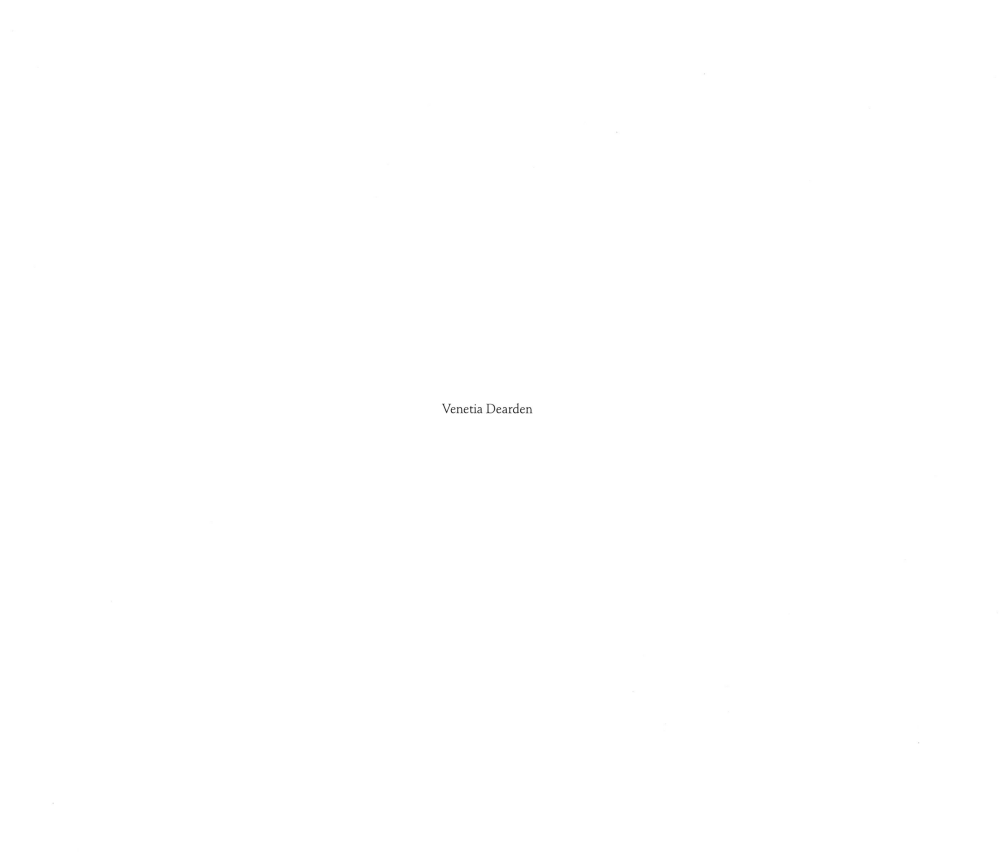

Venetia Dearden

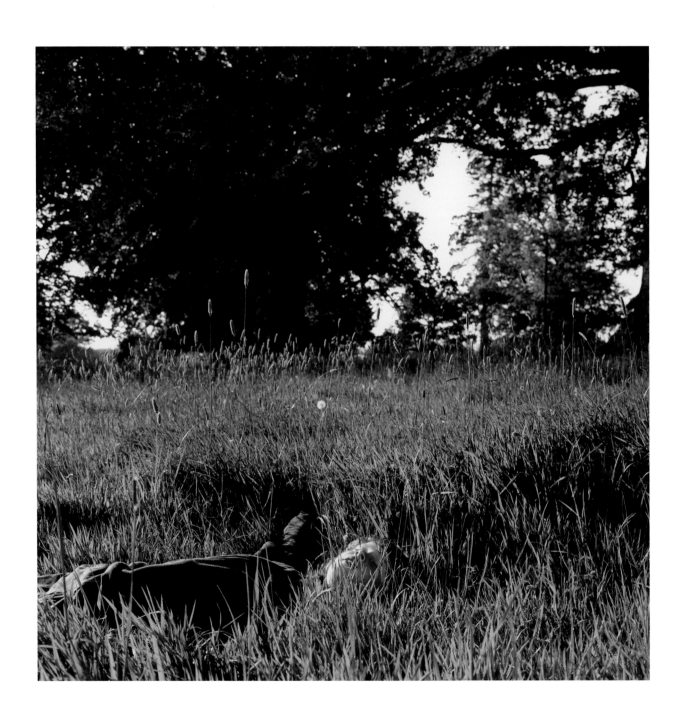

VENETIA DEARDEN

Somerset Stories   Fivepenny Dreams

KEHRER

4   INTRODUCTION

Venetia first showed me her photographs from Somerset in 2005. The premise was simple – to travel the highways and byways of this quintessentially English county to meet the people and document an identity and sense of self in harmony with the land.

On Venetia's journey through Somerset the people she meets and the places she pauses at form the experience she relates in this book. The story is as much a sensory journey as it is a description of a place. Her photography has an ability to "take you back" to a time and a place of a memory and a feeling. Her portraits are created with sensitivity and an effortless ability to tell her story. And so the Somerset I see and feel in this book is one that is abundantly positive. I am instantly seduced by Venetia's heavenly mix of country air, an abundance of nature and the light that shines and bathes the photographs in this book.

Maybe it's because I am a suffering Englishman that I have developed a heightened weather-sense. I can fully appreciate the moment the sun pokes through the cloud and drizzle on an otherwise grey day. I can feel the evening glow of sun on my face in a picture of an open field. But I know that I love these photographs because I see and feel the warmth and the freshness in them. And, as I know only too well, the sun will not last long; rain will follow soon.

Each turn of the pages introduces us to a new character with a relationship to the story as a whole as well as to each other separately. Each person has their own history and yet they tell us about something else as well. The clues to each person's life are in every photograph: the home, the cardigan, the toys, the animals, even a bookshelf. These objects help us build a picture of the who and what it is we think we are looking at. But the message of the image and the book is not of many independent instances, it is a shared message of intertwined existence and identity. The sunlight is perhaps the best motif for this as it is but one sun, felt in many lives.

When I read the photographs in this book I create mini fictions of my own to connect the people and places. I see that the people do not only fit into each other's stories as co-stars in the larger story of Somerset. These girls, boys,

women and men can also become each other. Only time separates a stooping old lady and a party of schoolchildren sleeping on the floor of their trailer at the county fair. An age apart it may seem but they are also part of each other in who they were and who they may become. The young girl awake on the floor of the trailer looks at the photographer while her friends sleep alongside. This image speaks gently of a blissful awareness of time. "It is moments like these that stay with you throughout your life", they say. In this book they seem to last forever.

This book is both the story of the people and their relationship to Somerset and Somerset's own story. Venetia's choice of subjects mixes elements that often divide and define society, age and class, with moments of life that actually bond us together. Here age is not a number but a measure of life and experience, and those everyday discoveries are what can make a life special. Similarly in Venetia's Somerset, resistance to age does not seem futile, it is a way of respecting the unstoppable flow of life yet savouring each moments and making it possible to last forever.

A theme of resistance is probably overall what makes Somerset special in the minds of many of the other English. Somerset's resistance to unnecessary change, has helped preserve its values of love and natural worth. Sadly these principles are not so much in vogue around my parents' place in Sussex. New build country cottage housing and superstore shopping developments conspire to eradicate history and the rural ways of life. Even in the cities we increasingly fear the homogenisation of our local shops and neighbourhood character by the big monotone brand merchandisers. In these photographs Venetia has captured the spirit of Somerset's resistance to this unnatural change.

The warmth and freshness of Venetia's photographs show us a loving land of interwoven histories, and by making it her story she has introduced us to new friends whilst paying homage to the spirit that makes Somerset special.

Jon Levy,
Editor FOTO8 Magazine

Early one morning I walk through the dappled shadows of Cockmill Lane, stepping over banks of wild garlic into a field where a cluster of dwellings nestle in an arboretum. I follow a paved path through long grasses scattered with toys and plant pots, lined with fruit trees, to an open front door. Lisa is pregnant with her third child and the midwife has just been to visit her at her home: an octagonal 'low-impact dwelling', made with woven ash poles and covered with waterproof canvas. Joel puts the kettle on as Lisa shares her excitement of being a mother again, 'My children are brought up in an amazing environment with fresh air. I can plant food; they can pick fruit off the trees. They can touch everything. Feel it all. I'm living here for my children, because it's a safe place for them to explore the wonderland out there."

On a blustery autumn afternoon at Fivepenny Farm about thirty miles to the West. Ari, Chloe and Pip are wrapped in colourful knitted garments as they run semi feral on their land, intermittently tending to the chickens, pigs and their patch of sweet peas. Jyoti is bagging up freshly picked organic vegetables for the weekly market and tells me about the success of this 'two family farm' that she and her partner, Dai, share with their friends, Olly and Kerry. Although both families manage their own individual smallholdings, they take the strain off their ambitious endeavours by sharing the basic running costs and offering support when needed. Their innate dedication to their beliefs and dynamic energy infuses me with a great sense of hope. "We are striving to create something beneficial that endures for the next generation and beyond", Olly tells me. I walk up to the entrance of the modest weather-boarded house Dai built for his family and step over a mound of abandoned muddy boots, past Minnie the dog, into the cosy interior where Ele, aged eleven, welcomes me with a tray of warm freshly baked biscuits.

My passion and curiosity for Somerset has been fuelled by my long-term connection, and recent disconnection with this area of the West Country. Seduced by its arcane essence I am compelled to return again and again to explore my relationship with the landscape and the people living here. It is reassuring to witness the pioneering spirit of those living on and within the resources of their surroundings, but the preservation of this quality of rural life is tenuous. Whilst land has become a commodity, there is a growing realisation of the detrimental effect we humans can have on our environment.

In the face of economic and ecological changes globally, a younger generation is responding and adapting to their parents' ideas of progress. Despite the increasing numbers of people moving to the West Country, Somerset somehow manages to retain its acceptance of diversity, and continue to nurture those close to the land. I want simply to capture intimate moments in families striving to create a way of life they believe in and draw attention to basic human qualities. My journey takes me through seasons, rituals, gatherings and day-to-day life in Somerset. I witness a sense of belonging and identity within these rich bonds of family and community.

Tom and Becca are part of a fading horsedrawn community in the West Country and are on a quest to live in direct contact with their environment. With their children, horses, and goats in tow, they move with the opportunity of work setting up temporary camps wherever they are welcome. Tom talks about freedom, "Nothing beats it, when we're moving, on the road, wagons packed, animals on board. We are the Kings of the Road! That's freedom". But this freedom does not come without compromise. "It's philosophy become manifest, but not a romantic way of life, not today. It's hard to live on the road when there is no free land. Even the verges are owned. It's difficult to find work. The farms don't want itinerant workers today".

At the end of the summer I am at the Priddy Horse Fair on the Mendips, an event attended by horse and sheep dealers, fair-goers, traders, tinkers, revellers and tourists from across the country. Across a vibrant crowd enjoying the evening sun at the village pub and I see Debbie, sitting on a wall surrounded by her family, splitting with laughter, glistening with gold adornments. A few weeks later, we are perched on the steps of her caravan in a concrete yard that is protected by chained Dobermans who run at anyone who is passing by. She has just shown me a recent television documentary that features her teenage daughters, celebrating their gypsy qualities. Her eldest daughter Charlene, aged sixteen, is settling into her first few weeks of motherhood and is tending to her caravan, carefully watering the decorative flower boxes and sweeping the patch it sits on. Debbie cracks another can and conjures romantic visions of her own childhood: life always on the move, the pride she felt growing up with her kind. The nostalgia heightens the sense of loss of a way of life, and the difficult decision to settle. "It's changed, its not the same as it used to be. I get nervous about the reception I am met with when I go out collecting tat, but that's

what I've always done and how I was taught to make a living. We are who we are, and I am proud of it. Whatever happens I know my children will inherit my values. That's what gives me hope. The inheritance of my values".

Kate, to me, is a reflection of the spirit of Somerset. Her family have been farming in the area for seven hundred years and against all odds she continues this legacy. She and her husband Simon wait patiently for planning permission to build a home on their sixty acres of land. They work night and day to sustain their small farm and large family. They hold their dreams in sight. "We're free range people! We are living the way we want to do and we're happy. I could have an easier life, but this is what I know. I'm bred for it'. Kate is standing in her boots, toddler firmly planted on her hip and a wounded hen under her spare arm. We have done the rounds of animal feeding, visiting the pens of rare chicken breeds and rescued calves. She walks me to the gateway where there is an honesty box on an old weathered cart laden with home produce. I drop a few coins into a jam jar in exchange for a bunch of colourful peonies. As I look back down the lane I can still see Kate showing Monzy and Mike how to gently remove strands of straw from the egg boxes before arranging them next to her piles of hand painted cards.

I journey home from Dreamers Farm through narrow lanes punctured by weathered gateways that offer breathtaking views through overgrown hedges. On rainy days you can cover great distances without seeing anyone. I grew up roaming for miles on horseback through these fields, woodlands and muddy bridle paths. Here I inherited a sense of freedom and possibility, and this personal photographic journey within the horizons of my homeland is testament to this spirit of Somerset. My favourite days are when dark grey clouds roll over the sky, layering, folding and dispersing, allowing the sun to diffuse through. The light is gentle, enveloping, soporific and reassuring. Sometimes towards the end of the day the light intensifies; the sun makes its final attempts to burst through before the night falls. These moments I greet with excitment; they offer discovery. The landscape is alive, even the shadows shine in this illumination; everything seems as one.

Venetia Dearden

14   *Early one morning*

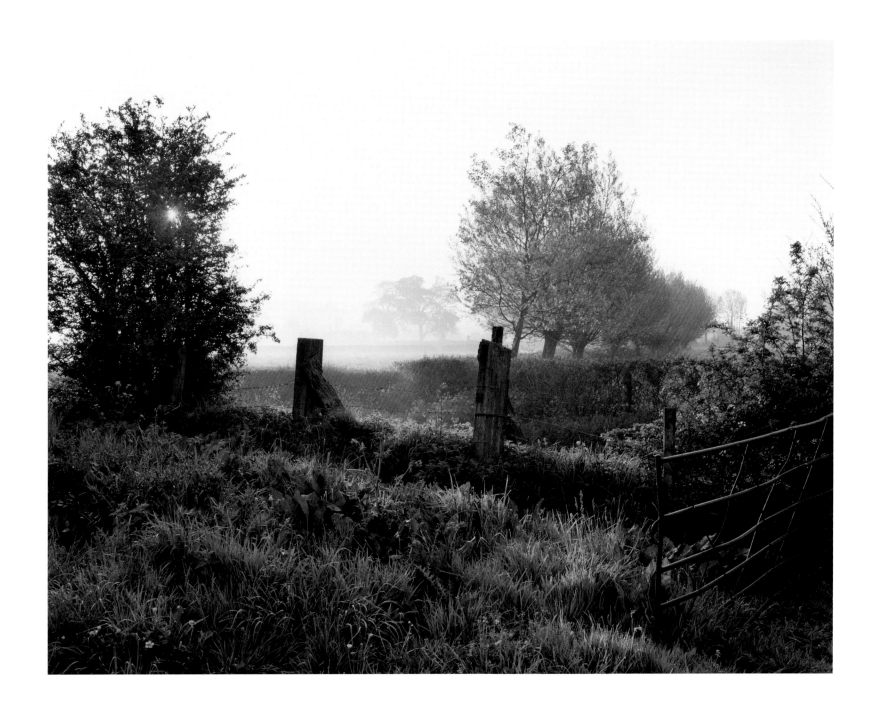

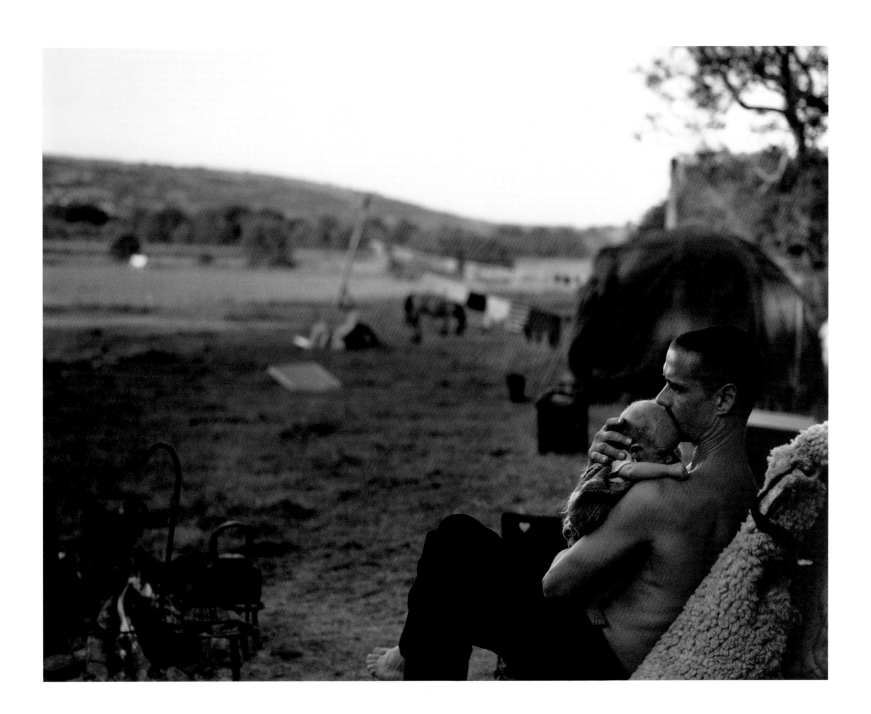

18   *Summer days*

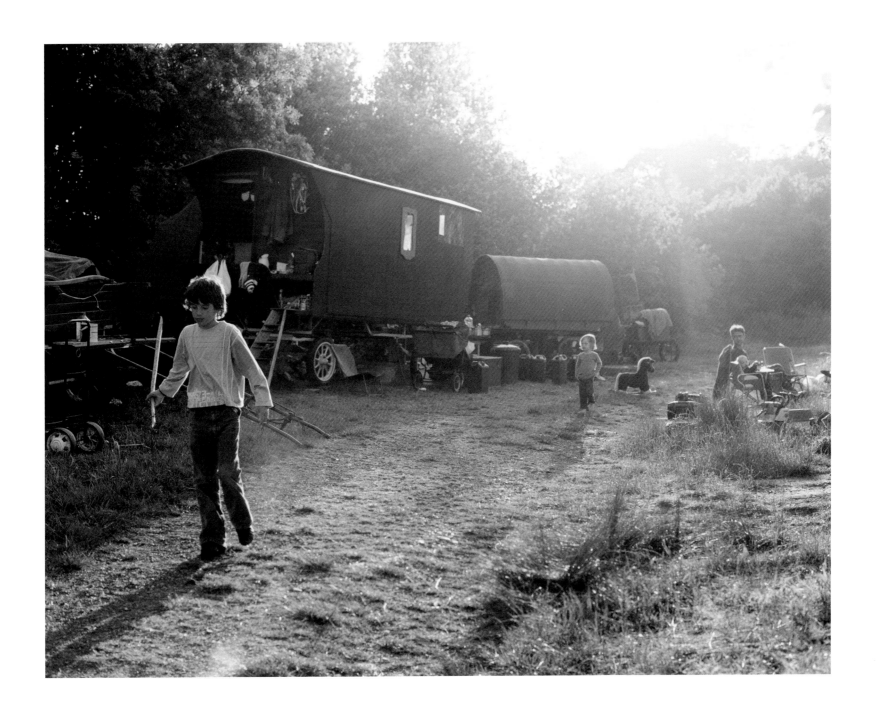

20   *Chloe and Minnie*

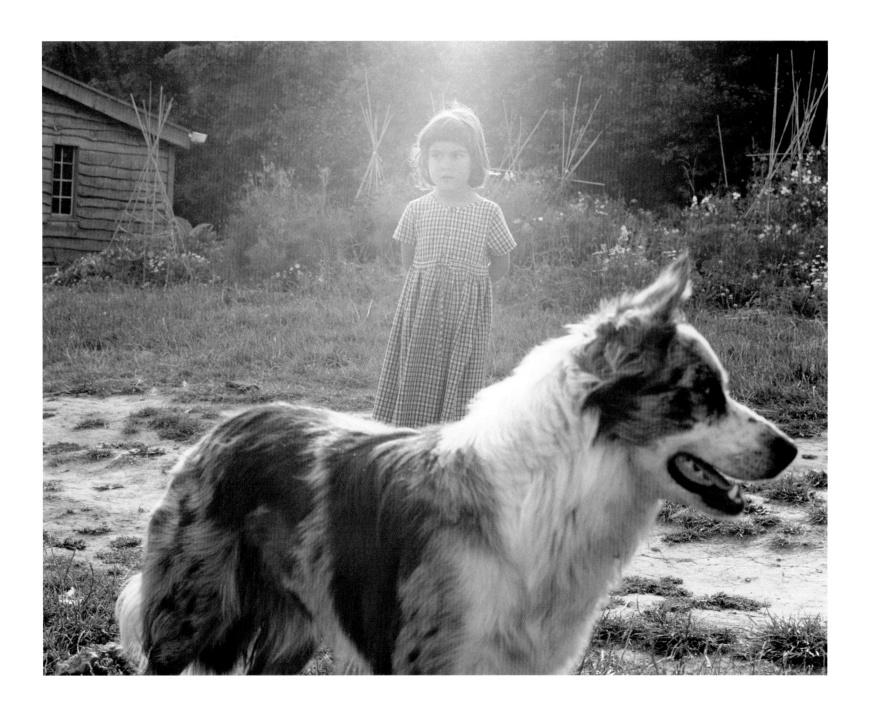

22   *Ele, Pip, Ari, Chloe at Fivepenny Farm*

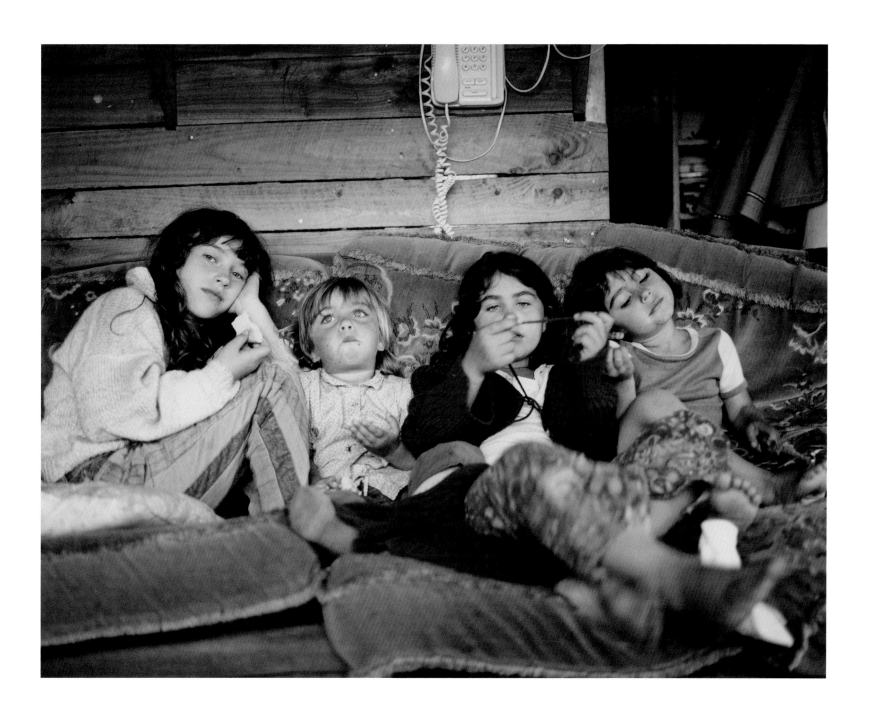

24   *Oisin and Kitty*

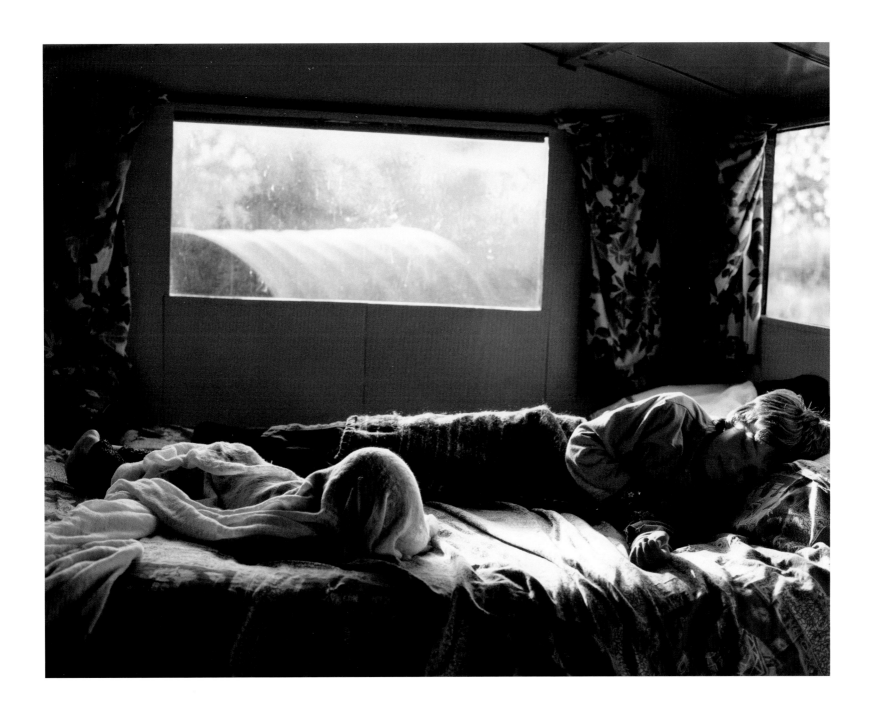

26   *Joyti gets ready for market*

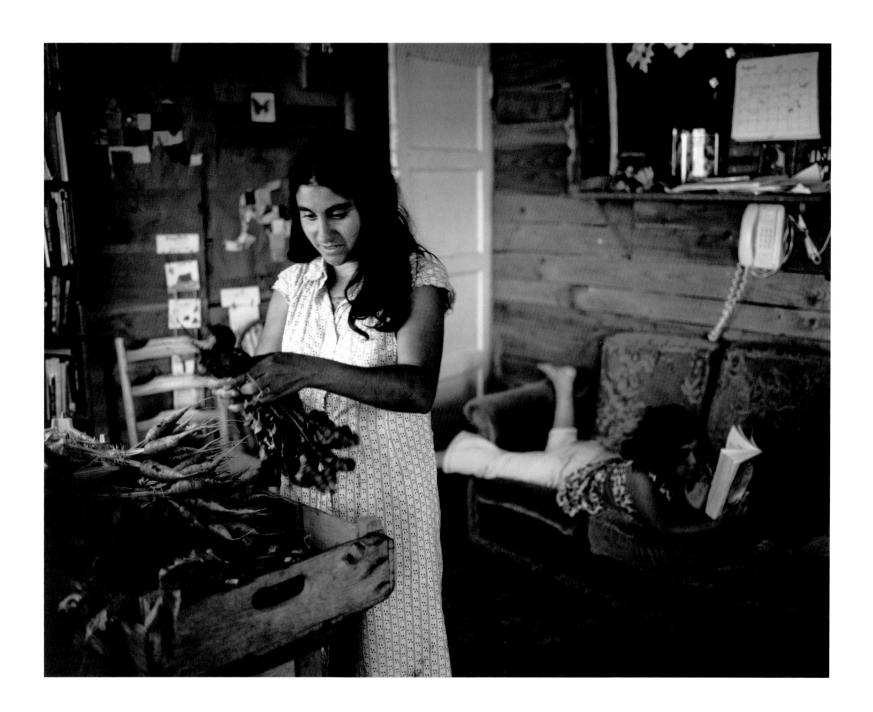

28   *Inside for tea*

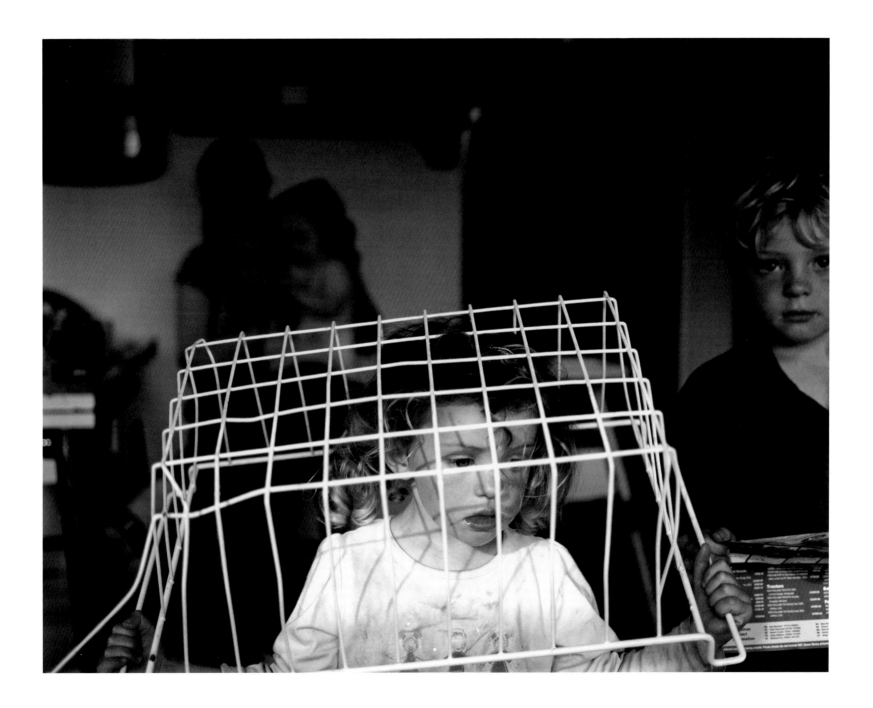

30   *Kate and Claudia, with Mikey, Monzy and Annabelle*

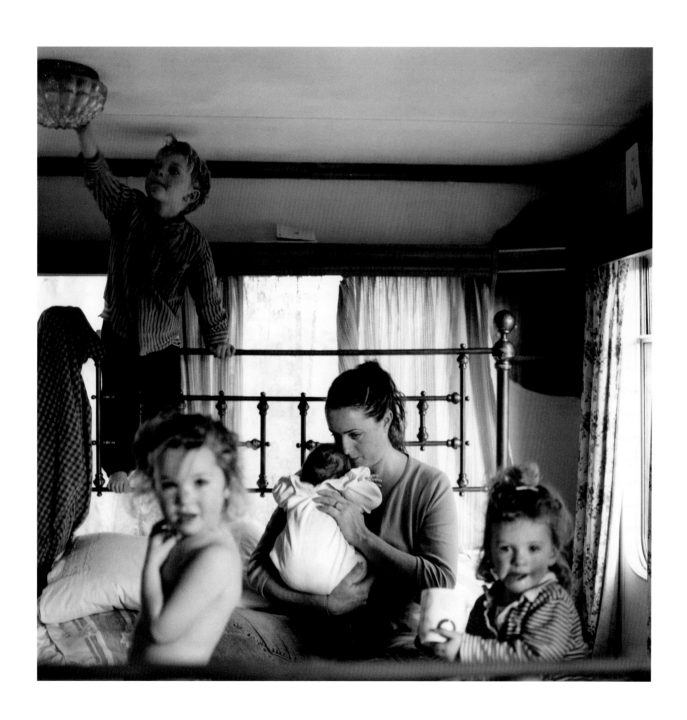

32   *Our home, Dreamers Farm*

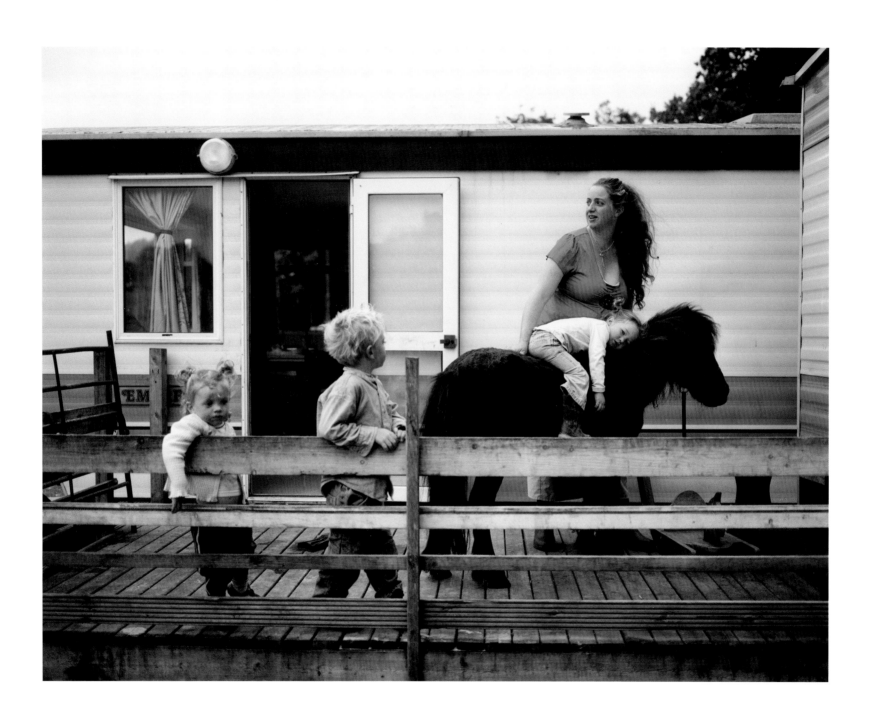

34   *Mikey*

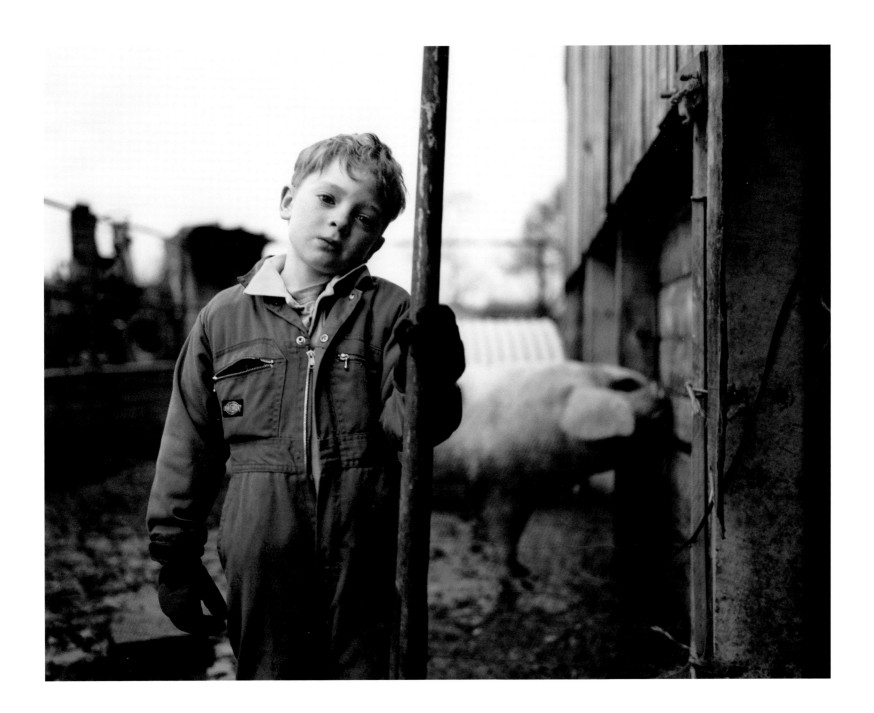

36   *Visiting Cathy*

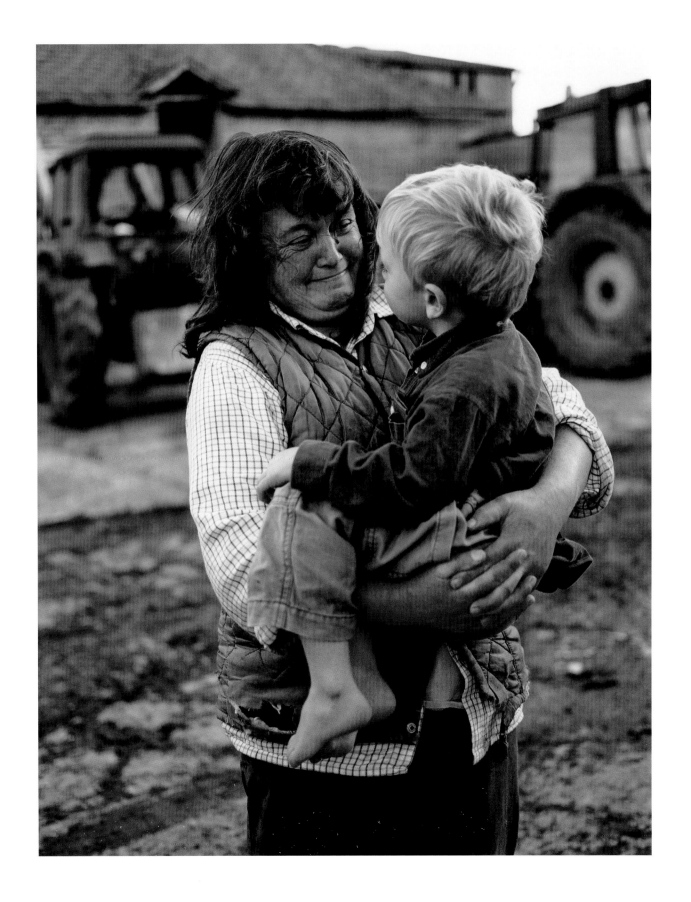

38   *Downpour at the orchard*

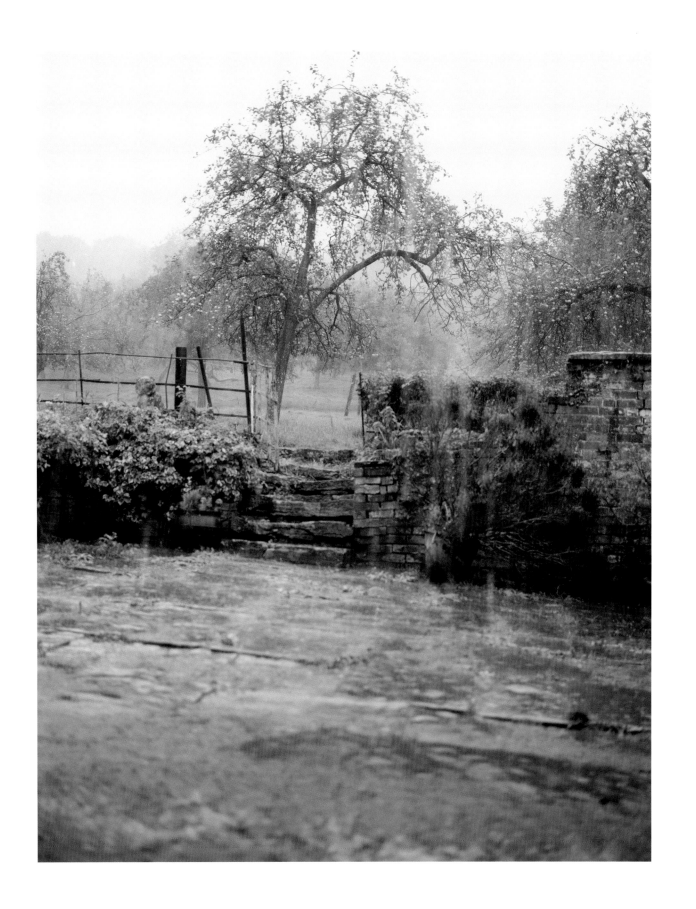

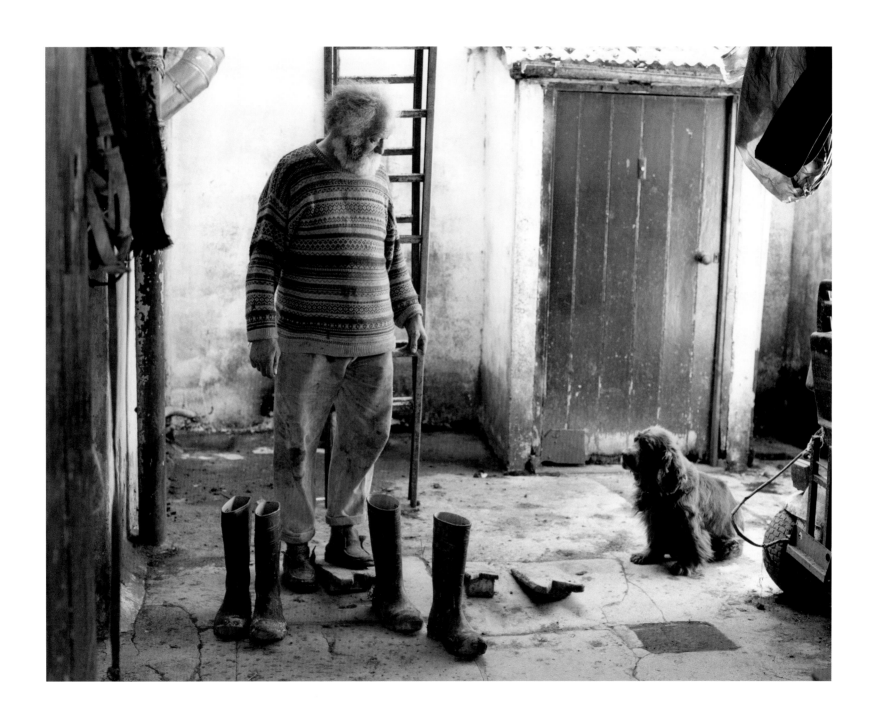

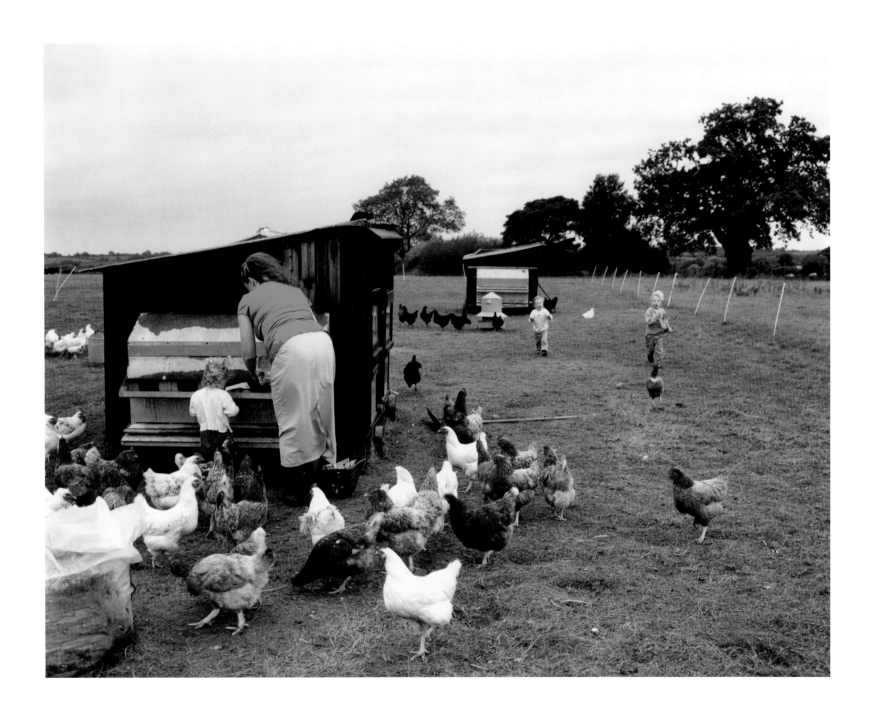

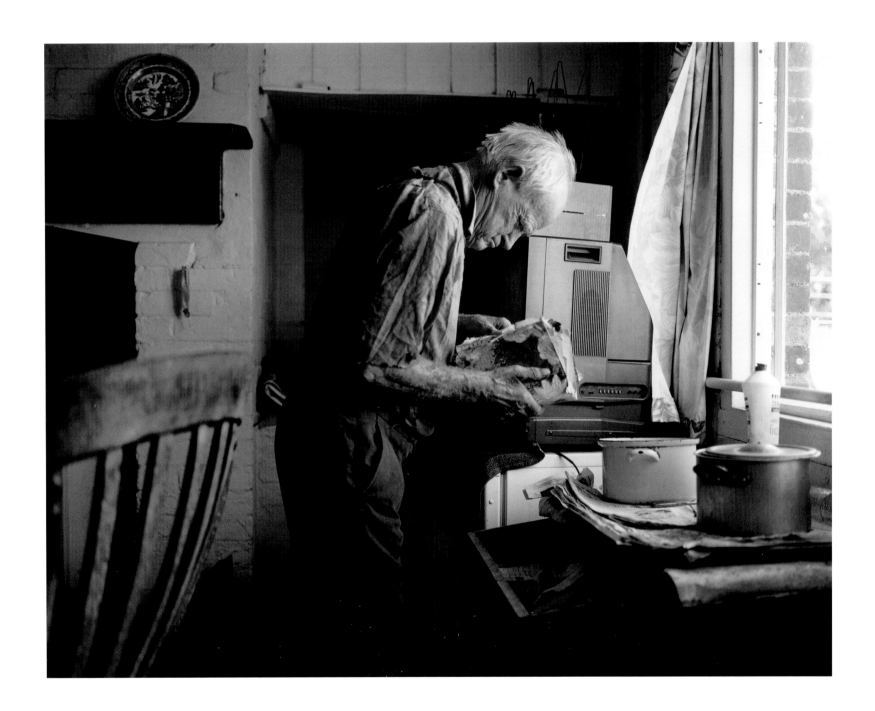

46   *Ele bakes biscuits*

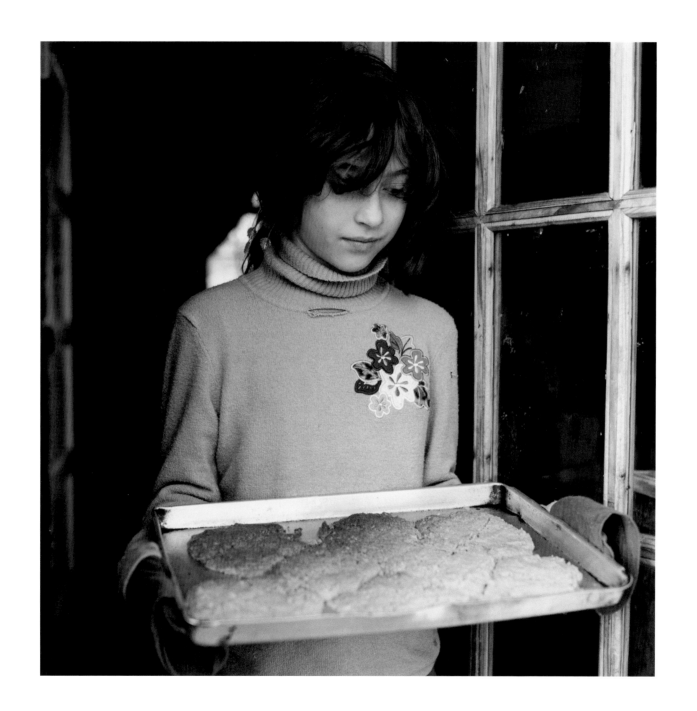

48   *Chloe and Pip weigh berries for jam*

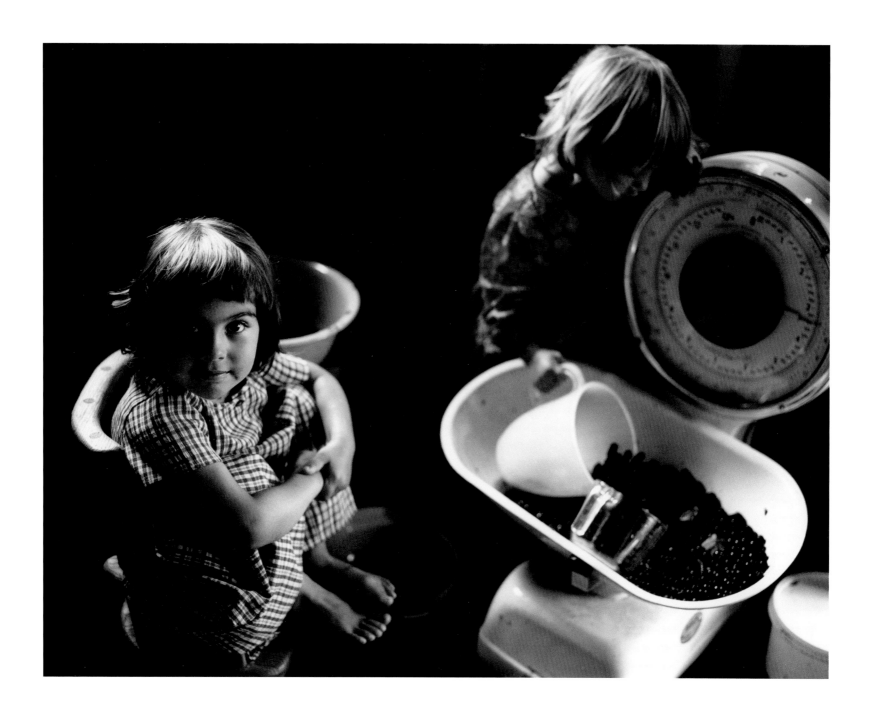

50   *After a muddy adventure*

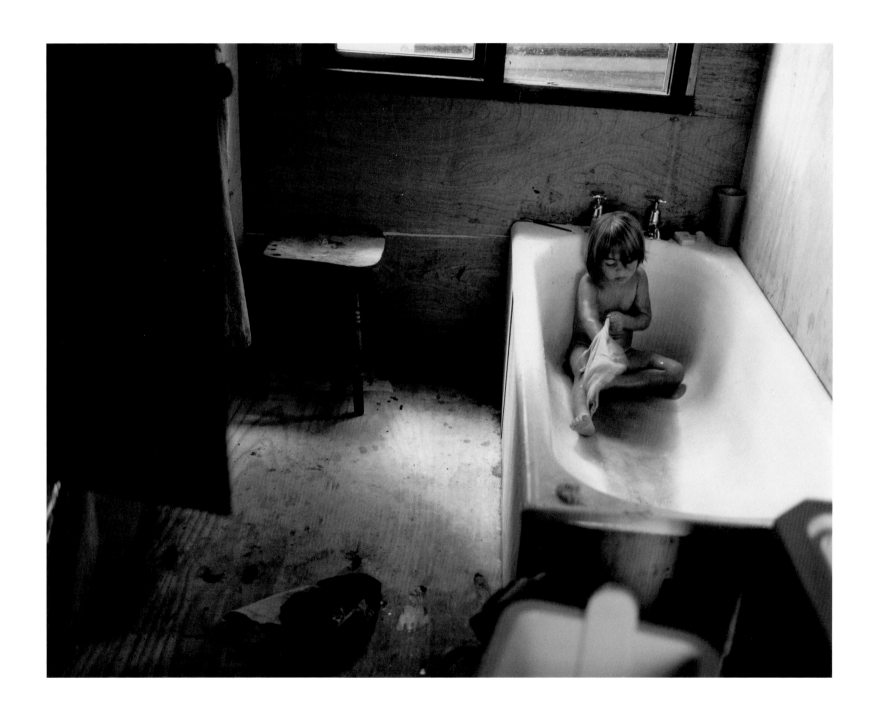

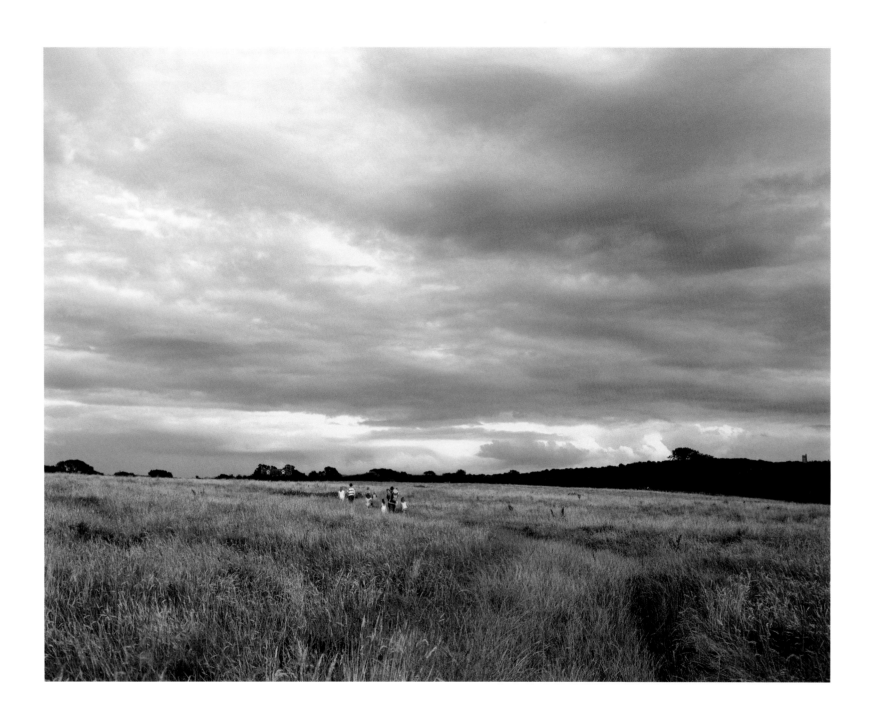

54   *Bella and Jai*

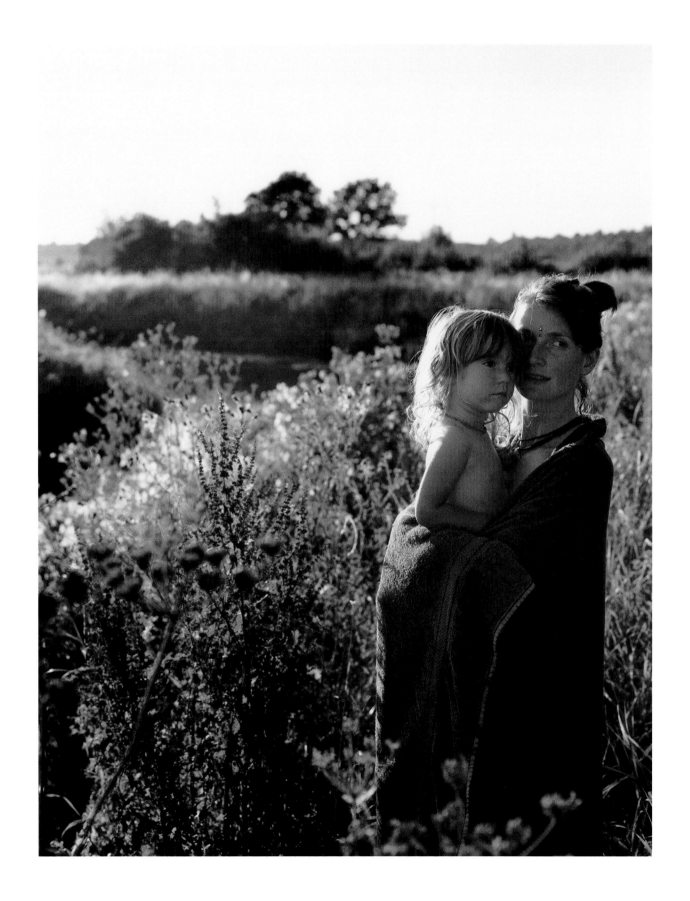

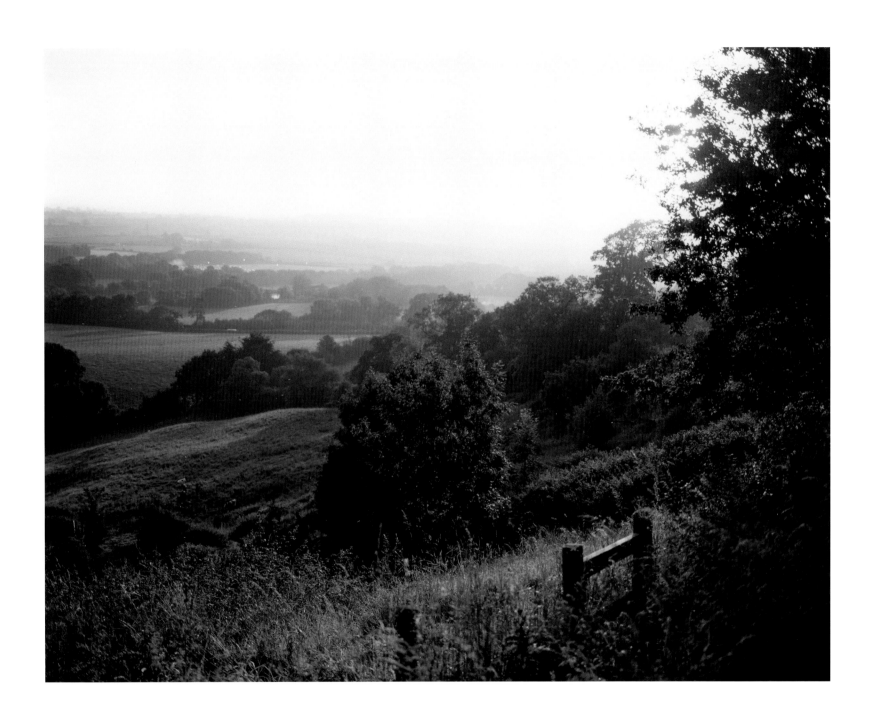

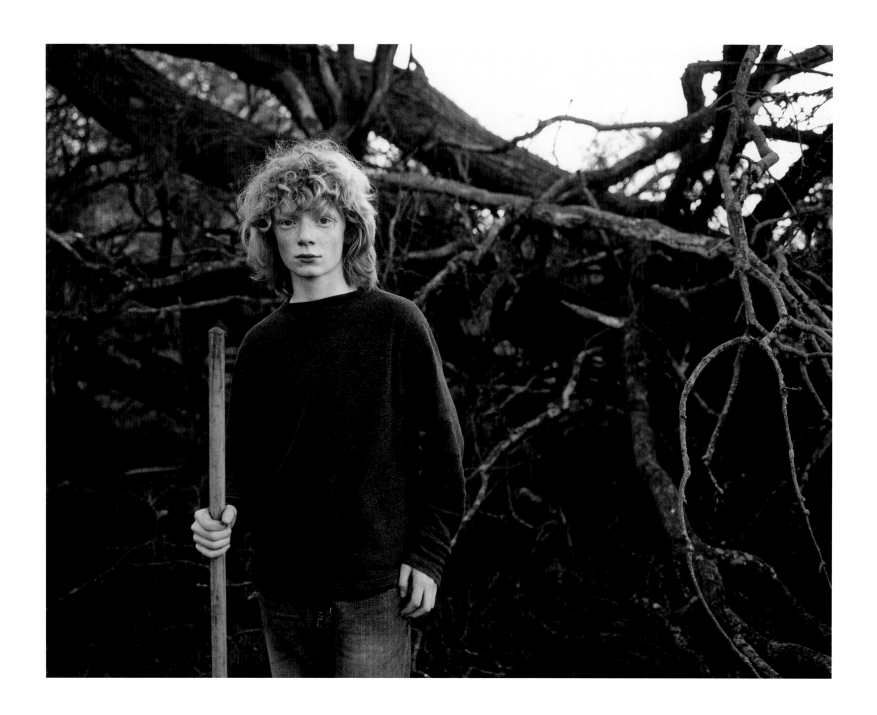

60   *Passing the afternoon*

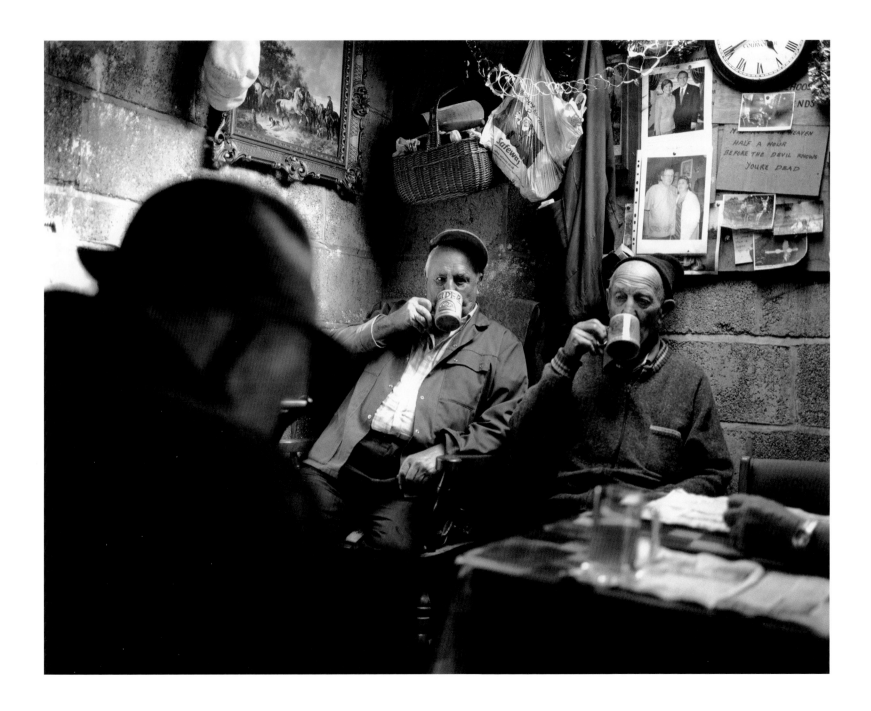

62   *Oisin and Arrow, Becca and Wolfie*

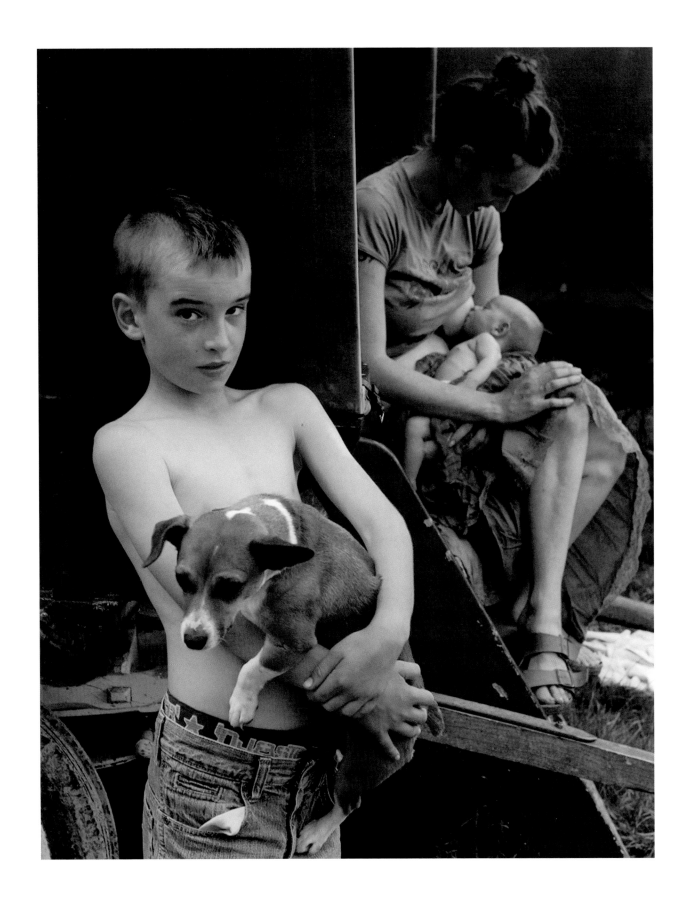

64   *Pip, Chloe and Evie*

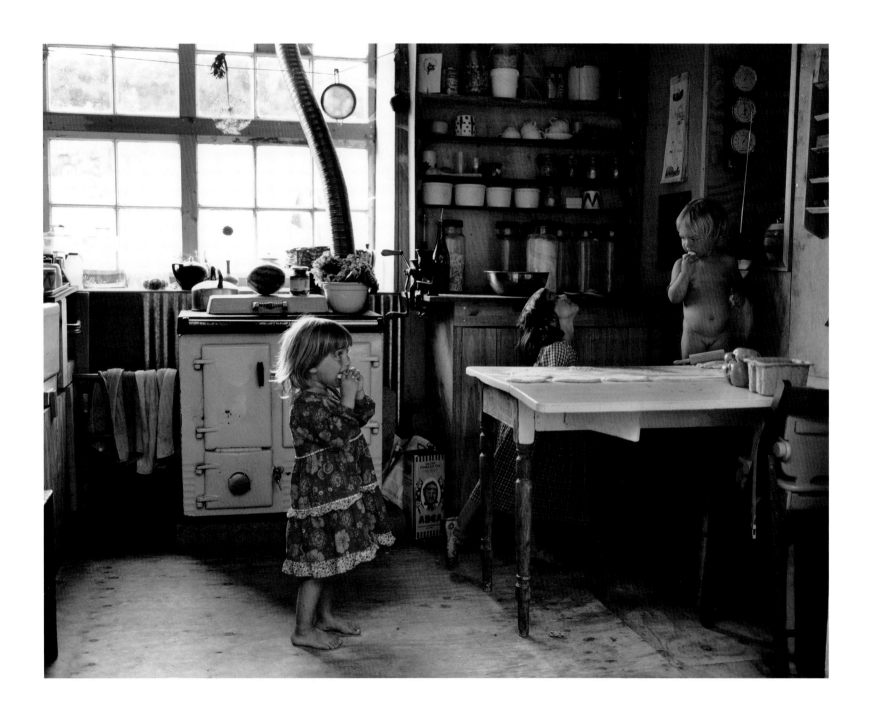

66   *Ari*

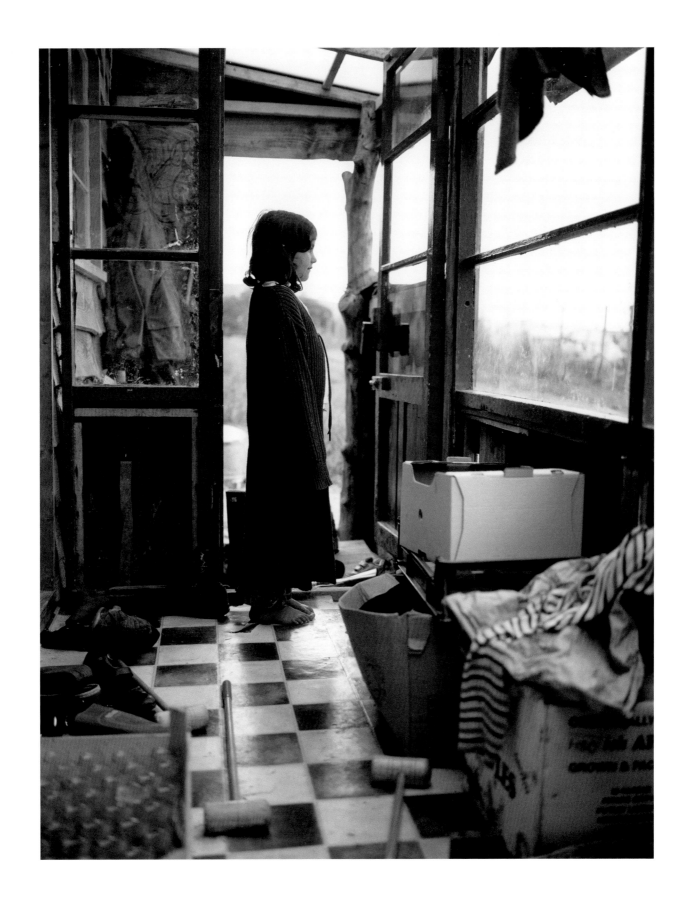

68   *Someone's calling*

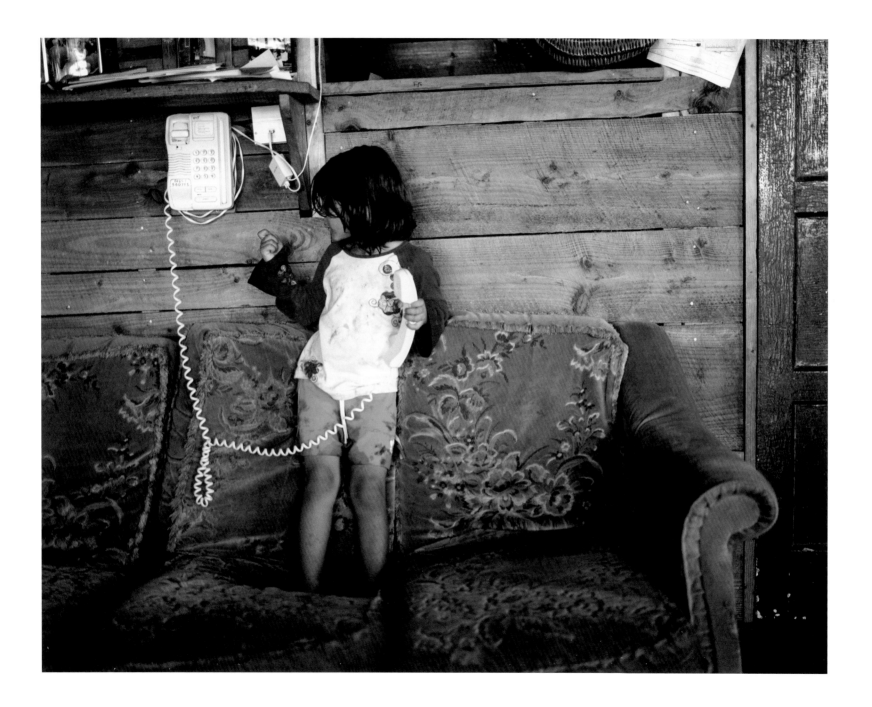

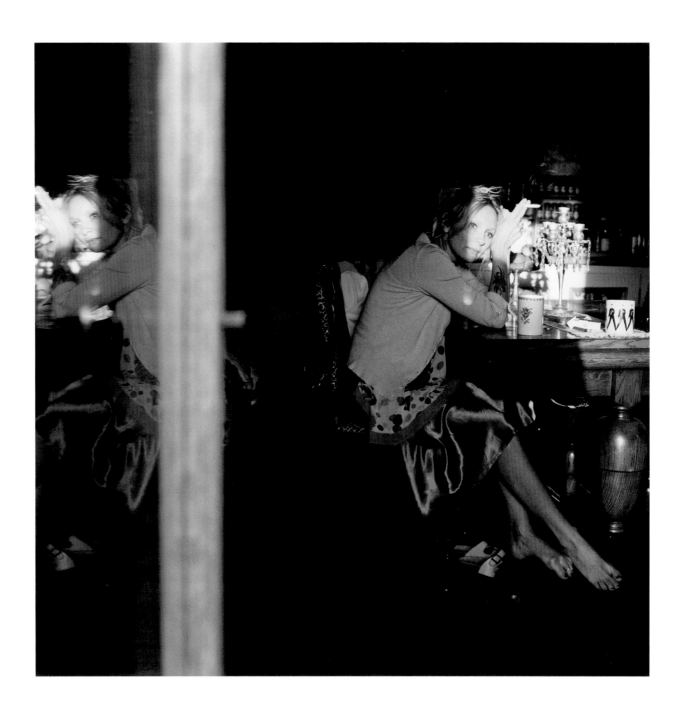

72   *Kelsey on the Carnival Float*

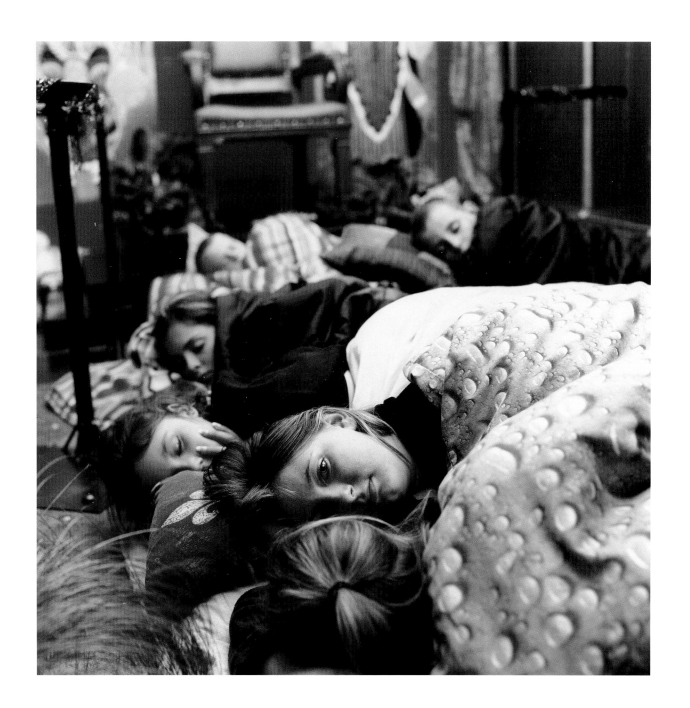

74 *River jumping*

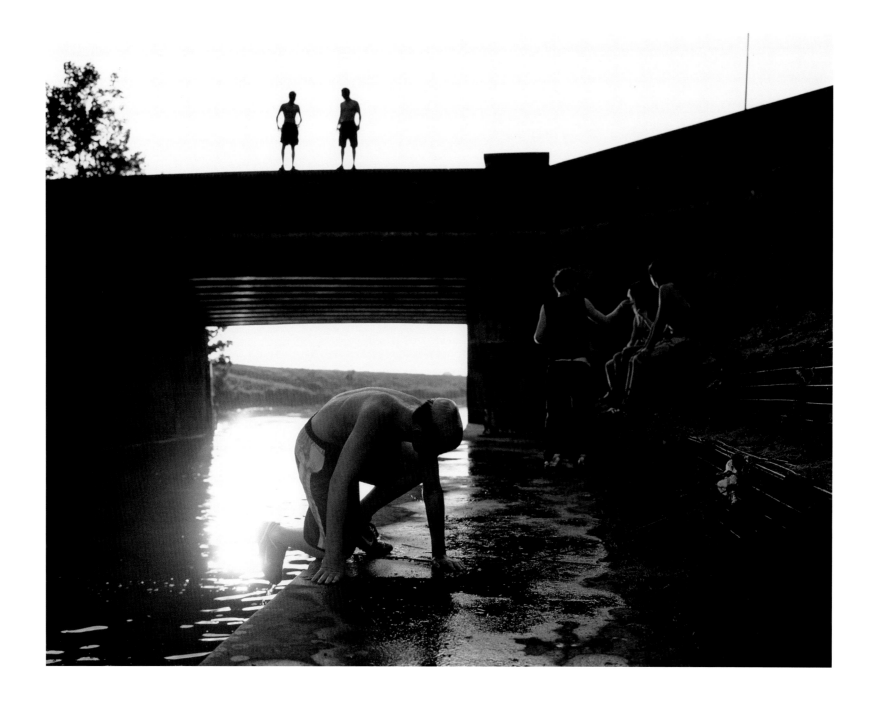

76   *Being with you*

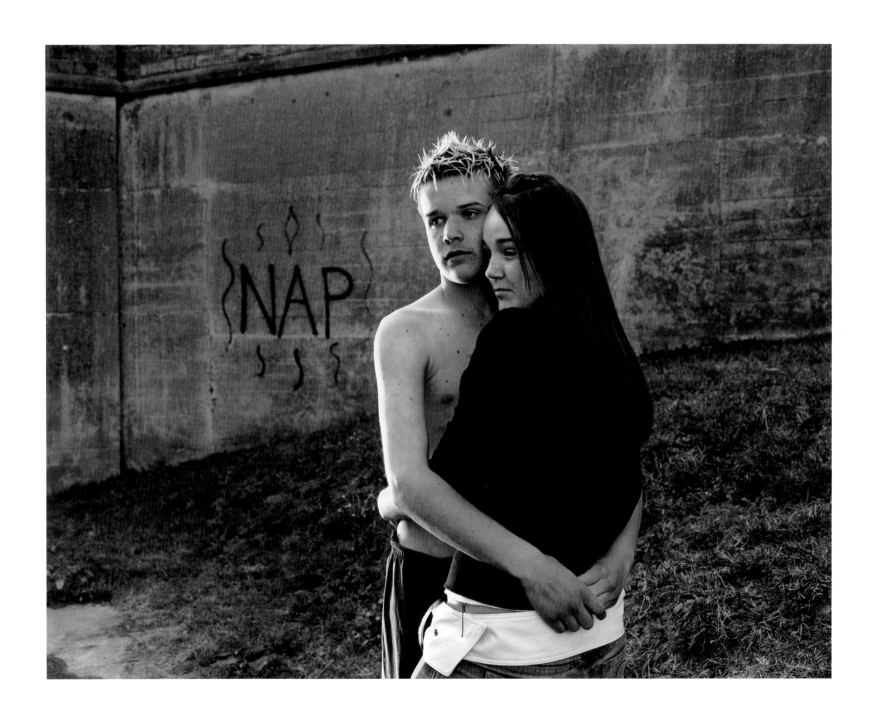

78   *Lisa and Joel*

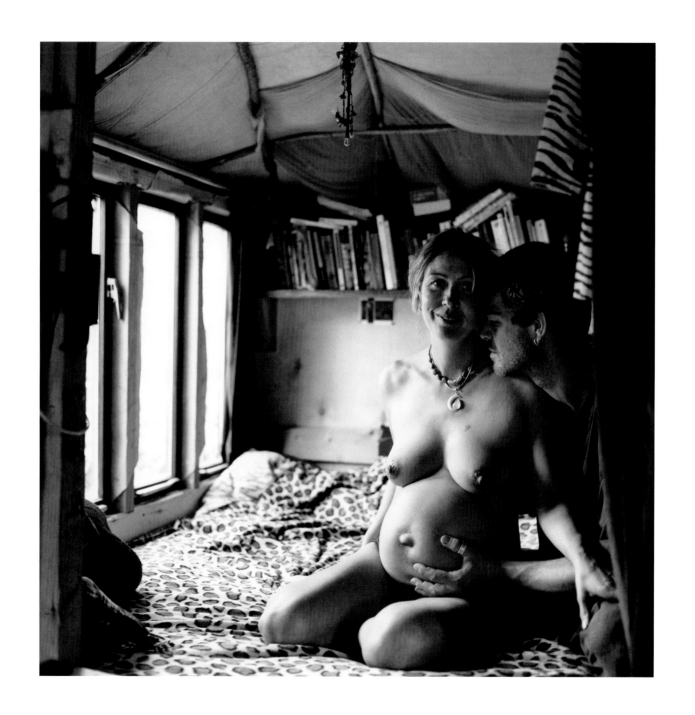

80   *Luke moves on*

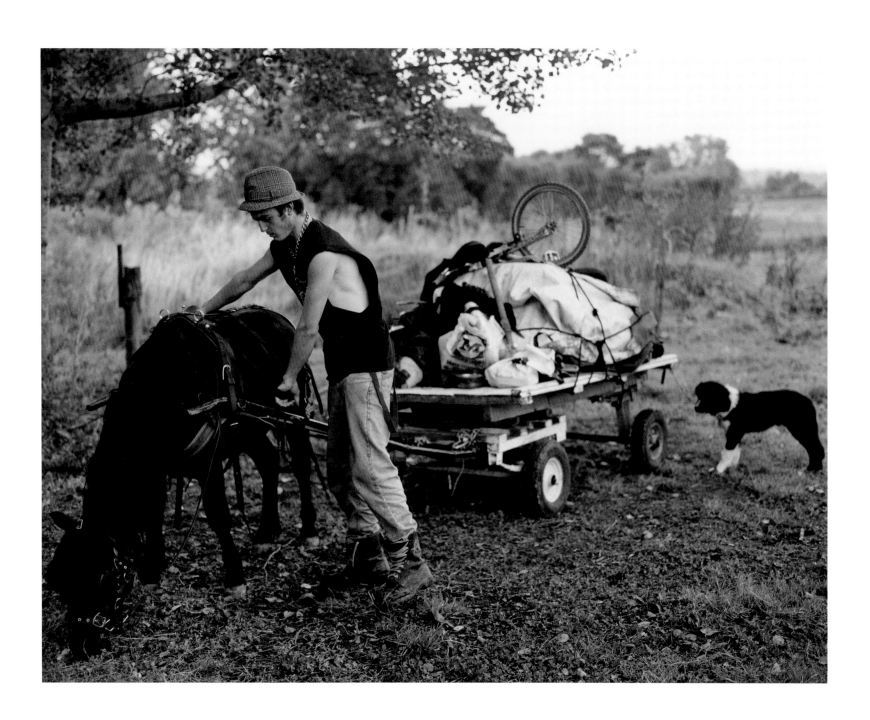

82   *This is where we live*

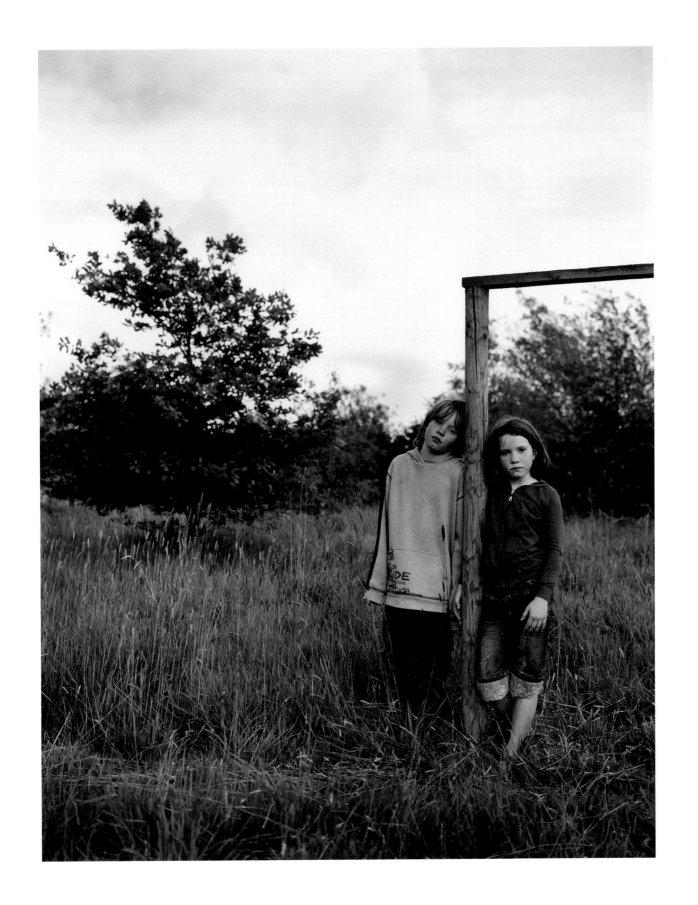

84   *Kerry and Gracie*

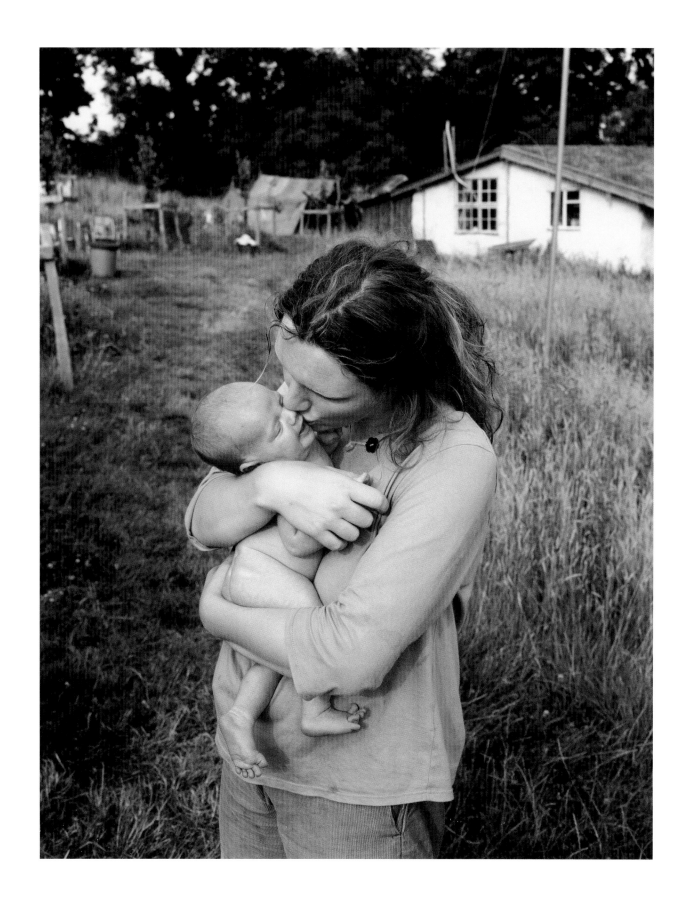

86 *Becca and Kitty*

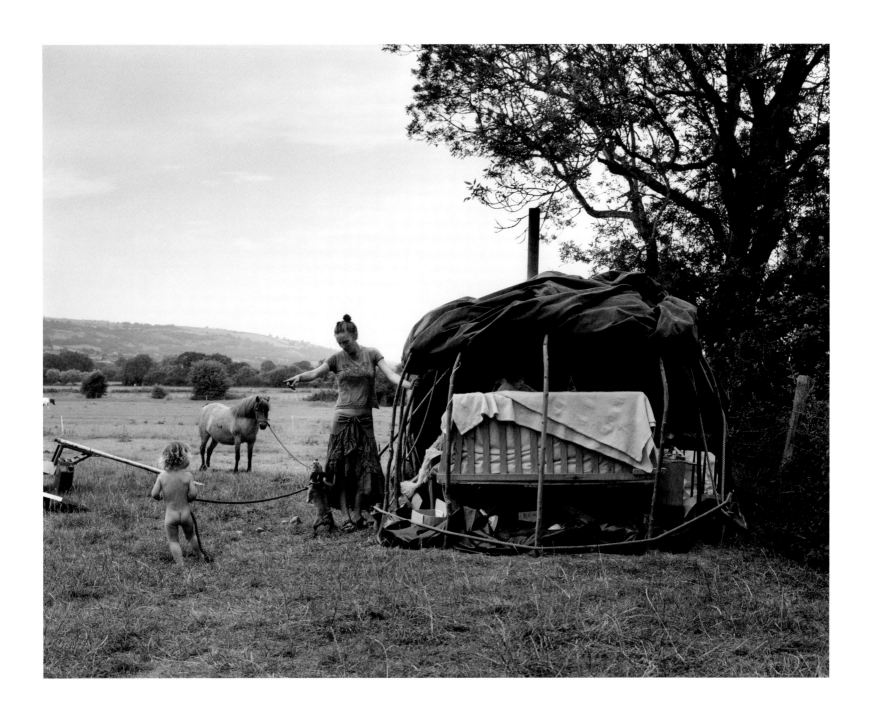

88   *Pip and the pigs*

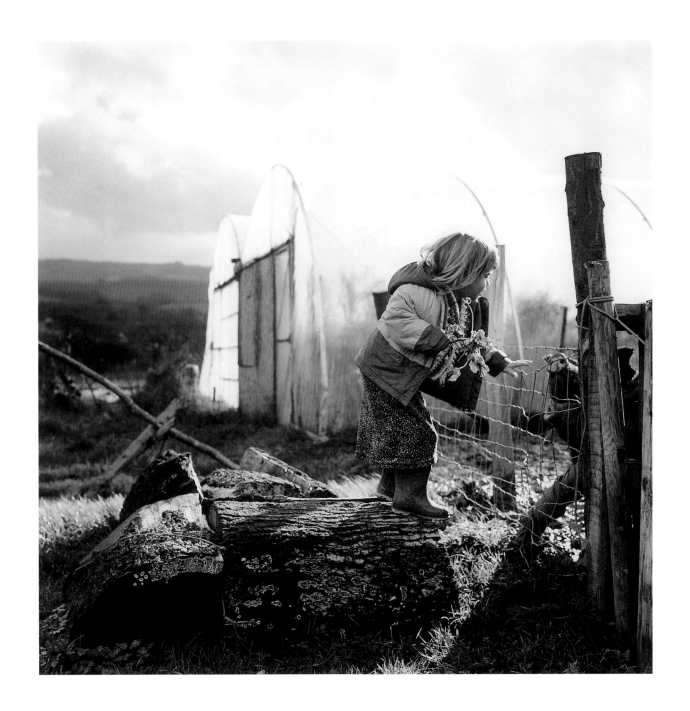

90   *Chris and Zeta*

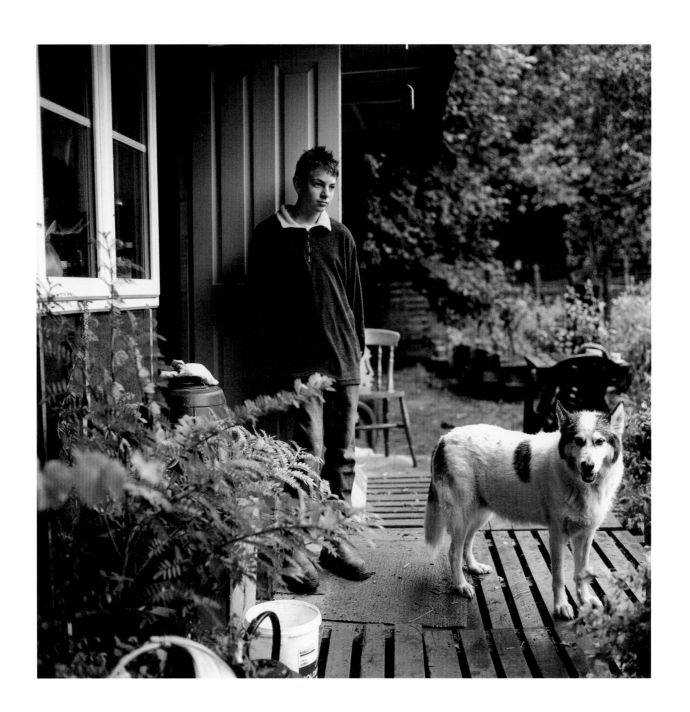

92   *Debbie*

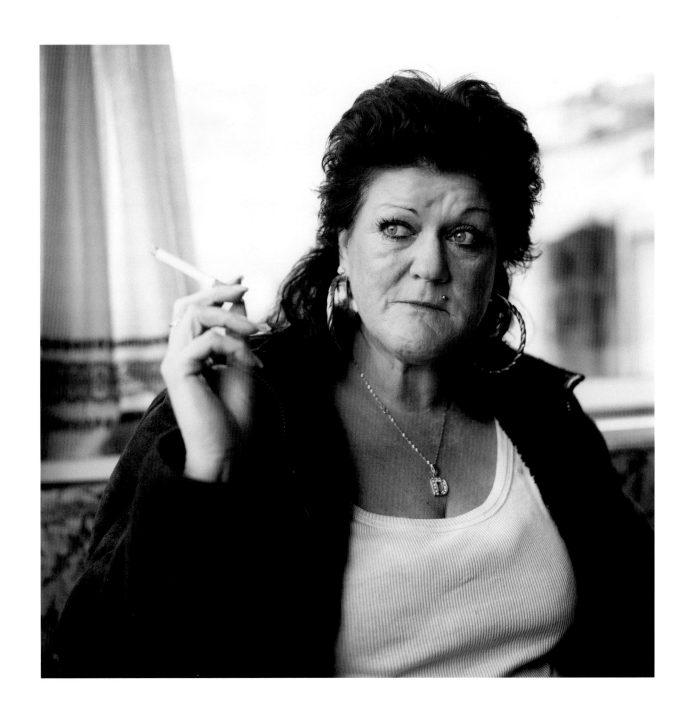

94   *Charlene in her Caravan*

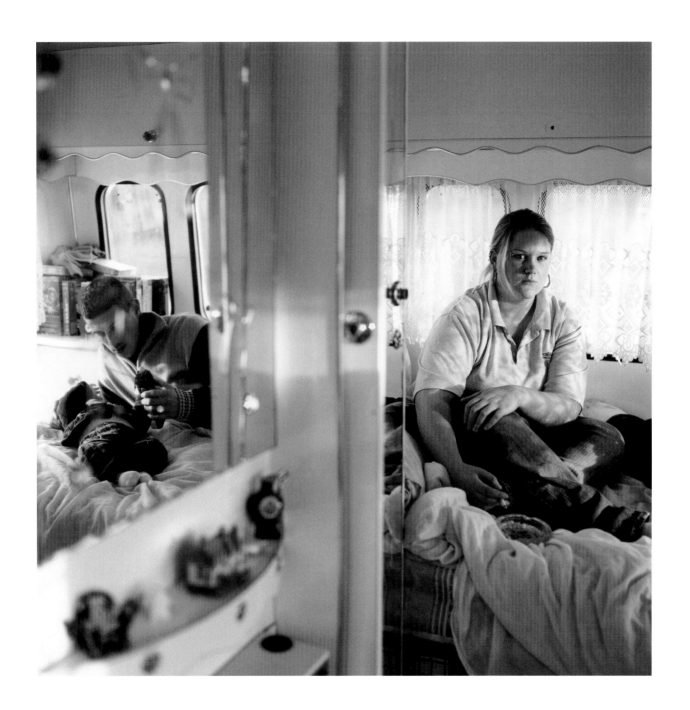

96   *Ewan and his metal detector*

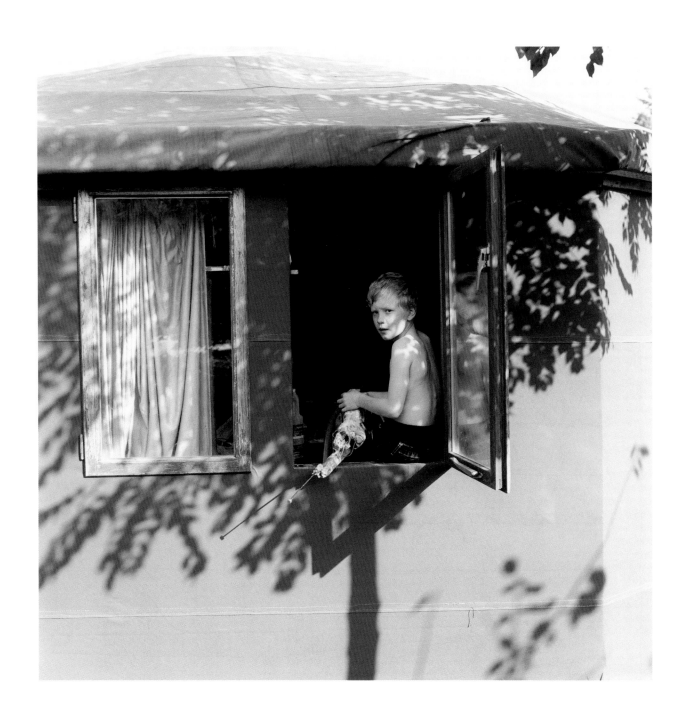

98 *The River Parrett*

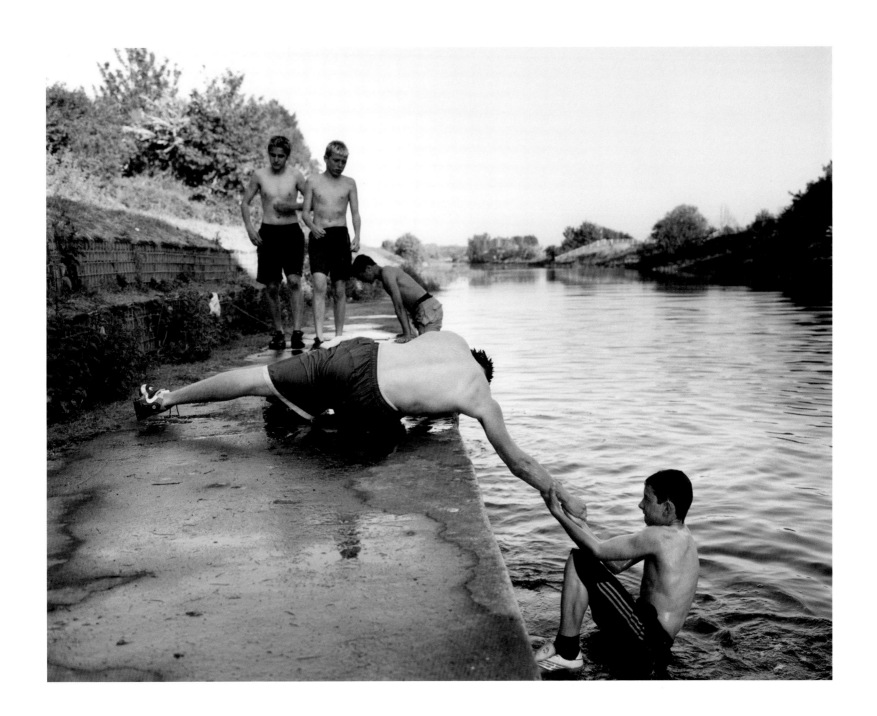

100   *The skatepark*

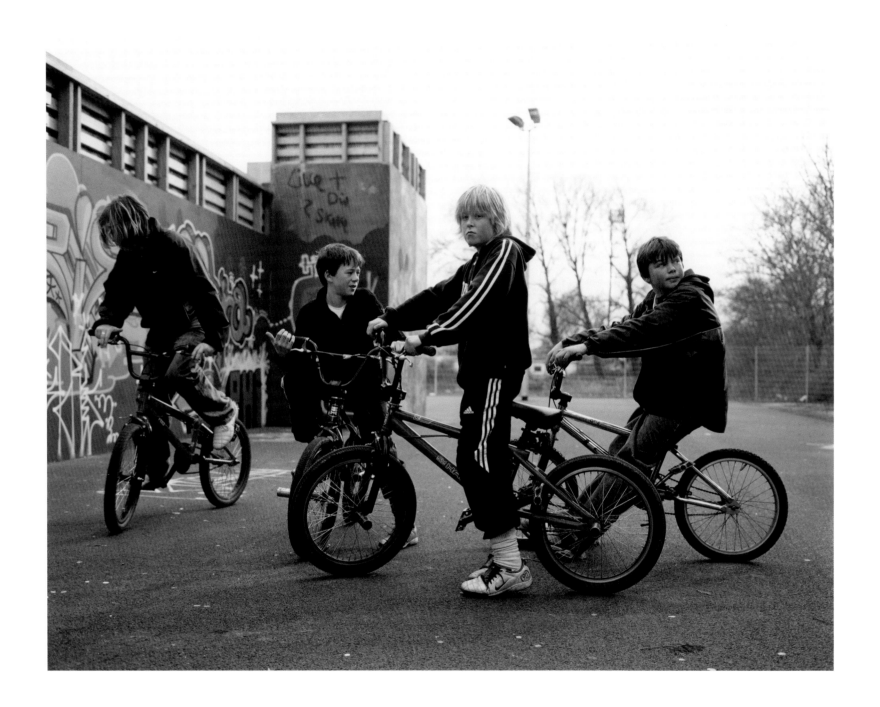

102   *Friday night*

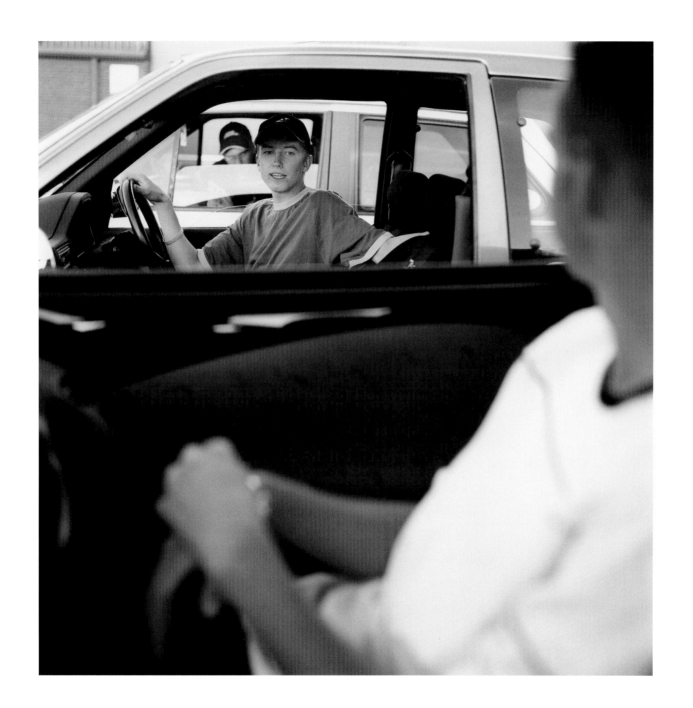

104   *Val and Sam*

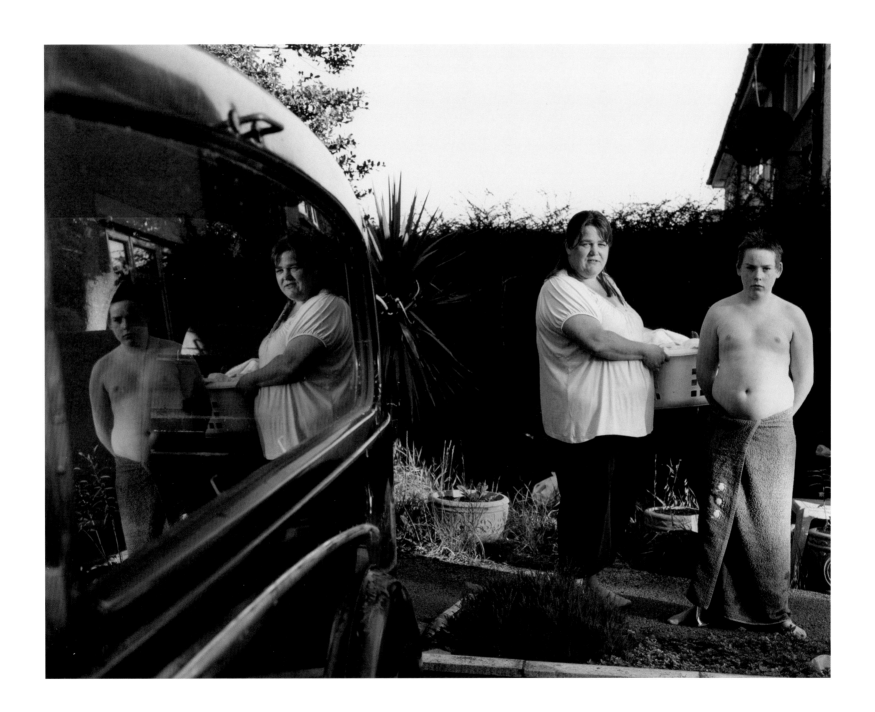

106   *Mercedes and Stuart*

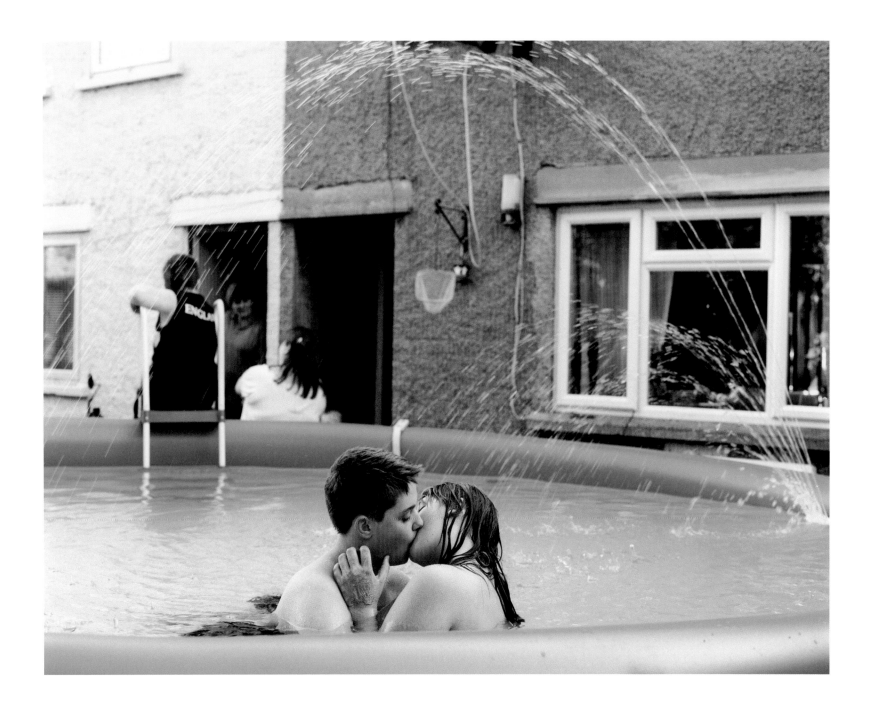

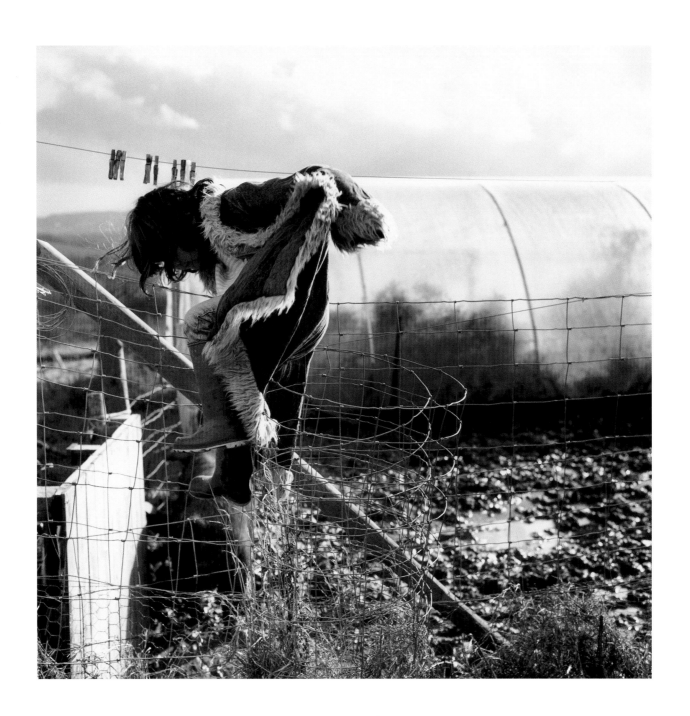

110   *Brian and his dogs*

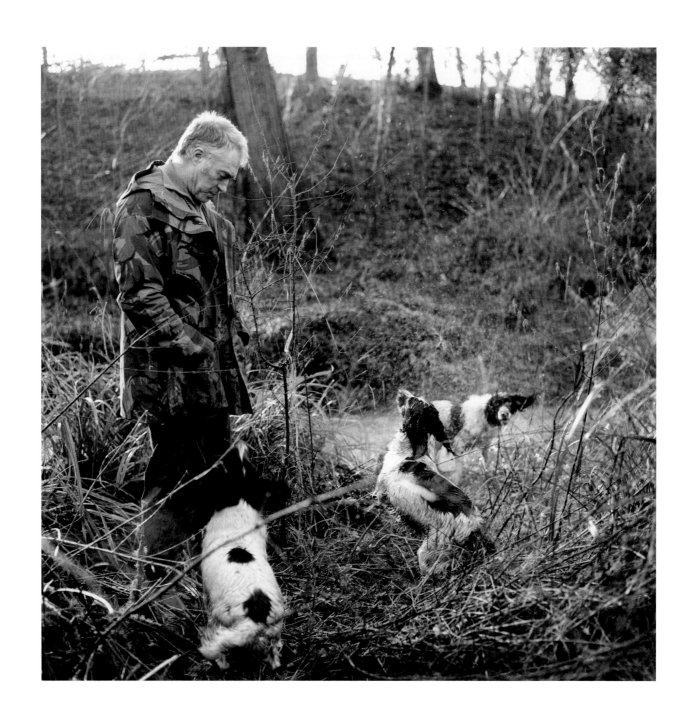

112   *Tom and Becca's winter camp*

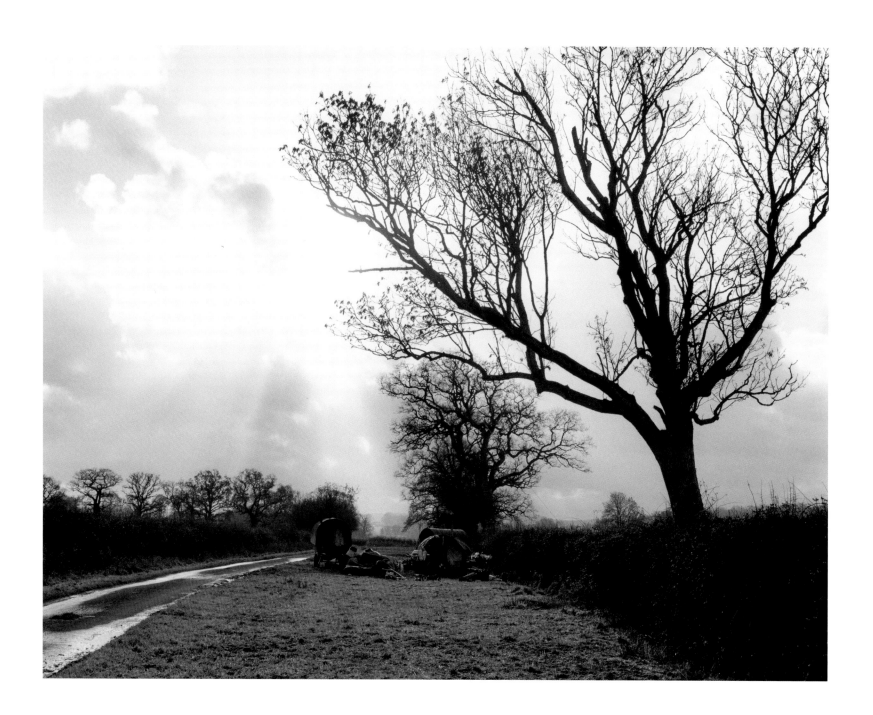

114   *Ez collecting wood*

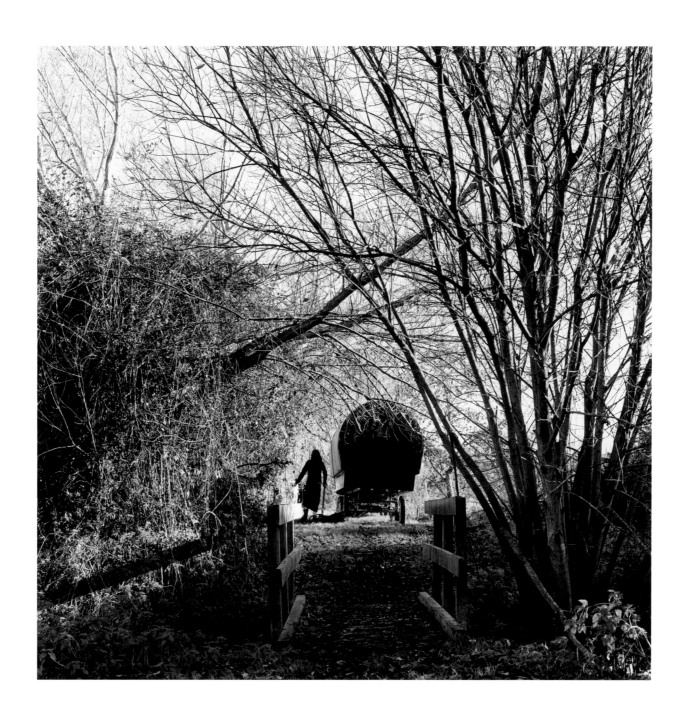

116   *Zoe*

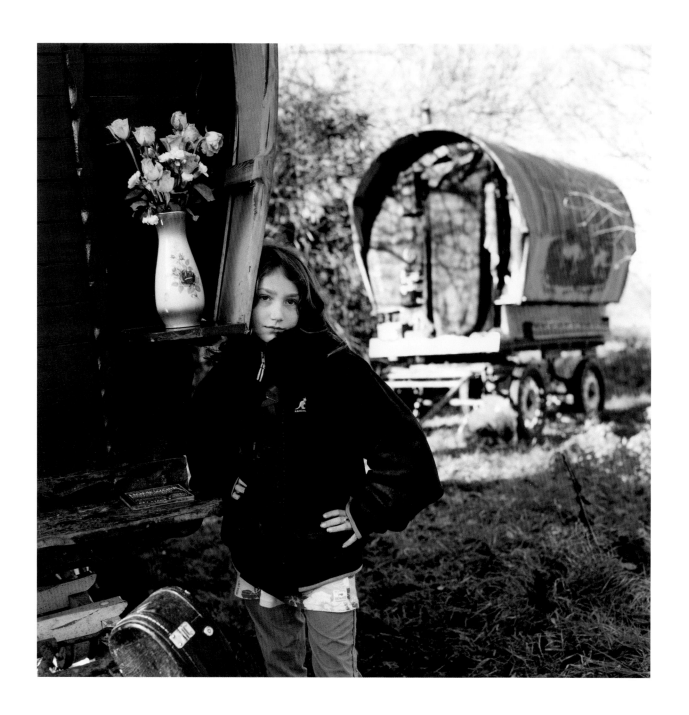

118   *Cinnamon Lane*

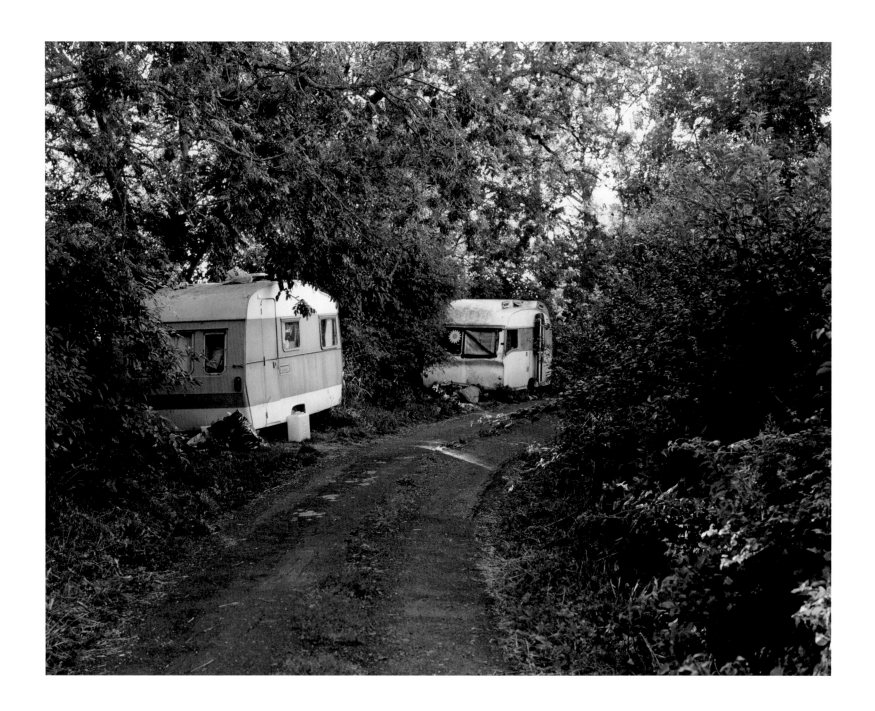

120 *A gentle moment*

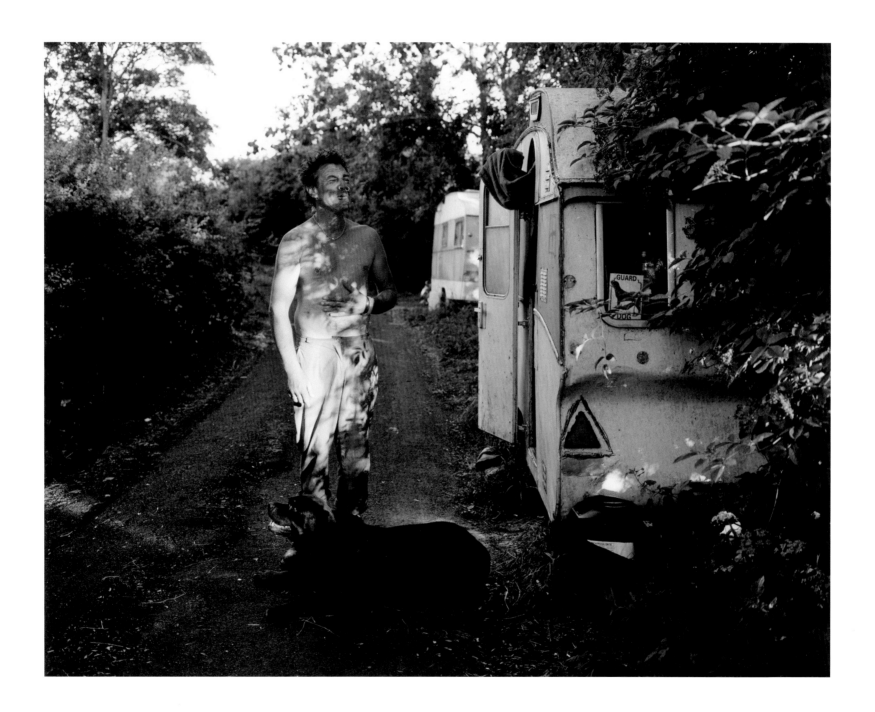

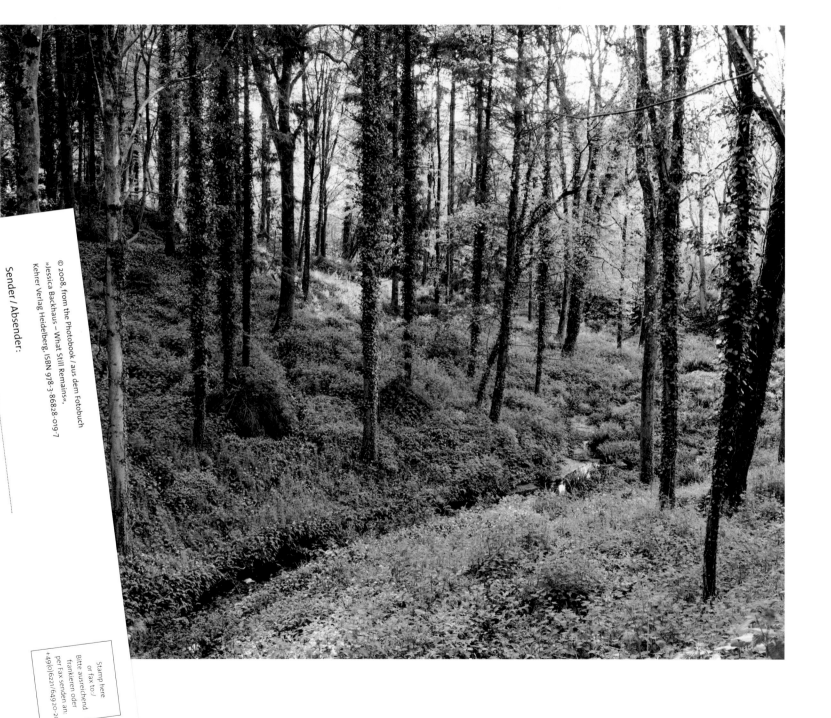

Sender / Absender:

Name / Name
....

Street / Straße
....

City, state, postal code / PLZ, Wohnort, Land
....

E-Mail
....

Phone, fax / Telefon, Fax
....

I would like to receive your current catalog
(as PDF file in foreign countries) / Ich würde gerne
Ihr aktuelles Verlagsprogramm beziehen:

☐ once / einmalig   ☐ each season / dauerhaft

⊞ K E H R ∃ R

Kehrer Verlag Heidelberg / Germany · www.kehrerverlag.com ·
contact@kehrerverlag.com · Phone / Telefon +49 (0) 6221 / 649 20–0
Distributor USA / Canada: Consortium Book Sales & Distribution /
Perseus Distribution · 1094 Flex Drive · Jackson, TN 38301-5070 ·

Kehrer Verlag Heidelberg
Heinsteinwerk
Wieblinger Weg 21
69123 Heidelberg
Germany

Stamp here
or fax to /
Bitte ausreichend
frankieren oder
per Fax senden an:
+49(0)6221/649 20-20

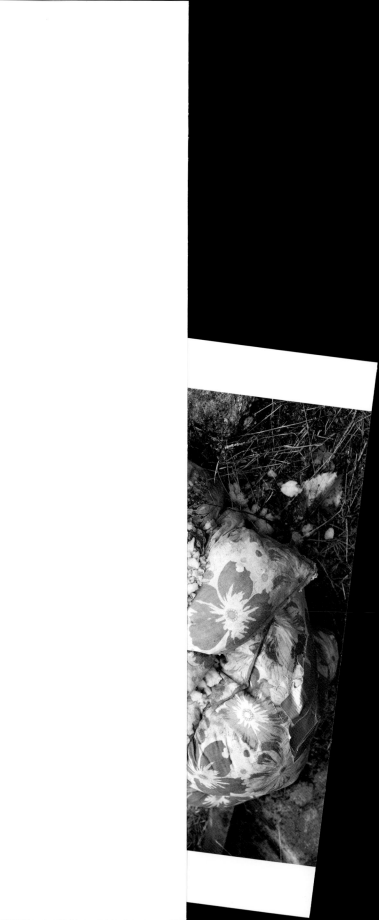

For my parents, Martin and Susie

126   BIOGRAPHY / ACKNOWLEDGMENTS

Venetia Dearden grew up in Somerset, the West Country of England. She completed a degree in Anthropology at Edinburgh University followed by a postgraduate degree in photojournalism at the London College of Printing. She has since travelled extensively, her work focused in Africa, Asia and South America, documenting social and humanitarian issues, facilitating workshops as a consultant for Photovoice and developing her passion for photographing people that continues to be published worldwide. Her ongoing work in Somerset has been widely acclaimed, (Art and Commerce Peek Awards, New York 2007 and ItsPhoto Awards, Trieste 2008) selected images have been shown at The National Portrait Gallery. Venetia Dearden lives in London where she is represented by Santucci & Co.

I would like to thank everyone in this book, for welcoming me into your lives and gifting me with your trust. A special thanks to Kate and Simon at Dreamers Farm, Jyoti and Dai at Fivepenny Farm, Joel and Lisa, Avril and Hedge, Tom and Becca, Frank Naish, The Stoodleys. To you and so many others who always greeted me open hearts, a warm brew and time to chat and share your insights. To Ele, Ari, Chloe, Pip, Osheen, Kitty, Cerys, Ewan, Marley, Mikey, Monzy, Annabelle and Claudia who took me through the doorways of your imaginations and made our natural environment an even more magical place than I already knew it to be.

My warmest thanks to Chris Ashman and the team at Artful Dodgers for your unfailing support, patience and encouragement. Medford Taylor, for your teachings and inspiration from the very beginning. Klaus Kehrer and Alexa Becker for believing in me. To Mulberry without whom the realisation of this book would not have been possible.

There are so many people I am eternally grateful to for the guidance, love and understanding that lights my way. Thank you all for these enduring friendships which are my greatest source of happiness and learning. To Martin, Susie, Harry, Barty and Jonny, you are my family and best friends. This is for you.

© 2008 Kehrer Verlag Heidelberg,

Venetia Dearden and Jon Levy

Contributions:

Jon Levy and Venetia Dearden

Proofreading: Kehrer Verlag (Tom Grace, Nicole Hoffmann)

Image processing:

Kehrer Design Heidelberg (Jürgen Hofmann)

Design and production:

Kehrer Design Heidelberg (cd / Katharina Stumpf)

Printed in Germany

Bibliographic information published by

the Deutsche Nationalbibliothek:

The Deutsche Nationalbibliothek lists this publication

in the Deutsche Nationalbibliografie; detailed bibliographic

data are available in the Internet at http://dnb.d-nb.de.

www.venetiadearden.com

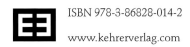 ISBN 978-3-86828-014-2

www.kehrerverlag.com   With generous support by Mulberry, London / Somerset, U.K.

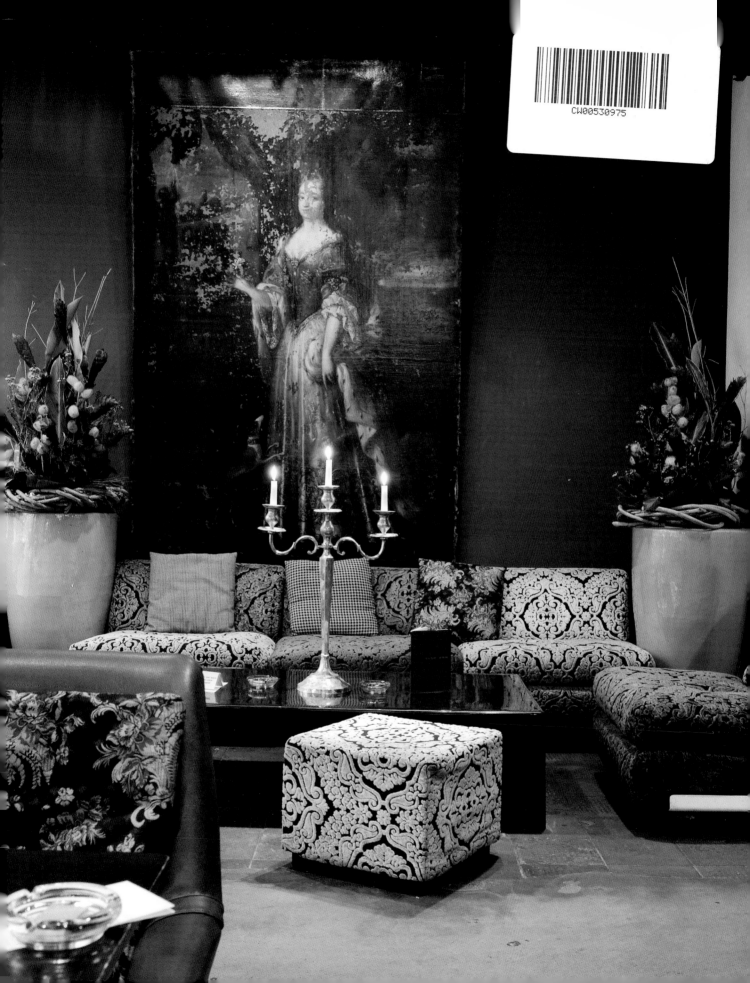

Hiltl.
Veggie
International.
A World
of
Difference

For my family, Rolf Hiltl

Hiltl.

Veggie

International.

A World

of

Difference

orell füssli

Recipes: Hiltl family and their team of cooks

Adapted and prepared by Barbara Elmer and Pascal Haag

Photos: Marie-Pierre Morel, Paris (recipes and restaurant), Felix Frey, Küsnacht (portraits pages 154 – 157).

Keystone (portraits pages 161, 164, 165, 170 middle)

Drawing of buffet, page 167, Ushi Tamborriello

History and portrait of the company and of the House of Hiltl: Urs Bühler, Zurich

Editor: Christina Sieg, Zurich

Publishing consultant: Gian Laube

Design and layout: Heiri Scherer, Scherer Kleiber CD, Lucerne

Design assistant: Luki Huber, Barcelona

Typesetting: Yves Scherer, Lucerne

English translation: Birgit Rommel, Weisslingen

English editor: Birgit Rommel, Weisslingen

Printed by Himmer AG, D-86167 Augsburg

ISBN 978-3-280-05380-5

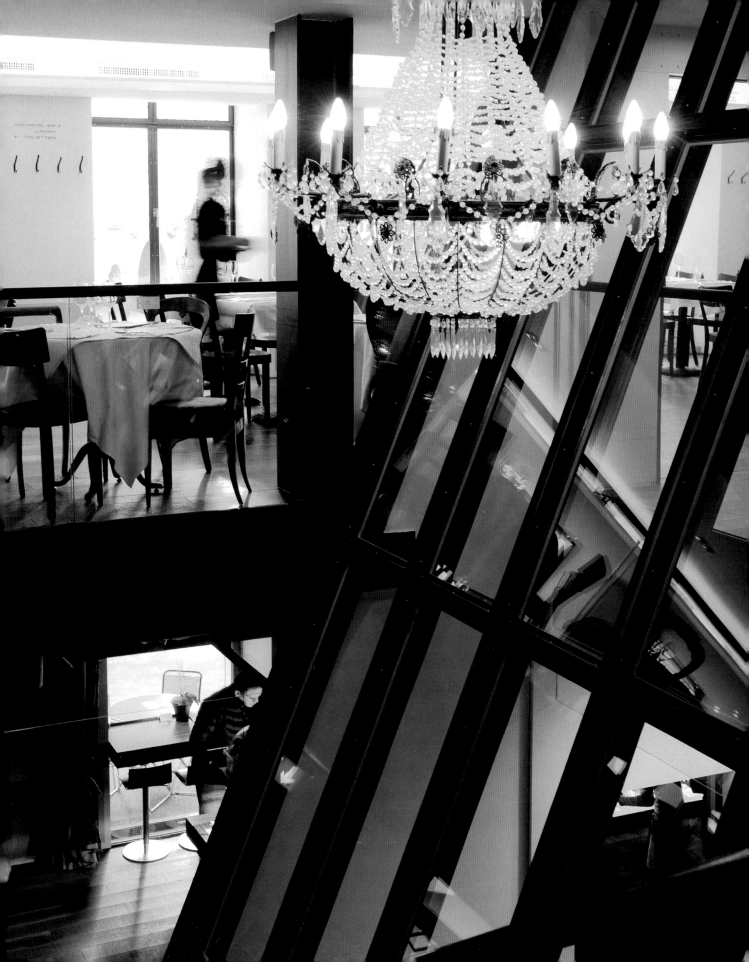

CONTENTS

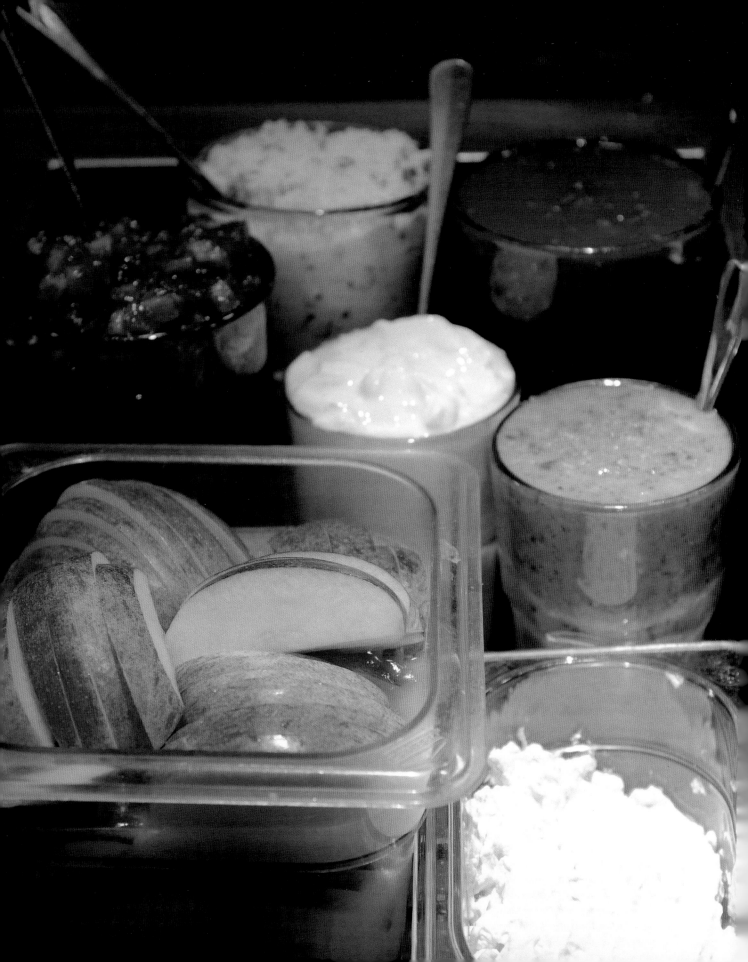

Talking to Rolf Hiltl

Why do we need another Hiltl cookbook?

Rolf Hiltl: We often receive e-mails, letters and phone calls from our guests asking about recipes for the meals they have enjoyed in our restaurant. The examples in this book have all been tried and tested thoroughly by Hiltl staff: They are either on our menu or available from our popular buffet. The Hiltl team doesn't stand still, we are always trying to improve and develop – and this also applies to our recipes and thus to our cookbooks.

Does one have to be a good cook to cope with these recipes?

We guarantee that they work. The procedures for most of the recipes have been kept as brief and simple as possible, though there are one or two that might even challenge the more experienced cook. Probably the most difficult thing will be to find some of the more exotic ingredients. But that is absolutely in line with our Hiltl tradition.

What type of cuisine – apart from vegetarian – do you personally prefer?

I have an affinity to Indian cuisine both through our family and our company history and because of its wide variety of spices; I'm fascinated by Thai cooking because of the interaction of sweet, hot and sour components; for me Italian food is the best of all, partly because it has so many vegetarian elements; and finally, when I was being trained at Zurich's Grand Hotel Dolder, I was introduced to the principles of Auguste Escoffier's classical cuisine française – it is certainly the basis of many a good cuisine.

You often choose to cook for your family. When you're cooking at home, are you somewhat pedantic in your approach or are you more the disorganized type?

In our kitchen at home I tend to be somewhat disorganized and at the same time I'm very spontaneous. I enjoy going to our local markets to buy what is in season. Or I simply use what happens to be in the fridge. I also like to start with a recipe and then develop variations. That usually works very well. After all, I'm a fully trained cook. I'd recommend that less experienced hobby cooks follow the recipes in this book closely.

Why do most Hiltl guests opt for the buffet when they could so easily place an a-la-carte order from the comfort of their table?

It really is true that we generate more than half our turnover at the buffet. It is a fast, uncomplicated and individual way of choosing your meal that goes well with our modern lifestyle. You get exactly what you see and you only pay for what you take; our female guests are great buffet fans – after all, women tend to have smaller appetites. Moreover, the buffet is a kind of meeting place where our guests talk to each other as they choose their food.

At weekends, the House of Hiltl is also a club with its own DJ and all the other amenities. What do you think your great-grandfather Ambrosius Hiltl would say if he were still alive today and wandered into the restaurant in the middle of a party at 2 a.m.?

First of all, he'd probably hold his hands over his ears – it can get pretty noisy during such nights. But seriously, he was a cosmopolitan, broad-minded person, he travelled a great deal, and loved to talk to his guests. I think he'd get used to it very quickly and he'd certainly be delighted that the House of Hiltl was so popular among young people.

Have any of your three children – Céline, Léna and Téo – shown any marked interest in cooking yet, so that you can already be sure that the Hiltl tradition will continue?

We'll see. Our children are free to choose what they want to do in the future. All three of them have cooked with me every now and then when I'm behind the stove at home and asked whether one of them would like to help. Our oldest daughter Céline, who is now twelve, has attended a cooking course for children in our cooking studio, which she enjoyed very much.

Interviewer: Urs Bühler

Enjoy!

Preparing food figures among the essentially human skills. Although not strictly a major subject in educational programmes, cooking is considered a fundamental cultural technique throughout the world. And not only is sharing a meal one of the most sensuous ways of pampering guests – it is widely regarded as the ideal way.

This is certainly true when the born host or hostess does the entertaining and cooking; nothing is too much trouble and everything seems effortless: Such people allocate the necessary amount of time to kitchen tasks but never so much that they neglect their guests; they use exquisite ingredients without repeatedly pointing out how exclusive these are; they decorate their dining table elegantly but never overload it; they are masters of time management although their guests are not aware that there is an underlying schedule.

Apart from this ideal type, there are various categories of no less charming hosts who, however, have not yet fully mastered the art of entertaining. Of course, we're not talking about people who don't take any trouble at all and, at best, give their guests baked beans on toast and, as dessert in April, some leftover Christmas cake. We're talking about more problematical cases. Such as those who are primarily entertaining their own ego. They say they need to spend five minutes in the kitchen and then they're swallowed up there for the next hour or so. They are working on a sumptuous meal and, with considerable aplomb, dish up masterpieces that bear witness to their virtuosity. They present roasted duck liver with sculpted wasabi ice-cream, a unique and innovative combination of flavours; they proffer a side dish based on the findings of molecular cuisine; they design patterns with balsamic vinegar around the edge of every plate; they even give their guest proper menu cards sprinkled with elitist French gastronomic terms. But woe betide the guests if any of these creations should turn out a flop! Then these culinary magicians will sulk for the next few hours – and spoil everybody's evening. Our suggestion for people in this category: Forget all the hassle and invite your next guests to sample a simple stew. You'll be amazed how they'll love it – and you!

At the other extreme there are those who call their guests guinea pigs right from the start and spend the rest of the evening apologizing: for an allegedly burnt pastry; for the dryness of the olive paste, even though a new recipe was used; for a wine that could, just possibly, be corked. Actually, without all the apologies, everything would have been fine. For some this defensive attitude is really their way of fishing for compliments, for others it is an inborn urge to belittle themselves. Whatever the explanation, it is awkward for the guests, who feel they have to keep contradicting. Then there is the category of surly hosts and hostesses. On the surface they seem quite different from the defensive ones, but the reasons for their surliness are similar. They slap dishes on the table as if they wanted to remind their guests that etymologically the term "guest" originally meant "enemy". And the words "enjoy your meal" will never cross their lips. One has to be fairly sensitive to recognize that this rough and ready approach is adopted to conceal their hang-up about their cooking skills. The theory being that if the guests don't expect great food then they won't be disappointed. Oddly enough, the compliments such cooks receive are often all the more effusive. Obviously there are no grounds for the qualms they had that their efforts in the kitchen would all be in vain. Our suggestion for both these categories is that they rid themselves of the preconceived notion that their guests only accept their invitation in order to savour their cooking. It simply is not true. They come because they enjoy the company!

However different they may be in their approach to entertaining, most people turn to cookbooks for ideas on what to serve their guests. And even today, with an ever increasing number of recipes available on the Internet, cookbooks have lost none of their appeal. Nothing can replace the fascination of a book in which stains and grease spots mark your favourite recipes, a book you leafed through for hours during sleepless nights, a book that makes your mouth water just by reading it. Naturally, this current cookbook targets all the categories described above. But it will give most pleasure to people who believe in a straightforward approach to cooking – in a combination of ingredients that may be unusual, but never merely for show; in creating a dish that is subtle, but not gimmicky. Above all, however, this collection of Hiltl recipes is for people who are convinced that the perfect menu does not necessarily call for a traditional roast or a filet of beef cooked according to the aficionados of low-temperature cooking. It is for people who want to master the art of cooking a meal composed of ingredients often still considered basic or relegated to side-dish status. In brief, the art of vegetarian cooking. And such a meal can be a revelation. Knowing this, you can look forward to receiving your guests in a few hours time while you are preparing just such a meal. You can look forward to sitting at table and enjoying their company while they enjoy their food. It is this prospect which makes entertaining your guests both a challenge and a pleasure.

Urs Bühler

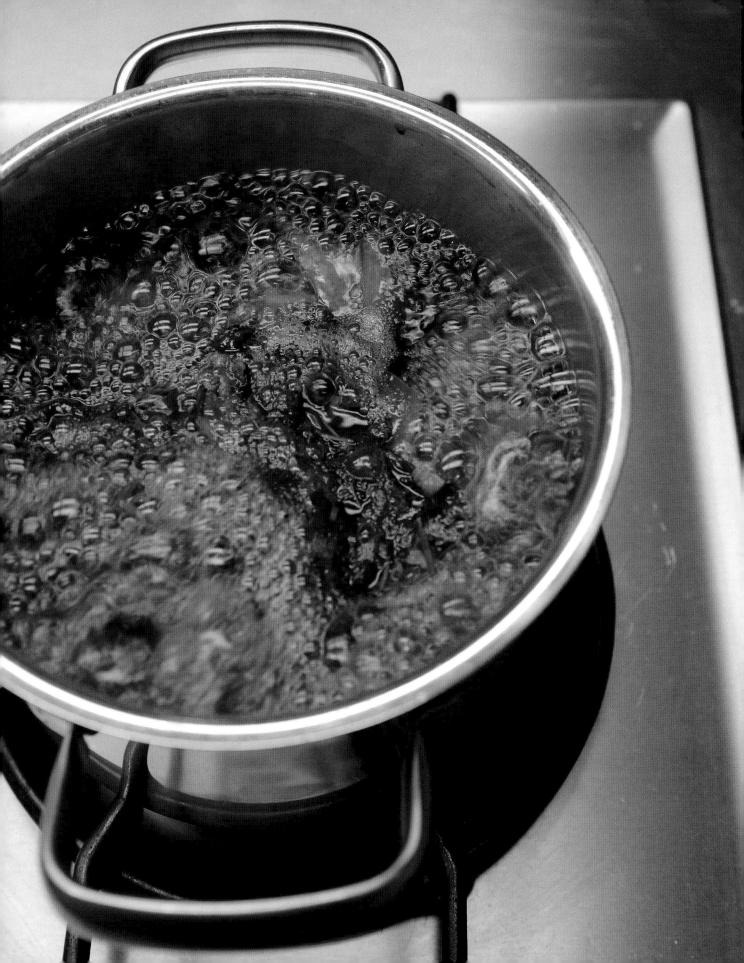

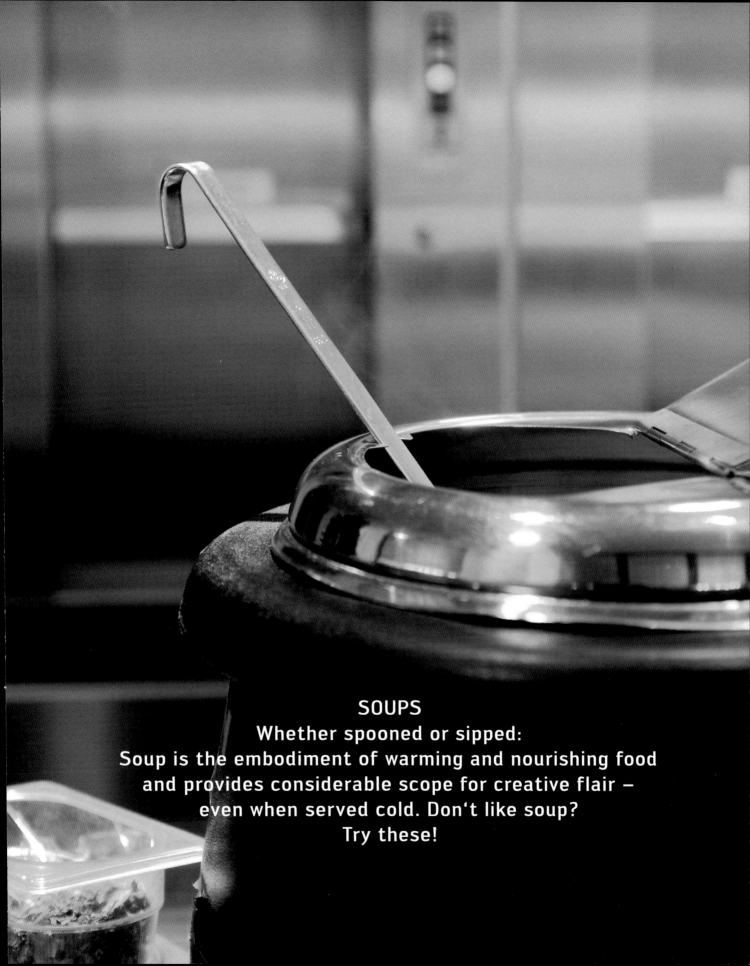

SOUPS
Whether spooned or sipped:
Soup is the embodiment of warming and nourishing food
and provides considerable scope for creative flair –
even when served cold. Don't like soup?
Try these!

Tomato & Orange Soup
Pascal's secret recipe

serves 4

500 g tomatoes
15 g cooking butter
1 onion, chopped
2 tbsp tomato puree
2 tbsp flour
3 sprigs fresh basil
1 l vegetable stock

400 ml fresh orange juice
2 tbsp brown sugar
2 bay leaves
2 cloves
10 black peppercorns
1 stick cinnamon

250 ml cream
sea salt, freshly milled pepper

gl/mi/on

Snick the top of the tomatoes, plunge them briefly into boiling water, slip off their skins and then dice.

Heat the butter and cook the onions till soft. Add the tomato puree and sauté for 5 minutes. Then add the diced tomatoes and, over a gentle heat, sauté for a further 5 minutes.

Dust with flour, add the basil, and then the stock. Stir until the soup comes to a boil and leave to simmer for 15 minutes.

In a separate saucepan bring the orange juice, sugar and spices to the boil and, over a low heat, reduce by about one half. After 10 minutes remove the cinnamon.

Pour this reduction through a sieve into the soup and blend with a wand mixer. Add the cream and bring up to simmering point. Add salt and pepper to taste.

Our tip: Serve the soup with cinnamon foam. Heat 300 ml milk to 69 °C and blend for 2 minutes. Place a swirl of foam on each serving and sprinkle with a little ground cinnamon.

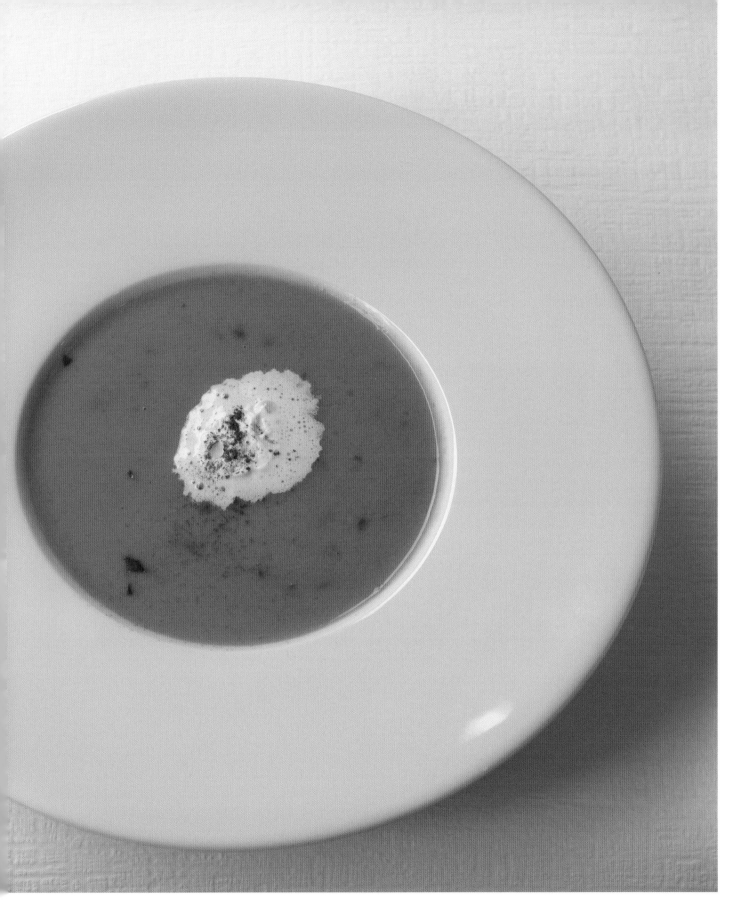

Chilled Melon Soup

with mascarpone and
fresh mint

serves 4

800 g ripe cavaillon melon, peeled and
deseeded

800 ml cold vegetable stock

250 g plain yoghurt

200 g mascarpone

$^1/_2$ bunch fresh mint, chiffonade cut

1 pinch freshly ground black pepper

1 tsp salt

2 pinches cayenne pepper

sea salt, freshly milled black pepper

a few sprigs fresh mint

mi

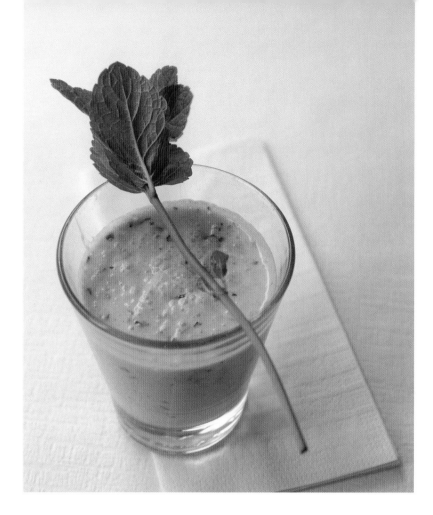

Dice the melon. Place in a blender with all the other ingredients and
blend thoroughly. Pass through a sieve and season to taste with salt
and pepper. Chill for 1 – 2 hours. Serve with fresh mint leaves.

Our tip: Melons are ripe if they give off a noticeable melon fragrance and if they yield to slight pressure.

Mint belongs to the Lamiaceae family. Mints are aromatic, bushy perennials that prefer a temperate climate. They have wide spreading underground rhizomes; their leaves and stems are often downy. There are some 20–30 species and countless varieties. Peppermint leaves contain up to 2.5 % of essential oils, mainly menthol (about 50 %), menthone (10–30 %), and menthyl esters (up to 10 %). Jasmone (0.1 %), an aromatic substance, substantially enhances the value of the oil. Mint has long been a popular garden plant. In 812, Charlemagne required three mint species to be planted in gardens in his empire: Water mint *(mentha aquatica)*, spearmint *(mentha spicata)*, and its subspecies horse mint *(mentha longifolia)*. Mint species and cultivars used as culinary herbs often have names that indicate a flavour similar to other plants such as apple mint, pineapple mint, basil mint, bergamot mint, orange mint, chocolate mint.

There are many other well-known mint species such as: Moroccan nana mint, field (also wild or corn) mint, pennyroyal, Corsican mint, and large apple mint, also called foxtail, hairy or woolly mint.

Chiffonade is a culinary technique for cutting herbs or leafy green vegetables into long, thin strips. This is generally accomplished by stacking the leaves, rolling them tightly, then cutting across the rolled leaves with a sharp knife to produce fine ribbons. Chiffon is French for "rag". Formerly this cutting technique was used to prepare rags for further processing in paper mills. Today chiffon is used to describe a fine, sheer fabric – usually silk – with a slightly puckered surface. It can be packed tightly and takes up very little room.

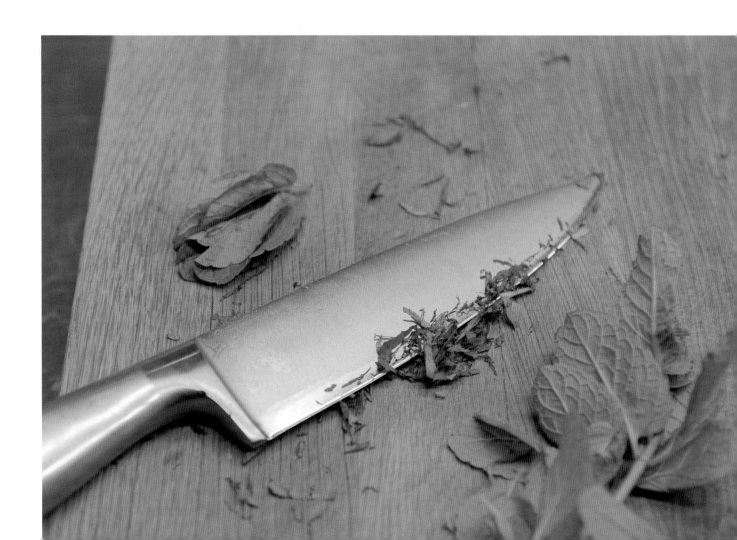

Harira Soup

Rachid's recipe

serves 4

30 g brown lentils

1 small carrot
1 potato (75 g)
50 g leeks
250 g very ripe tomatoes
1/2 onion in wedges
1 clove garlic, halved
1 sprig parsley
1 sprig fresh coriander

2 tbsp olive oil
3/4 tbsp tomato puree
1/2 tsp brown sugar
1/2 tsp ground cumin
3/4 tsp paprika
1/2 tsp ground ginger
2 pinches ground coriander
1 pinch saffron powder
1.2 l vegetable stock

25 g fine noodles
1/2 tbsp lemon juice
sea salt, freshly milled pepper

1/4 bunch fresh coriander, finely cut

ga/gl/on

Pick over the lentils, wash and drain them then, adding a pinch of salt, cook until soft. Coarsely grate the carrot and potato. Halve the leeks lengthwise, wash and cut into fine slices. Snick the top of the tomatoes, briefly plunge them into boiling water, cool them under cold water, slip off their skins, then deseed and dice them. Chop herbs coarsely.

Heat the oil, sweat the onion wedges and garlic halves. Add the vegetables and diced tomatoes and, over a low heat, soften them slowly for 10 minutes. Add the tomato puree, sugar, all the spices and herbs and sauté for a further 5 minutes.

Pour in the vegetable stock, and leave to boil for 30 minutes. Blend the soup very thoroughly, add the noodles and cook until al dente.

Add the cooked lentils. Bring the soup to simmering point and season to taste with lemon juice, salt, and freshly milled pepper. Serve garnished with the cut coriander.

Our tip: Harira is commonly eaten in Morocco and during Ramadan is served at the beginning of the evening meal. A swirl of sour cream may be added just before serving.

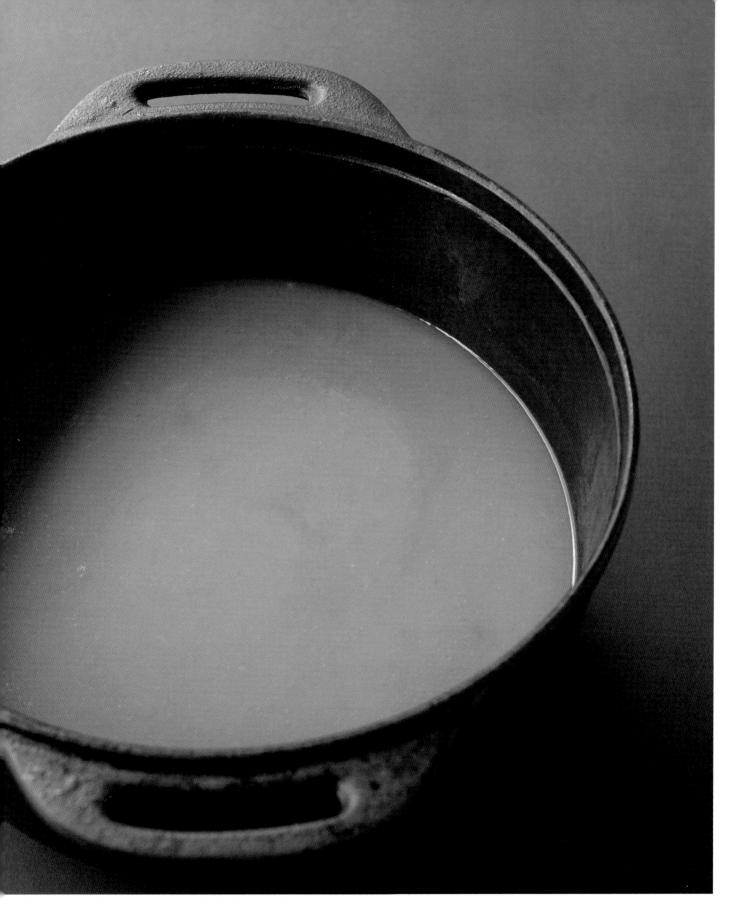

Fennel & Absinthe Soup

with fresh dill

serves 4

50 g celeriac, peeled
100 g carrots, peeled
400 g fennel

20 g cooking butter
1 onion, chopped
1/2 tsp ground caraway seeds
2 whole star anise
1.5 l vegetable stock
100 ml absinthe
2 1/2 tbsp sour cream
1/2 bunch fresh dill, chopped
sea salt, freshly milled pepper

a little sour cream

ce/mi/on

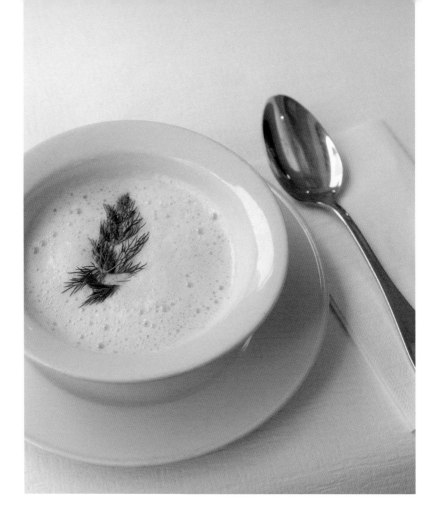

Cut all the vegetables into 1 cm dice. Melt the butter, add the onions and sauté. Add the vegetable dice and the ground caraway seeds and sauté for a further 10 minutes. Add the star anise, pour in the stock and bring to the boil. Add half the absinthe and continue boiling until the vegetables are soft.

Remove the star anise, puree the soup with a wand mixer and then pass through a sieve. Add the remaining absinthe, the sour cream and the chopped dill. Season to taste with salt and pepper, then whisk the soup until it is nice and frothy.

Garnish with a swirl of sour cream and some dill fronds.

Our tip: Pernod can be used instead of absinthe. It is milder in taste. The soup can also be made without alcohol, in which case more dill should be used.

Absinthe is a spirit made from wormwood *(Artemisia absinthium)* and its medical use can be traced back to ancient times. It was first produced on a large scale as a distilled alcoholic beverage in the modern sense in Val de Travers in canton Neuchâtel, Switzerland, at the end of the 18th century. Absinthe, with its fine bitter taste, is steeped in grande and petite wormwood, angelica root, hyssop, and lemon balm. Anise, star anise, and fennel seeds are further important ingredients. A characteristic feature of absinthe is that when water or ice are added it takes on a milky opalescence; this effect comes from the essential oil anethole found in anise. From its early beginnings at the Val de Travers distillery, absinthe consumption spread through Continental Europe and, by the middle of the 19th century, absinthe was a popular (addictive) drink known as *la fée verte* (the Green Fairy). Because of the thujone content in wormwood, absinthe was banned in almost all European countries at the beginning of the 20th century and listed as a psychoactive drug. Thujone is a neurotoxin which, if the dosage is sufficiently high, can cause disorientation and epileptic cramps. Thereupon the Pernod company changed the recipe and continued to sell its product as an aniseed drink – without wormwood.

Since 1998 production and consumption of absinthe with a limited thujone content has again been permitted in Switzerland and in all EU countries. Moreover, scientists today question whether the high thujone content in absinthe was, in fact, dangerous. They believe that the health damage attributed to thujone was caused by the high alcohol content or by poor quality spirits.

There are various rituals for preparing absinthe; they all call for an absinthe glass and spoon. Apart from the classic French ritual, the Czech or modern Bohemian method has now become popular: a shot of absinthe is poured into an absinthe glass and a sugar cube placed on an absinthe spoon (or a fork) resting on the glass. The sugar is soaked in absinthe and ignited. As soon as the sugar begins to caramelize the spoon is dipped into the absinthe to quench the flames and iced water is immediately added so that the absinthe will not reignite (a ratio of 50:50). If the absinthe contains enough anise, it will then turn milky, which connoisseurs call the *louche* effect.

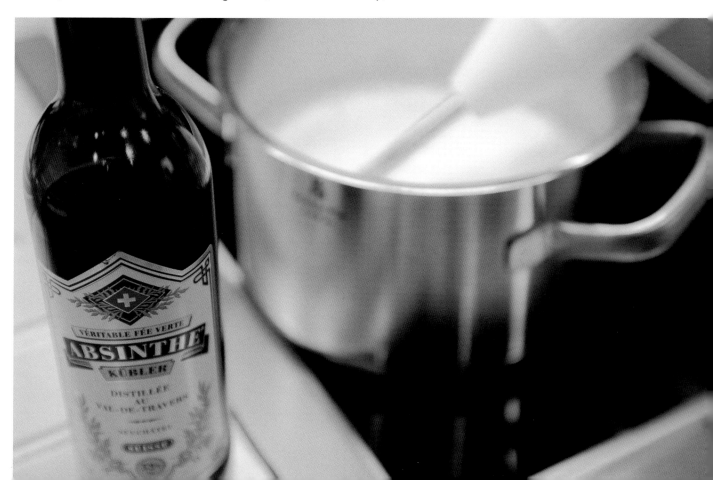

Homemade Vegetable Stock

the basis for soups and sauces

makes 3.5 litres

1 small leek

1/4 small savoy cabbage

1/2 fennel bulb

2 onions, unpeeled

1/2 small celeriac

1 carrot

2 tbsp oil

1 tbsp whole black peppercorns

1 tsp fennel seeds

1 tsp brown mustard seeds

1 tsp caraway seeds

2 bay leaves

4 sprigs parsley

1 small sprig rosemary

1 sprig tarragon

1/2 tsp lavender flowers

4 l water

2 tbsp sea salt

ce/on

Wash all the vegetables and chop coarsely. Heat the oil in a saucepan. Sauté the carrot, fennel, onions and celeriac till they are slightly browned. Add the chopped cabbage and the spices and cook until the spices develop their fragrance. Add the herbs and pour in the water. Bring to a boil and leave to simmer for 45 minutes. Stir in the sea salt. Pour the stock through a sieve and fill into sterilized glass bottles. Seal immediately and leave to cool.
Unopened the stock will keep in the fridge for at least 2 weeks.

Our tip: This stock can be used as the basis for soups and sauces as well as for deglazing. The onion skins give the fond its attractive brown colour. If onions do not agree with you, the stock can be made without onion and / or celeriac — but it will be paler in colour. Instead of this stock, you can use organic vegetarian bouillon or stock in powder or paste form.

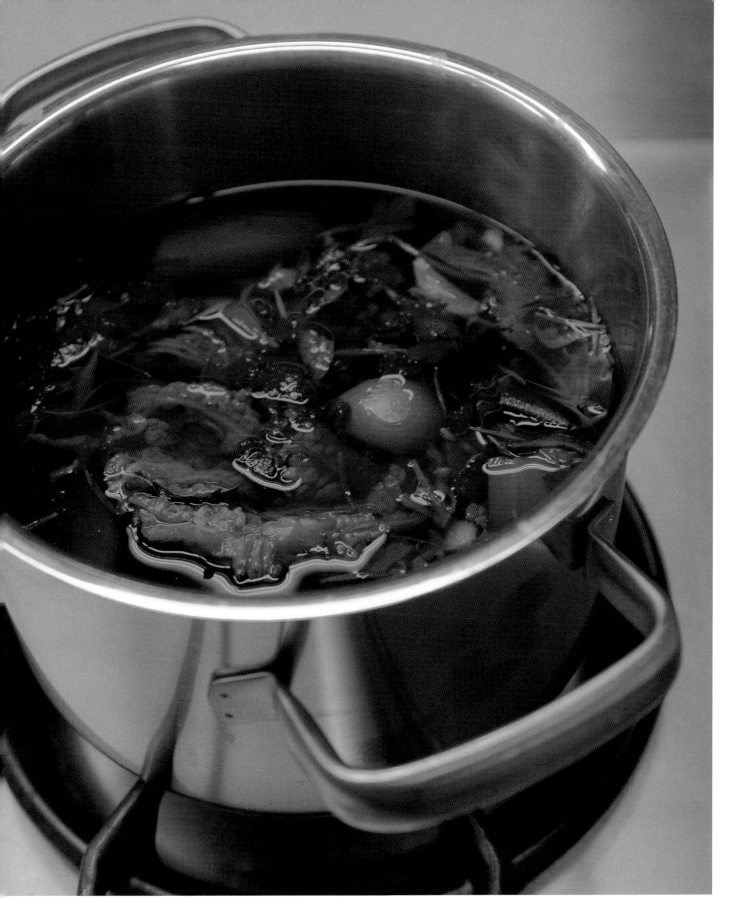

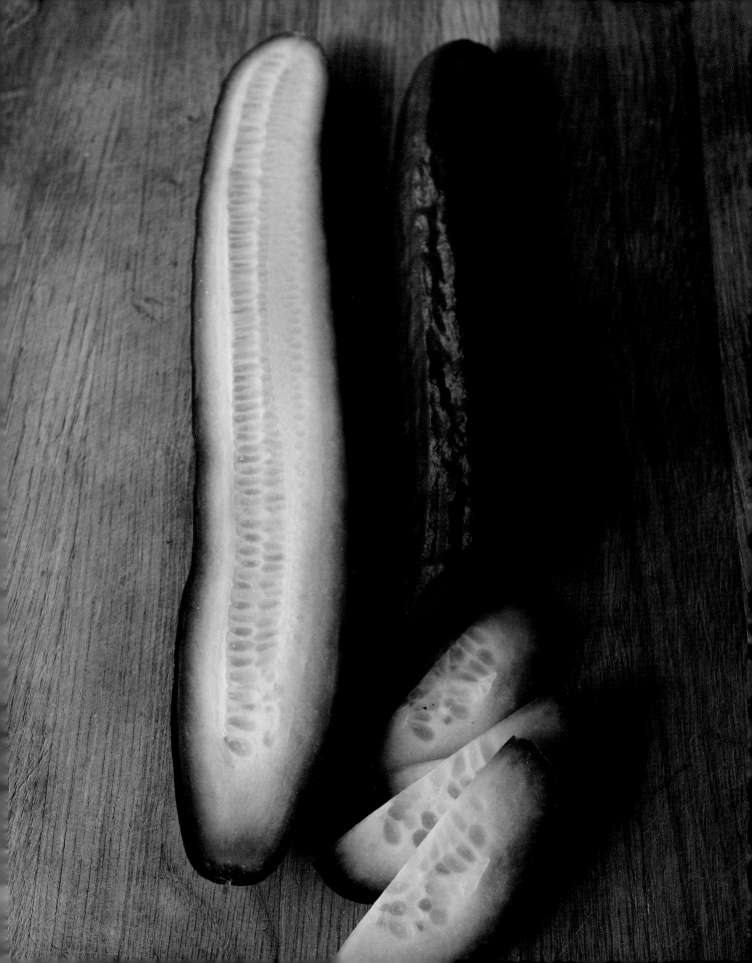

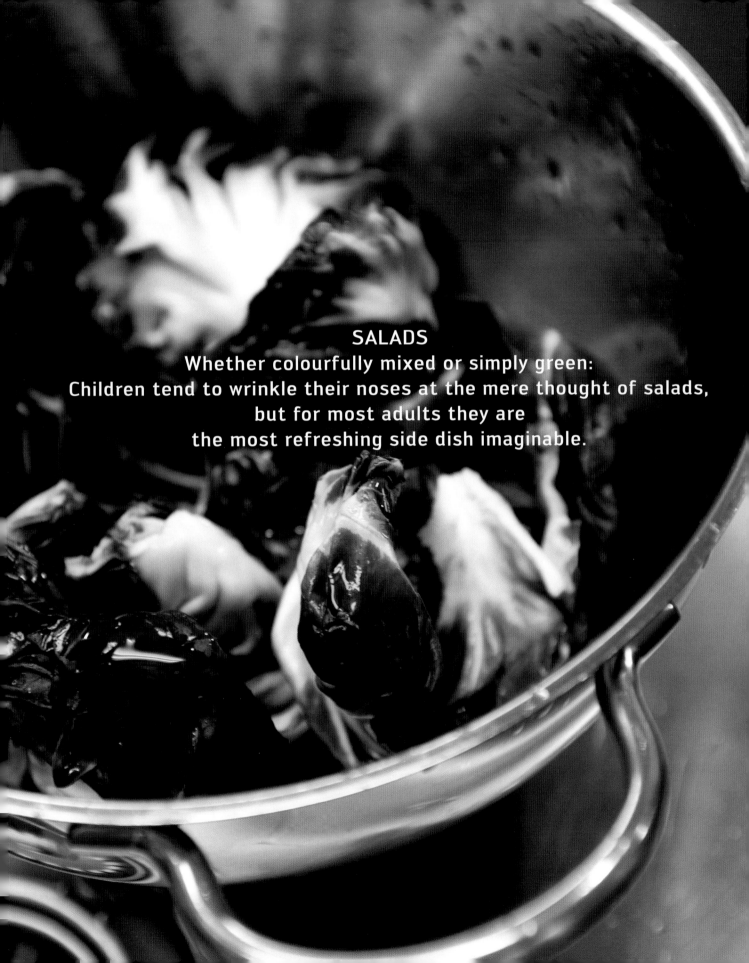

SALADS

Whether colourfully mixed or simply green:
Children tend to wrinkle their noses at the mere thought of salads,
but for most adults they are
the most refreshing side dish imaginable.

Salade Niçoise
Hiltl's interpretation of this classic

serves 4

Dressing:

4 sprigs parsley

4 tbsp balsamic vinegar

5 tbsp red wine vinegar

1 tbsp Dijon mustard

1 1/2 tsp sea salt

freshly milled black pepper

150 ml olive oil

600 g small potatoes

250 g french beans

100 g salad leaves

100 g capers

200 g black olives, pitted

2 tomatoes

4 eggs, hardboiled

1 onion, in rings

eg/on

For the dressing, chop the parsley. Blend the balsamic vinegar, red wine vinegar, mustard, parsley and pepper. Add the olive oil, stirring continuously.

Boil the small potatoes for approx. 20 minutes until just tender, leave to cool slightly and cut into quarters lengthwise. Cook the beans in slightly salted water until just tender, drain and immediately plunge into iced water to cool. Drain and, if necessary, cut in half.

Wash the salad leaves, shake dry and tear into bite-sized pieces.

Mix the potatoes, beans, leaves, capers and olives in a bowl. Before serving, add the dressing and toss.

Cut the tomatoes into wedges, quarter the eggs lengthwise and halve each quarter. Place the mixed salad in the centre of four plates, arrange the egg and tomato wedges around the salad, and garnish with the onion rings. Serve immediately.

Our tip: In early summer use new potatoes.

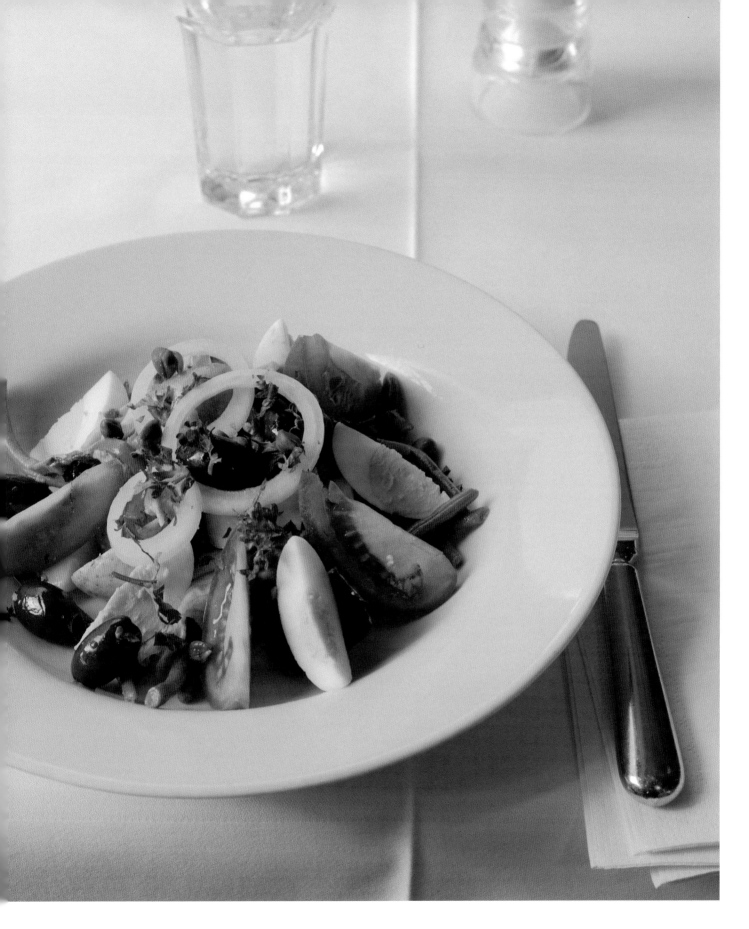

Asian Noodles Salad
with green chillies

serves 4

450 g rice noodles

2 l boiling water

250 g San Marzano tomatoes

100 g carrots, peeled

100 g spring onions

40 g sesame seeds, hulled

Dressing:

2 small green chillies, deseeded

150 g fresh pineapple, peeled

150 ml light soy sauce

150 ml sunflower oil

3 tbsp sesame oil

1 1/2 tsp sea salt

2 lemons, juice

6 tbsp rice wine

1 1/2 cloves garlic, chopped

90 g fresh ginger, chopped

3 tbsp tomato ketchup

1 tbsp brown sugar

ga/gl/on/so

Place the rice noodles in a bowl and cover with the boiling water. Set aside for 30 minutes and then drain thoroughly. Halve the tomato lengthwise, deseed and cut into narrow strips crosswise.
Cut the carrot into julienne sticks. Wash the spring onion, halve lengthwise and cut diagonally into fine slices. Add to the noodles and mix well.
Toast the sesame seeds in a dry, non-stick pan and add to the noodles.
Chop the chillies and pineapple and purée together with the other sauce ingredients. Pour the dressing over the noodles, mix thoroughly and serve immediately.

Our tip: The sauce can be made without garlic; instead, use more fresh ginger (a total of 150 g).

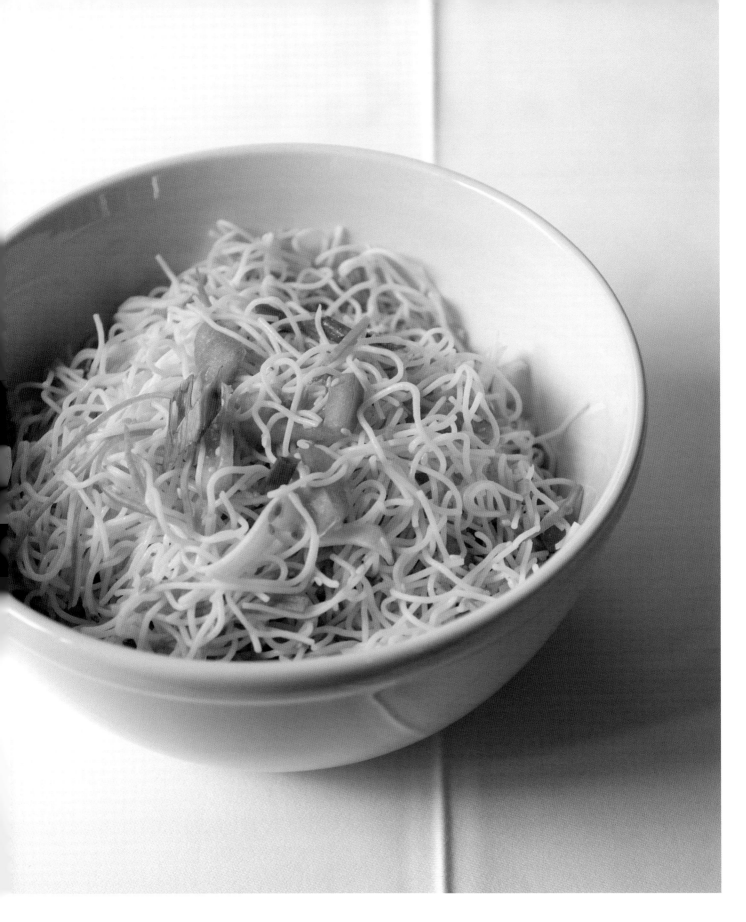

Wakame & Cucumber Salad
a taste of the sea

serves 4

Dressing:

10 g butter

10 g fresh ginger, grated

1 1/2 tbsp brown sugar

200 ml light soy sauce

4 tbsp lemon juice

6 tbsp sesame oil

1 cucumber, washed

1 green pepper

1 bunch fresh mint

1 bunch fresh coriander

30 g wakame seaweed, dried

200 g shiitake mushrooms, fresh

2 tbsp groundnut oil

1/2 tsp sea salt

horseradish sprouts

gl/mi/so

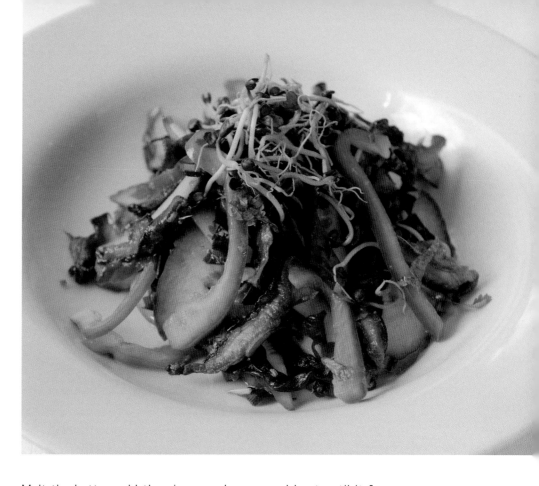

Melt the butter, add the ginger and sugar and heat until it forms a golden-brown caramel. Remove from the heat. Pour in the soy sauce, lemon juice and sesame oil and warm gently until the caramel melts. Halve the cucumber lengthwise and cut diagonally into thin slices. Halve the washed pepper, deseed and cut into fine strips. Chop the mint and coriander finely.

Soak the seaweed in cold water for about 10 minutes, place it in a sieve and drain. Cut off the hard stems of the shiitake mushrooms and discard. Slice the caps finely.

Heat the groundnut oil in a frying pan and fry the mushrooms, sprinkle with a little salt and mix with the cucumber slices, pepper strips, herbs and seaweed. Add the dressing, arrange on plates and garnish with the horseradish sprouts. Serve immediately.

Our tip: Wakame gives the salad its tangy flavour. It is available from health-food stores and in Japanese and Korean shops.

Algae

Algae For our ancestors edible seaweed was nutritious food, and it is still commonly eaten in Japan, China, and on the coasts of North, Central and South America. In France and Ireland dulse, sea lettuce and some types of kelp are regarded as culinary specialities.

According to type, dried seaweed contains 10 – 40 % protein, 1 – 5 % fat, 2 – 8 % dietary fiber (roughage), 15 – 35 % dietary minerals. Edible seaweed is a major source of iodine.

Nori, a red seaweed, has been cultivated off the Japanese coast for centuries. Dried and processed into sheets, it is commonly used as a sushi wrap. The traditional Welsh and Irish laver bread is made from laver, a seaweed very closely related to nori.

Dulse is also a red seaweed. It grows in the mid intertidal zone of the Atlantic, where the water is cold. It is used in soups and salads and, after soaking briefly, it can be eaten uncooked. This tender sea vegetable is particularly rich in iron, fluorine and vitamins B6 and B12.

Sea lettuce is a green seaweed that grows in shallow water. It is often found attached to rocks by a hold-fast, but can also be free floating in stagnant tide pools. In France sea lettuce, either fresh or rehydrated, is used to marinate fish and to line steamers; it is also added to salads, soups, cakes and pastries.

The brown seaweed **wakame** (shown below) is considered a delicacy in Japan, and is second only to nori in popularity. Today it is also farmed in Brittany and thrives in strong currents in the low tide zone. Mekabu, the flowering sprout of the wakame plant, is stronger in flavour and requires considerable cooking time.

Hijiki is another brown seaweed. It is particularly sought after because of its firm structure, unmistakeable flavour and slight sweetness. Hijiki always needs to be reconstituted. Firm, fleshy and glistening, this seaweed cooked with carrots and onions adds another dimension to soups, stews and noodle salads. Its calcium content is 10 times higher than that of milk.

Harvested in the Pacific, **arame** has a mild, delicate flavour. Unlike other sea vegetables it has little taste of the sea. Instead, with its mannitol content, it has a distinct sweet flavour. It needs to be soaked briefly before use and, even if lightly cooked, it still retains its black colour. Arame is rich in iodine and should therefore be used very sparingly.

Kombu is a brown seaweed belonging to the *Laminaria* genus, which thrives in the cold coastal waters of Japan. All *Laminaria* species are commonly called kelp. As they all have a high iodine content, they are not admitted as food in some countries (such as Germany) although they have been approved as a bath additive. Kombu contains more minerals and vitamins than any other edible seaweed. In Japan kombu is used to flavour dashi, the basic stock for many Japanese soups.

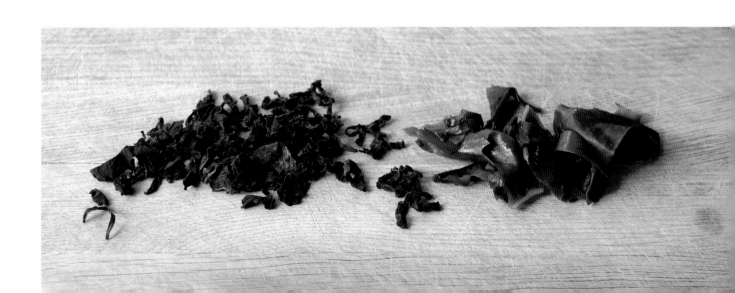

Caesar Salad
with smoked tofu

serves 4

Dressing:

200 ml sunflower oil

1–2 tbsp lemon juice

1 egg

2 tsp Dijon mustard

8 tbsp plain yoghurt

1 clove garlic, crushed

3 tbsp parmesan

sea salt, freshly milled black pepper

5 slices sliced bread

20 g cooking butter

250 g smoked tofu

2 tbsp sunflower oil

4 eggs, hardboiled

4 heads romaine lettuce

(hearts and tender leaves)

30 g parmesan, grated

1 lemon, in wedges

ch/eg/ga/gl/mi/so

For the dressing place the sunflower oil, lemon juice, egg and mustard into a narrow, tall mixing glass. Using a wand mixer, blend for 30 seconds without moving the wand, then draw it up once.

Mix the yoghurt, crushed garlic and parmesan into the mayonnaise, blend briefly and add salt and pepper to taste.

Cut the sliced bread into 1 cm dice and fry in the cooking butter until the croutons are brown and crispy. Drain on kitchen paper. Cut the tofu into 1 cm dice, fry in hot oil until golden and drain on kitchen paper. Peel the hardboiled eggs and cut into 8 wedges. Wash and drain the romaine lettuce, tear into bite-sized pieces and toss with the parmesan, croutons, and tofu cubes. Just before serving add the dressing, arrange on 4 plates, and garnish with the egg and lemon wedges. Serve immediately.

Our tip: Part-time vegetarians use bacon instead of smoked tofu.

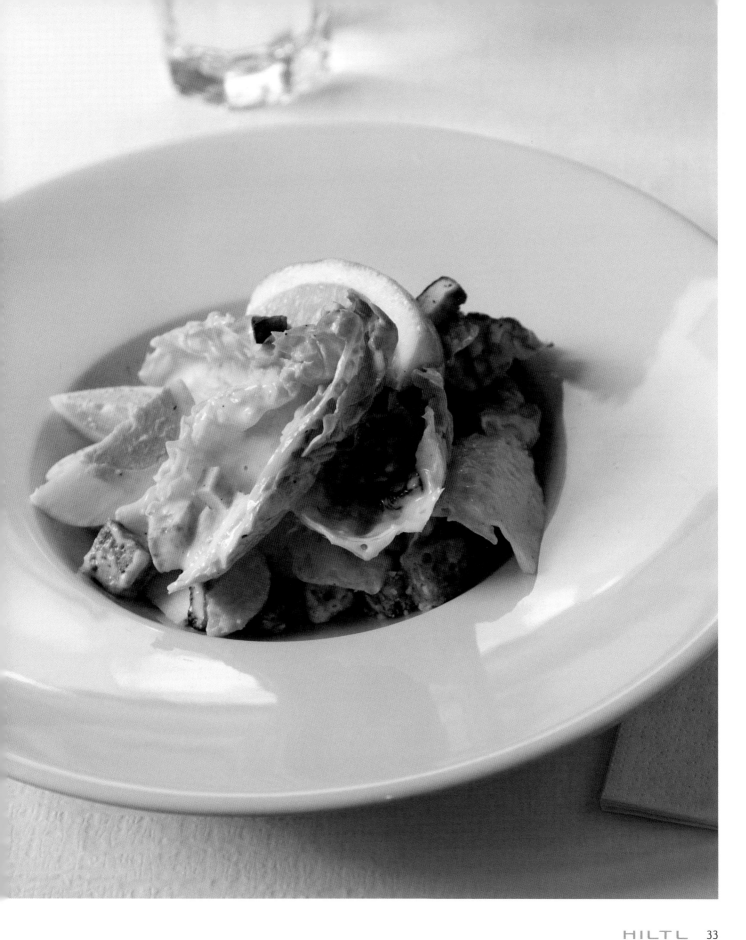

Italian Tofu Salad

with fresh herbs

serves 4

600 g plain tofu

Marinade and dressing:

7 tbsp white balsamic vinegar

70 ml olive oil

3 tsp sea salt

3/4 tsp freshly milled black pepper

4 sprigs fresh oregano, chopped

4 sprigs fresh thyme, chopped

4 sprigs fresh marjoram, chopped

4 fresh sage leaves, chopped

4 San Marzano tomatoes

120 g black olives, pitted

so

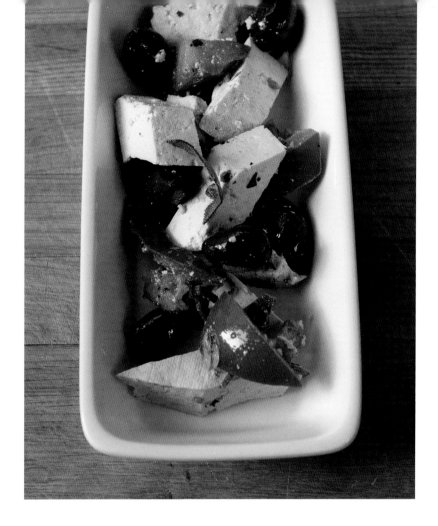

Cut the tofu diagonally to form 2 cm rhombic shapes.

Mix the balsamic vinegar with the olive oil, salt, pepper and chopped herbs. Marinate the tofu overnight in the sauce.

Quarter the tomatoes lengthwise and cut the quarters diagonally into 2 cm pieces. Mix the tomatoes and olives with the marinated tofu and serve.

Our tip: Use a fine textured, medium firm tofu for this salad. We use white balsamic vinegar so that the tofu retains its light colour.

Cambozola Salad
with cranberries

serves 4

Dressing:
2 tbsp honey
1 tsp sea salt
freshly milled black pepper
50 ml cider vinegar
100 ml grape seed oil

300 g mixed salad leaves
400 g pears, halved lengthwise
2 tbsp lemon juice
250 g cambozola cheese
150 g sliced bread
15 g cooking butter
200 g walnuts, coarsely chopped
4 sprigs Italian herbs, chopped

1 spring onion
300 g dried cranberries
400 g black grapes

gl/ch/mi/nu/on

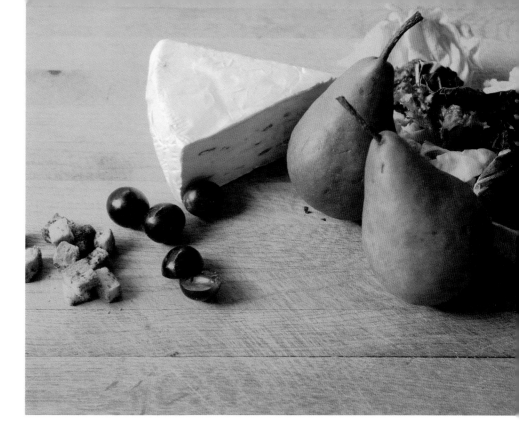

For the dressing, mix the honey, salt and pepper with the vinegar in a bowl and, stirring continuously, add the grape seed oil. Wash the salad leaves, drain and tear into bite-sized pieces. Core the halved pears and cut lengthwise into thin slices. Mix with a little lemon juice.
Cut the cambozola into 1 cm dice.
Cut the sliced bread into 1 cm dice and fry in the cooking butter until the croutons are brown and crispy. Drain on kitchen paper. Mix the salad leaves with the sliced pears, chopped nuts, diced cambozola, croutons and chopped herbs.
Just before serving add the dressing and toss. Arrange on four plates. Cut the spring onion diagonally into rounds and scatter over the salad together with the cranberries and grapes. Serve immediately.

Our tip: Ready-for-use mixed salad leaves with radicchio rosso, endive and frisee go particularly well with this dressing.

Chicory & Chestnut Salad
with fresh figs

serves 4

180 g mixed salad leaves

400 g chicory

2 red apples, halved

2 tbsp lemon juice

400 g chestnuts, peeled

10 g butter

200 g brown sugar

200 ml white wine

Dressing:

100 ml white balsamic vinegar

3/4 tbsp Dijon mustard

50 ml hazelnut oil

100 ml sunflower oil

1/2 tsp sea salt

freshly milled black pepper

3 fresh figs

60 g whole hazelnuts

mi/nu

Wash the salad leaves and drain thoroughly. Wash the chicory, remove 12 leaves, and set aside for the garnish. Halve the remaining chicory heads, cut out the core, and slice the chicory crosswise into fine strips. Mix with the salad leaves.

Quarter the apples and core. Cut into thin slices, toss in a little lemon juice and add to the salad leaves. Blanch the peeled chestnut and drain. Melt the butter in a small saucepan, add the sugar and caramelise. Remove from the heat and pour in the white wine. Add the chestnuts and cook over a medium heat until soft. Set aside to cool. Drain the chestnuts and reserve the cooking liquid.

For the dressing, blend the balsamic vinegar, mustard and cooking liquid in a bowl. Add the two oils, stirring continuously. Season to taste. Toss the leaf salad, chicory, apples and chestnuts in the dressing. Place four chicory leaves in a star shape on each plate, and arrange the mixed salad on top.

Trim the figs and cut into eight wedges. Arrange on the salad together with the whole hazelnuts. Serve immediately.

Our tip: Use deep-frozen, peeled chestnuts. Peeling fresh chestnuts takes a lot of time and effort.

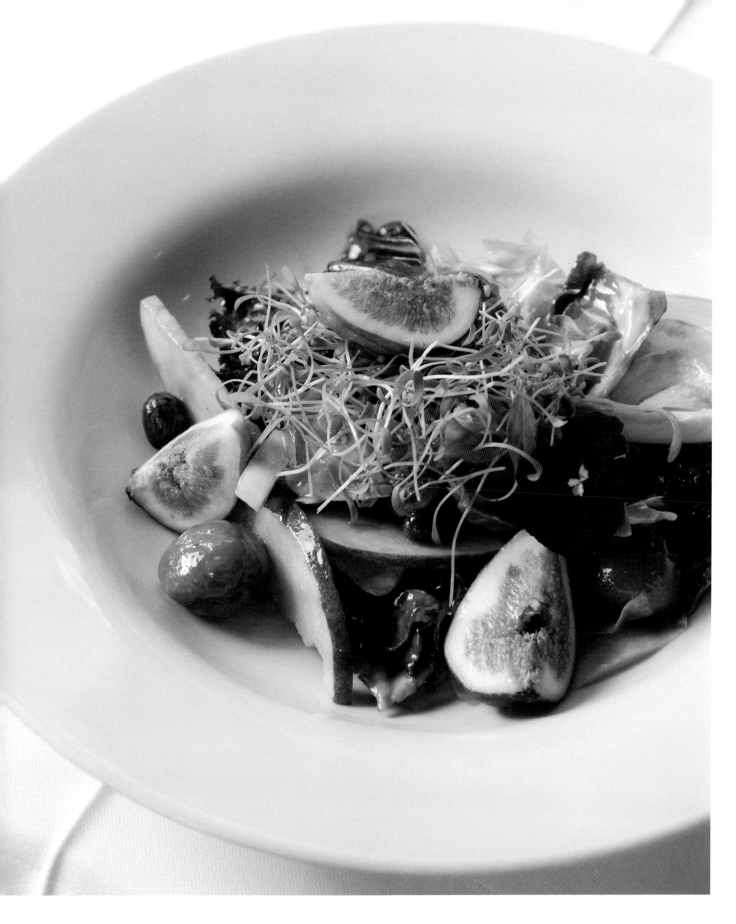

Celery & Star Fruit Salad
with pomegranate seeds and five spice powder

serves 4

Dressing:

5 tbsp white wine vinegar

50 g crème fraîche

1 tsp Dijon mustard

1 1/2 tsp five spice powder

4 tbsp sesame oil

8 tbsp sunflower oil

sea salt, freshly milled black pepper

3 star fruit (carambolas)

8 celery stalks

4 tbsp cashew nuts, roasted

1 ripe pomegranate

ce/mi

For the dressing, thoroughly mix the white wine vinegar, crème fraîche, Dijon mustard and five spice powder in a bowl and, stirring continuously, gradually add the two oils. Then add salt and pepper to taste. Wash the star fruit and cut into 2 mm slices. Wash the celery stalks and slice diagonally. Reserve the leaves for the garnish. Chop the cashew nuts very coarsely. Mix the cashews, celery and star fruit slices with the dressing and leave for 10 minutes.

Halve the pomegranate and, over a bowl, pound each half until the seeds come loose. Arrange the salad on plates, garnish with celery leaves; just before serving, scatter the pomegranate seeds over the salad.

Our tip: Pomegranates are ripe if their skin is slightly brown and somewhat rough to the touch. Their juice stains strongly. Five spice powder is a traditional spice mixture available in Chinese stores.

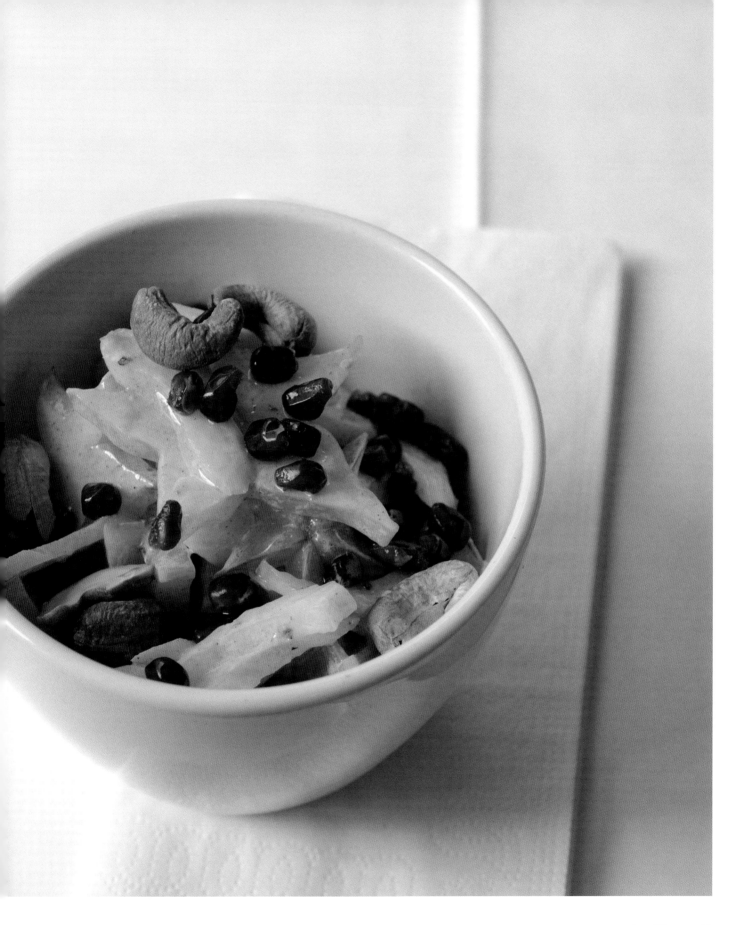

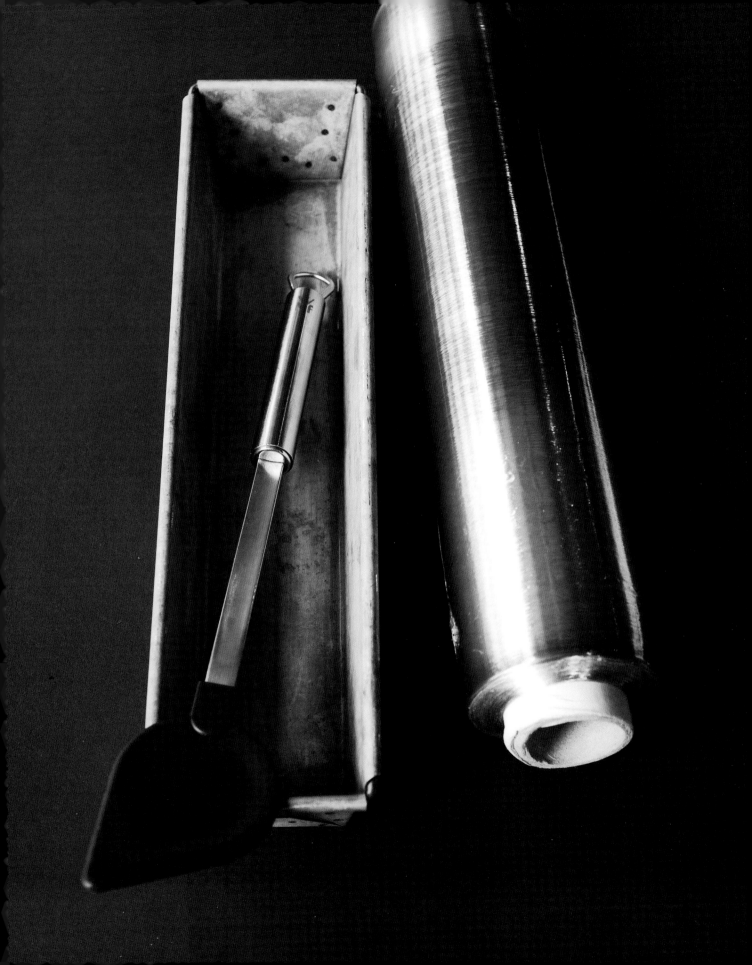

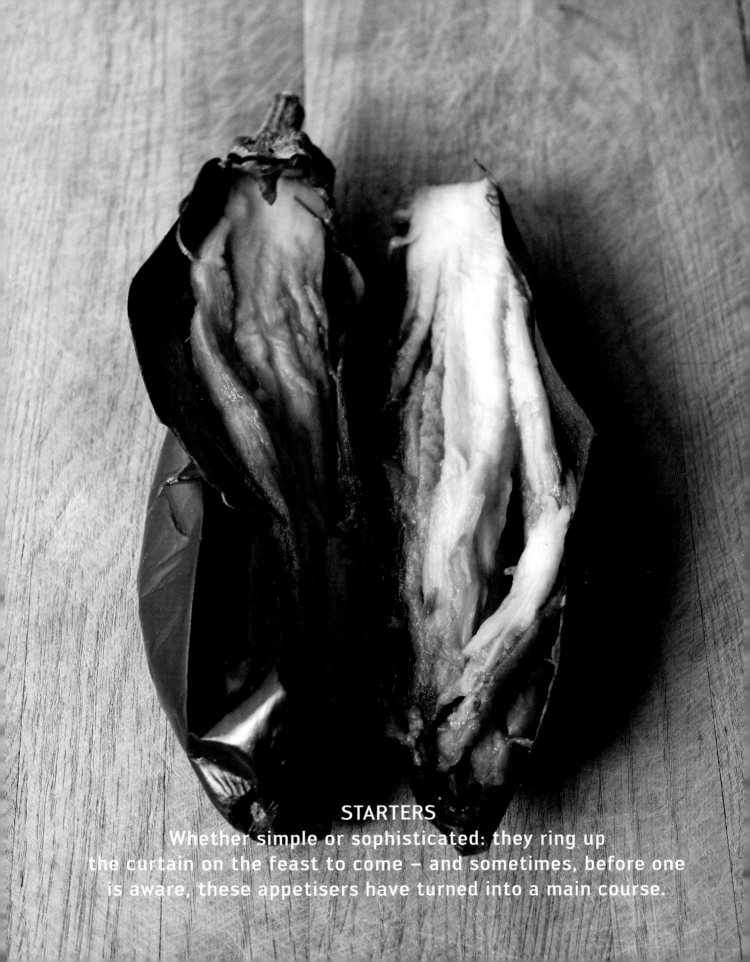

STARTERS

Whether simple or sophisticated: they ring up
the curtain on the feast to come – and sometimes, before one
is aware, these appetisers have turned into a main course.

Puff Pastry Triangles with Mushrooms
with fresh edible sprouts

serves 4

125 g puff pastry
1 egg yolk

220 g mixed mushrooms
(button, shiitake, oyster mushrooms)
1 spring onion
2 tbsp oil
200 ml brandy
70 g cherry tomatoes, halved
sea salt, freshly ground black pepper

a little Thai cress or other
edible sprouts

eg/gl/on

Roll out the puff pastry 3 cm thick and cut out four acute angled triangles with a side length of 16 cm. Refrigerate for 15 minutes. Place on a baking tray lined with baking paper and brush with egg yolk. Using a fork, make a diagonal line pattern in the yolk.

Preheat the oven to 220 °C. Place the triangles on a baking sheet and bake on the centre shelf till brown, leave to cool and then cut them open. Clean the mushrooms and cut into slices or strips. Split the spring onion and cut diagonally into fine strips.

Heat the oil in a stainless steel frying pan and fry the mushrooms over a high heat. Add the brandy and, using an extra long match, set alight. Take care not to get burned.

Take the pan off the heat, add the cherry tomatoes and spring onions, return to the heat and sauté briefly. Add salt and pepper to taste.

Place the puff pastry bases on four plates, arrange the mushrooms on them and place the upper half of the triangles on top. Garnish with Thai cress.

Our tip: Instead of mixed mushrooms, use chanterelles or porcini mushrooms.

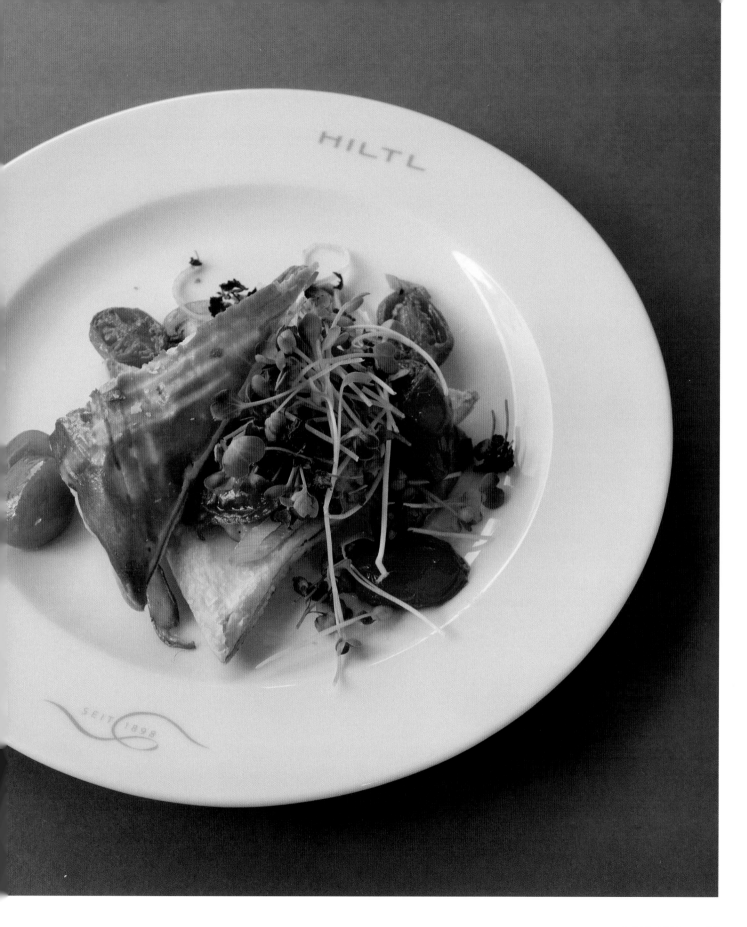

Stuffed Jalapeños
Hiltl's interpretation of jalapeño poppers

serves 4

16 jalapeños
180 g double cream cheese
1/2 lime, juice
1/2 tsp sea salt
1 pinch freshly ground black pepper
1 drop Tabasco

Coating:
300 g white flour
300 g breadcrumbs
4 eggs
1 tsp sea salt

1 l oil for deep frying

ch/eg/gl/mi

Wash the jalapeños, make an incision lengthwise and deseed carefully. The jalapeños must stay intact. In a bowl, mix the cream cheese with the lime juice, salt, pepper and Tabasco. Using a teaspoon, fill the jalapeños with this mixture.

Place the flour and the breadcrumbs in separate soup plates. Break the eggs into a further soup plate, season and then beat with a fork. Turn the stuffed jalapeños in the flour, then in the egg and finally in the breadcrumbs. Make sure while working that each jalapeño is fully coated with each ingredient. Draw the jalapeños through the egg and the breadcrumbs once again. Remove any egg-breadcrumb lumps that form on the breadcrumb plate.

Heat the oil in a tall cast-iron saucepan to 180 °C and fry the jalapeños until they are golden. Drain on kitchen paper and serve immediately.

Our tip: Do not deep-fry the jalapeños too long as they are liable to burst open and then the cheese would leak out. Serve the jalapeños with fresh guacamole (see recipe in Hiltl. Virtuoso Vegetarian – new revised and updated edition, 2006, page 24). In summer, the jalapeños served with a side salad make a light main course. Of course you could simply buy the jalapeños directly from the Hiltl buffet together with some Hiltl salad dressing from our takeaway.

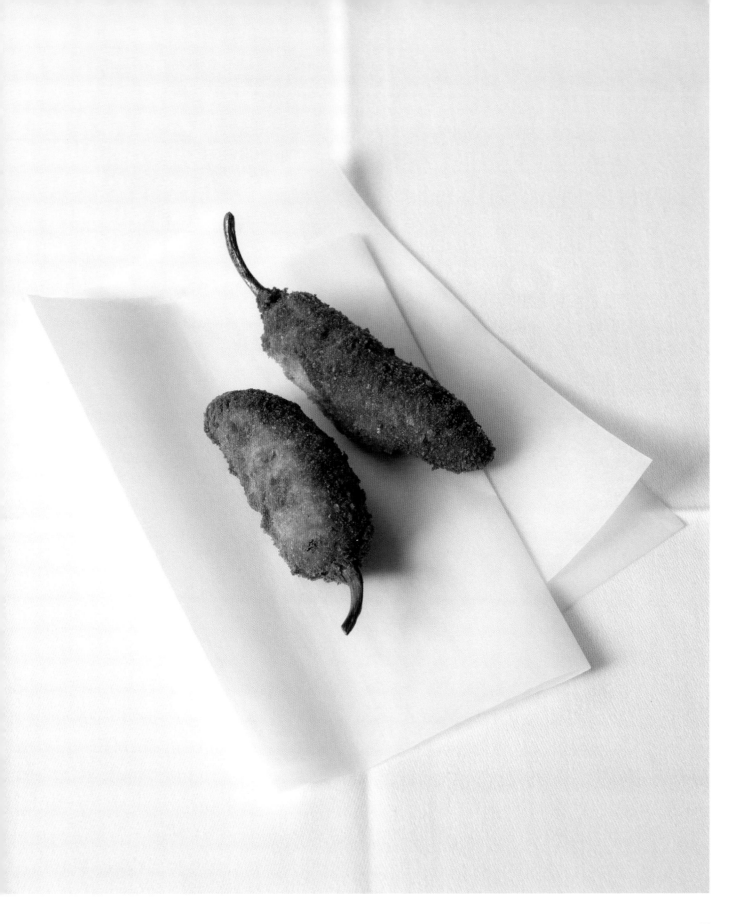

Crispy Tofu
in a spicy marinade

serves 4

360 g plain tofu

Marinade:
40 g soy sauce
20 g cornflour
160 g tomato ketchup
50 g Dijon mustard
1 pinch cayenne pepper
1 tsp madras curry, hot
4 tsp sea salt
20 g brown sugar
2 eggs

Coating:
250 g flour
200 g cornflakes
2 tbsp cornflour
4 tbsp soy sauce
2 eggs

1 l oil for deep frying

eg/gl/so

Cut the tofu into large slices 5 mm thick and halve diagonally. Mix all the ingredients for the marinade. Brush this mixture all over the tofu slices and leave to marinate overnight.

Place the flour in a soup plate, crush the cornflakes slightly in your hand and place in a second soup plate.

Break the eggs into a soup plate, stir the cornflour into the soy sauce, add to the eggs and beat with a fork.

Turn the marinated tofu slices in the flour, then in the egg and finally in the cornflakes. Make sure while working that each tofu slice is fully coated with each ingredient. Crispy tofu must be prepared just before deep frying because the cornflakes cling better to the tofu if they are really dry.

Heat the oil in a tall cast-iron saucepan to 160 °C and fry the crispy tofu slices until they are golden. Drain on kitchen paper.

Our tip: We serve crispy tofu with a salad bouquet in a cucumber ring, with a little more salad it makes a good main course in summer. Children love crispy tofu.

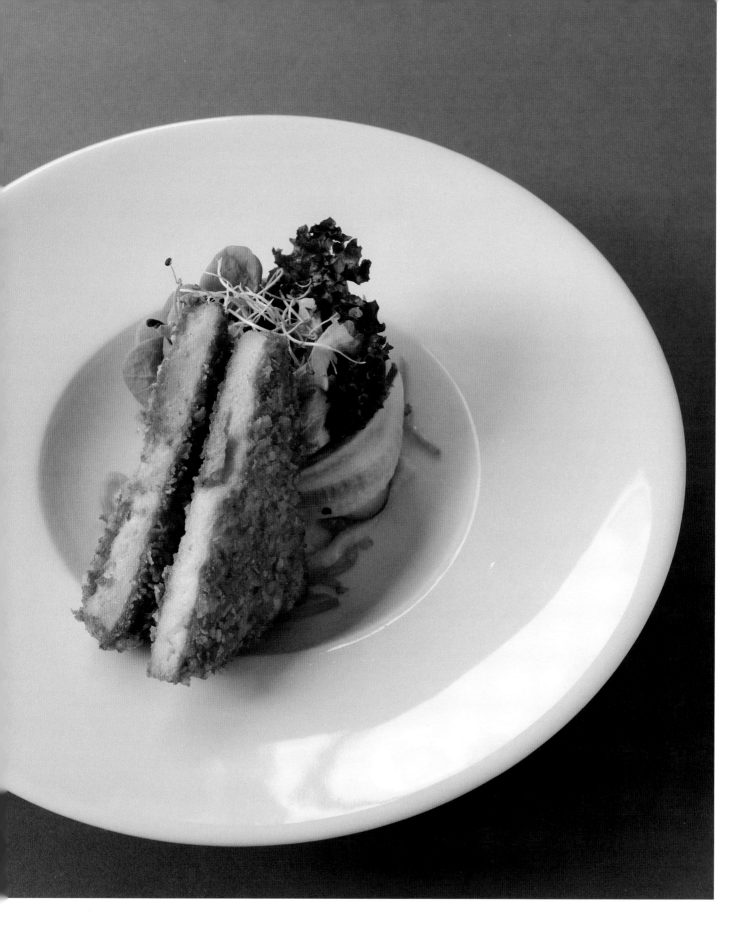

Aubergine Caviar
less pricey than the original

serves 4

1 kg aubergines

1/2 bunch fresh coriander, chopped

3 sprigs flat-leaf parsley, chopped

1 clove garlic, crushed

1 tsp ground cumin

1 tsp paprika

2 pinches cayenne pepper

2 tbsp lemon juice

3 tbsp olive oil

sea salt, freshly milled black pepper

ga

Preheat the oven to 200 °C. Place a cup of water in the oven and arrange the whole aubergines on a baking sheet and leave in the oven for 1 hour.

Remove the aubergines and allow to cool, halve lengthwise, scrape out the flesh and seeds with a soup spoon and place in a bowl. Blend the herbs and spices with the lemon juice and olive oil to form a paste, add to the aubergines and mix thoroughly. Add salt and pepper to taste. Well covered, aubergine caviar will keep in the fridge for 2 days.

Our tip: Serve aubergine caviar with pita bread or use as a topping for crostini.

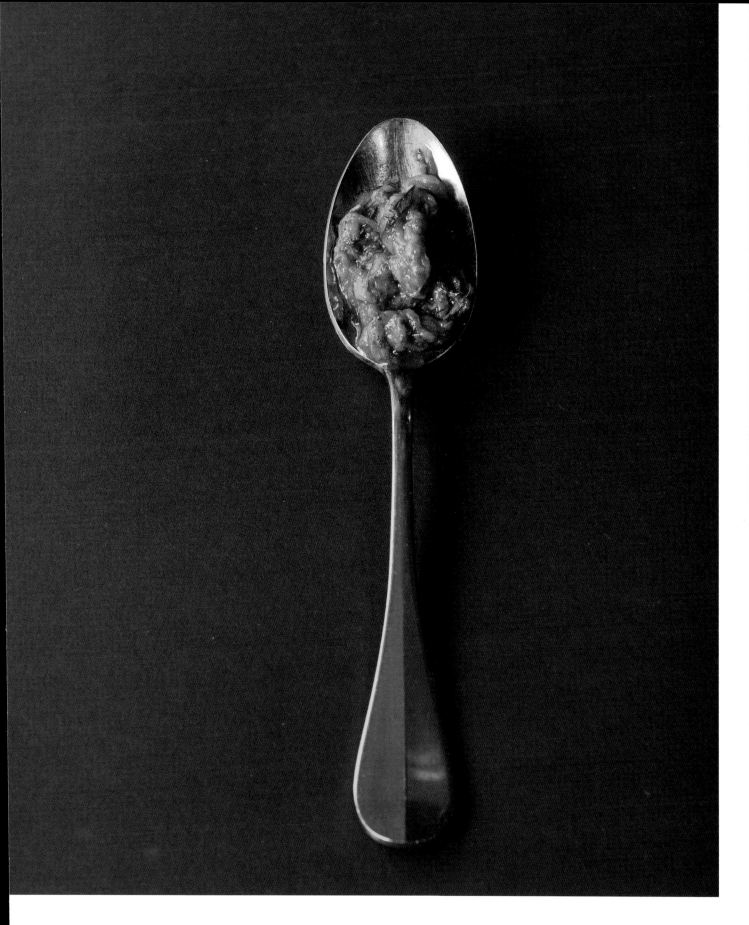

Date & Cheese Mousse
with fresh ginger

serves 4

1 small green chilli, deseeded

100 g dates, pitted

1 medium onion, chopped

$1/2$ tsp sea salt

2 tbsp brown sugar

3 tbsp lemon juice

$1/2$ bunch fresh coriander, chopped

1 tsp jeera, ground

1 tbsp fresh ginger, grated

2 tbsp tomato purée

2 tbsp sultanas, chopped

250 g brie

150 g double cream cheese

ch/mi/on

Chop the chilli, cut the dates into 5 mm dice and mix with the other ingredients. Cut the rind off the brie, chop the brie and mix with the date mixture.

Our tip: Serve as quenelles with salad. This mousse can also be used as a vegetable dip, a topping for crostini, and as a garnish for a cheese platter.

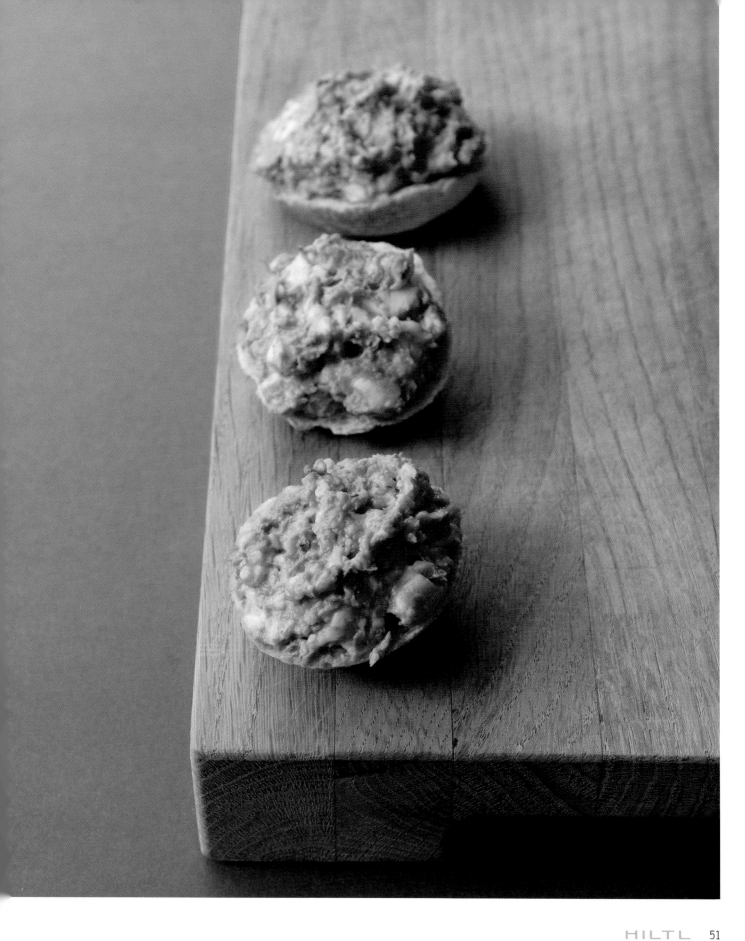

Lentil Terrine
with fresh truffles

serves 4

90 g red lentils

60 g beluga lentils

50 g vegetable brunoise

(celeriac, carrots, leeks)

10 g onions, finely chopped

120 ml cream

22 g agar agar

100 ml cold water

1 tbsp horseradish cream

2 tbsp truffle oil

1 tsp paprika

1 – 2 drops Tabasco

sea salt, freshly milled black pepper

1 walnut-sized fresh truffle

ce/mi/on

Pick over the two types of lentils separately, rinse, drain, cook al dente and drain again. Thoroughly mix the brunoise, chopped onion and cooked lentils in a bowl.
Bring the cream to a boil.
Stir the agar agar into the cup of cold water, pour into the cream and boil for 3 minutes stirring continuously. Add to the lentils and mix well. Add the horseradish cream, truffle oil and paprika, mix again and add Tabasco, salt and pepper to taste.
Line a terrine dish (25 x 6 cm) with cling foil as smoothly as possible, fill with the lentil mixture, press down firmly, cover and chill for 2 hours.
Turn out the terrine onto a chopping board and, using a knife dipped in hot water, cut into 2 cm thick slices. Arrange on plates and cover with shaved truffles.
Serve with a salad bouquet.

Our tip: Agar agar is a vegetarian starch made from red algae. For those who prefer a fruity flavour, serve the terrine with cranberry & apple sauce (page 123). In this case leave out the truffle oil and truffles, as the sauce would smother the truffle flavour.

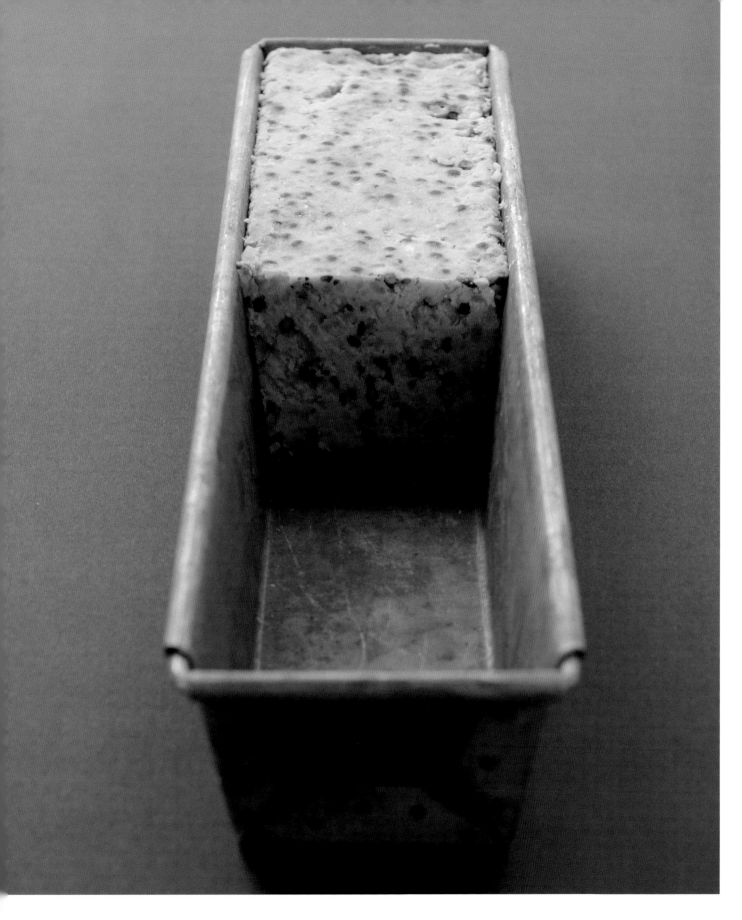

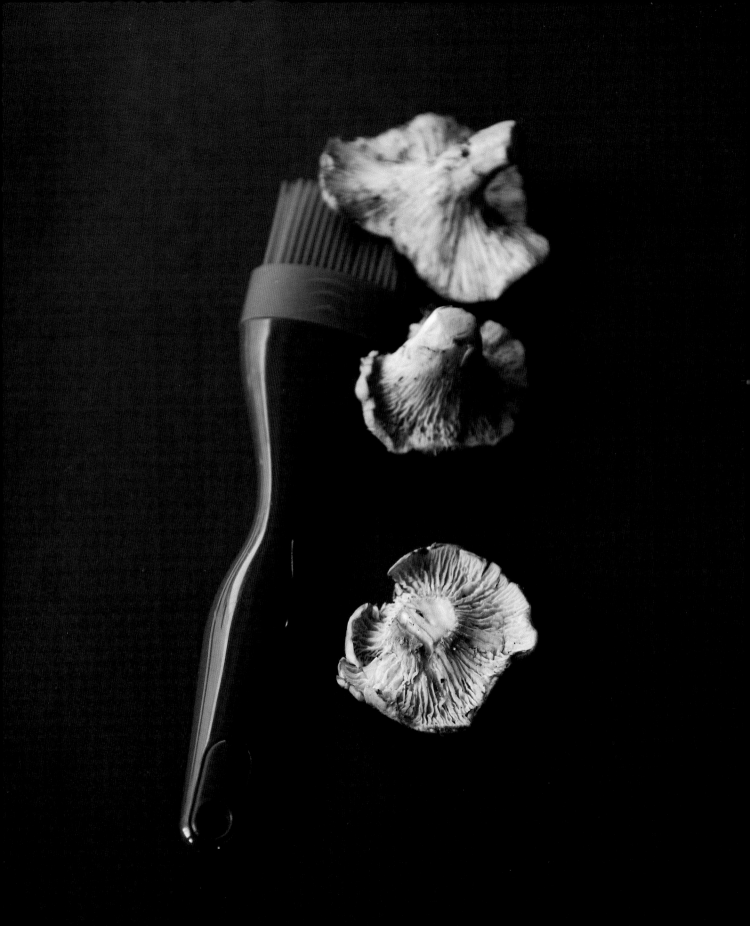

VEGETABLES & MUSHROOMS
Whether steamed or raw:
With just a little culinary skill whatever grows and
ripens in gardens, fields and forests
can become the focal point of any meal.

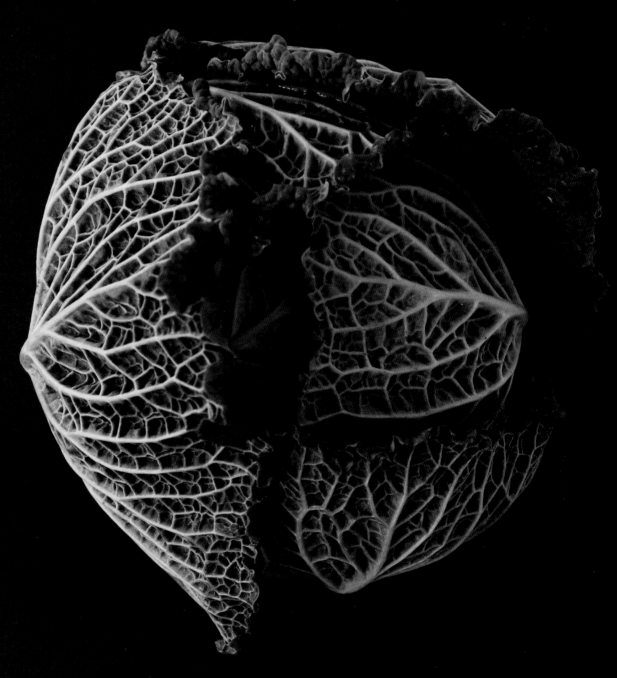

Indian Jalfrezi
recipe supplied by Joe from Madras

serves 4

150 g cauliflower, washed

1 carrot, peeled

1 medium courgette

1 small green pepper

2 onions, in rings

4 tbsp sunflower oil

1/2 tsp fennel seeds

1 bay leaf

1 tsp cumin seeds

1 star anise

1 small green chilli, chopped

1 clove garlic, crushed

2 pinches ground cardamom

1 pinch ground cloves

1/2 tsp ground ginger

2 pinches turmeric

1/2 tsp ground cumin

1 tsp garam masala

1 tsp ground coriander

1 pinch cayenne pepper

sea salt, freshly milled pepper

1 tbsp lemon juice

1 tbsp grated coconut

1 tbsp tomato purée

400 ml tomato juice

300 ml water

100 g peas, fresh or deep frozen

100 g plain yoghurt

sea salt, freshly milled pepper

1 bunch coriander, finely chopped

Divide the cauliflower into florets. Halve the carrot and courgette lengthwise and cut diagonally into 1 cm slices. Deseed the pepper and cut into 1.5 cm pieces.

Heat the oil, add the fennel seeds, bay leaf, cumin seeds and star anise, then sauté until they release their aroma and become fragrant. Add onion rings and sweat until soft.

Mix the chilli, garlic and remaining spices together with the lemon juice and grated coconut to form a paste.

Add this paste and the tomato purée to the onion rings and cook for a further 2 minutes. Pour in the tomato juice and reduce somewhat, add the water and simmer for 10 minutes. Blend the sauce with a mixing wand. Add the sliced carrot and cook al dente. Then add the peppers, cauliflower and sliced courgette. Simmer till tender.

Finally add the peas, bring to a boil and remove from the heat. Stir in the yoghurt and season to taste. Serve garnished with coriander.

Our tip: Serve with basmati rice (see recipe in Hiltl. Virtuoso Vegetarian – new revised and updated edition, 2006, page 116) or with chapati (see recipe in Hiltl. Virtuoso Vegetarian – new revised and updated edition, 2006, page 106).

ga/mi/on

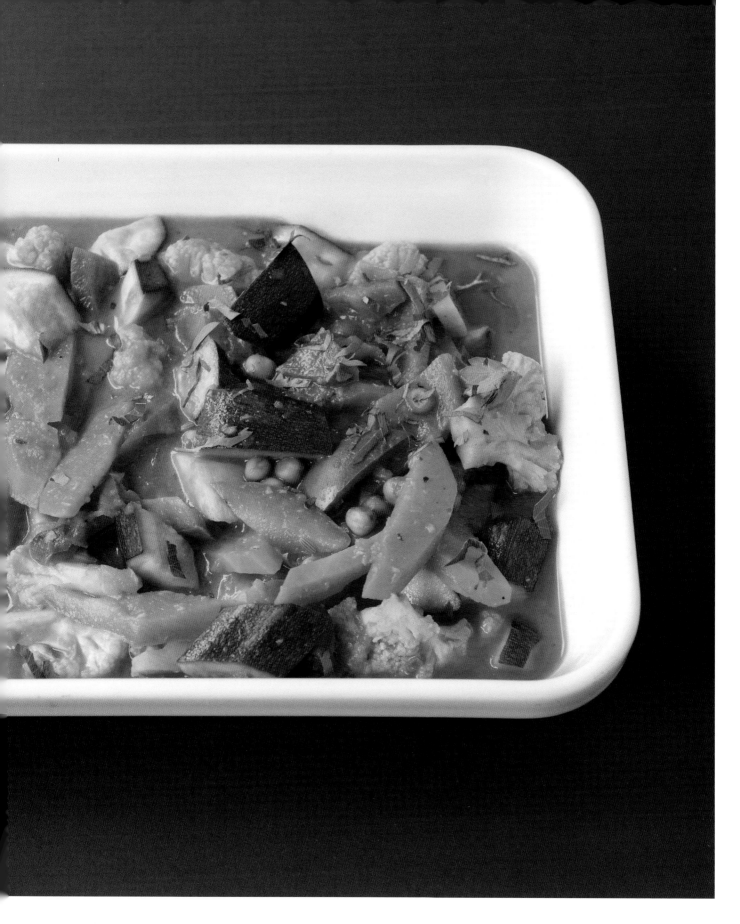

Fresh Chanterelles
with cognac sauce

serves 4

600 g fresh chanterelles

25 g cooking butter

100 g onions, chopped

1 tsp madras curry, mild

1 tsp black pepper, freshly milled

100 ml cognac

100 ml white wine

400 ml stock

30 ml cream

1 tbsp cornflour

4 tbsp white wine

sea salt, freshly milled pepper

4 tbsp fresh herbs, chopped

(parsley, a little thyme, chervil)

mi/on

Clean the chanterelles, if necessary halve or quarter them. Heat the cooking butter and fry the chanterelles over a high heat. Add the onions and sauté until transparent, add the spices.

Pour in the cognac and white wine, then add the stock and cream. Bring to the boil.

Mix the cornflour with a little white wine, stir into the sauce and simmer until the sauce has the desired consistency. Season to taste and garnish with the chopped herbs.

Our tip: Serve with Helmut's Caesar dumplings (page 102), rösti or tagliatelle. The chanterelles may be flambéed if desired, see page 72.

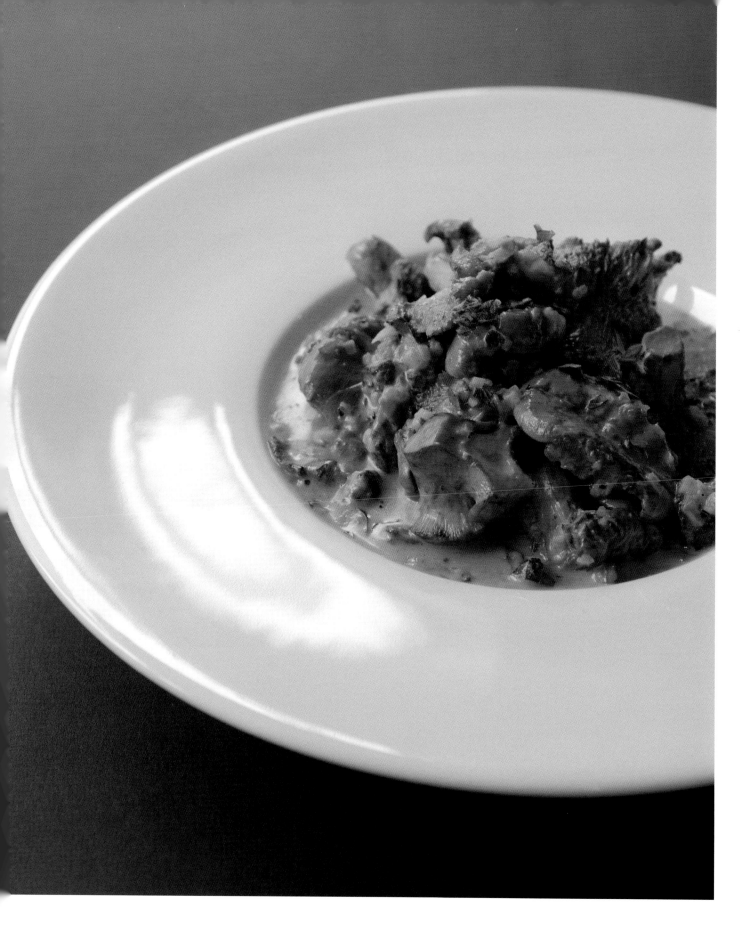

Feta & Saffron Artichokes

with fresh tomatoes

serves 4

650 g artichoke bottoms, deep frozen

2 tomatoes

2 tbsp olive oil

1 onion, chopped

20 g fresh herbs, chopped

(rosemary, thyme, oregano, marjoram)

25 g flat-leaf parsley

1/2 sachet saffron powder

2 tsp saffron threads

1/2 tsp freshly milled black pepper

200 ml white wine

600 ml vegetable stock

3/4 tbsp cornflour

350 g feta cheese

1/2 bunch flat-leaf parsley,

chiffonade cut

ch/mi/on

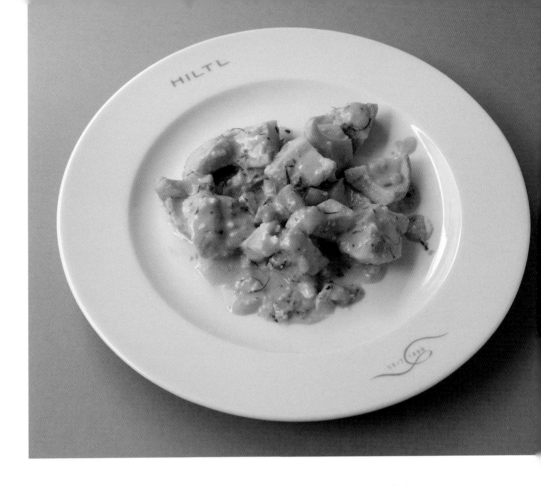

Cut the artichoke bottoms into six triangles. Snick the top of the tomatoes, plunge them briefly into boiling water, slip off their skins and then dice.

Heat the olive oil and sweat the onions. Add chopped herbs, saffron powder, saffron threads and pepper. Stir well.

Pour in the white wine and stock. Add the artichokes and simmer until tender. Mix the cornflour with a little water and stir into the sauce.

Crumble the feta and add to the sauce together with the diced tomatoes. Bring up to the boil.

Serve sprinkled with parsley chiffonade.

Our tip: Serve on spinach noodles.

Saffron from Switzerland

The saffron crocus belongs to the family of the Iridaceae and has been grown in the Orient for more than 3,500 years. The *Crocus sativus* was certainly cultivated by the early civilizations in Mesopotamia, "the land between the rivers" Tigris and Euphrates. There is no absolute evidence to pinpoint the origin of saffron, but it is assumed that it originated in either eastern Iran, western Himalaya or Kashmir. Certainly saffron was brought to Greece from these areas in ancient times; it was first documented there by Theophrastus (370 – 285 BC). From there saffron became popular in the Roman Empire. In the 8th century the Arabs introduced saffron cultivation into Spain and, via France, it was introduced into Switzerland. By the 14th century saffron was being planted in the village of Mund in canton Valais. It is assumed that either mercenaries or pilgrims acquired the crocus corms in Spain (knowing that by exporting them they risked the death penalty). The village of Mund is the only place in Switzerland where the age-old tradition of cultivating this prized and costly spice has been kept alive.

In Mund saffron is hand harvested from mid October and early November, with the main harvest between 20th and 30th October. It is a long, delicate job because the stigmas (each flower has three of them) have to be plucked out of the calyx by hand. They are then dried in a shady, airy place, where they lose 80 % of their weight. 390 saffron threads weigh about one gram; thus the stigmas of 120,000 flowers have to be harvested to yield one kilogram of saffron. Naturally, the price of saffron reflects the time and effort invested. Currently one kilogram of saffron costs between 14,000 and 15,000 Swiss francs (€ 9,000 – € 10,000, £ 8,300 – £ 9,000, $ 12,500 – $ 13,500). Going by weight, this makes saffron the world's most expensive spice.

Saffron from Mund is more pungent than any other saffron. This phenomenon has not yet been explained in scientific terms. It is assumed, however, that it is a result of the dual cultivation of the fields around Mund, which is unique. Winter rye is grown on the same fields as the saffron. The cereal is harvested between end July and early August – by hand with scythe and sickle. In this way air is introduced into the soil in which the saffron corms have been planted. The following year's rye crop is sown in September, before the saffron flowers appear. In winter, the shoots of the new winter rye will already have reached a height of about 10 cm and thus help protect the corms against the cold as they rest under the soil.

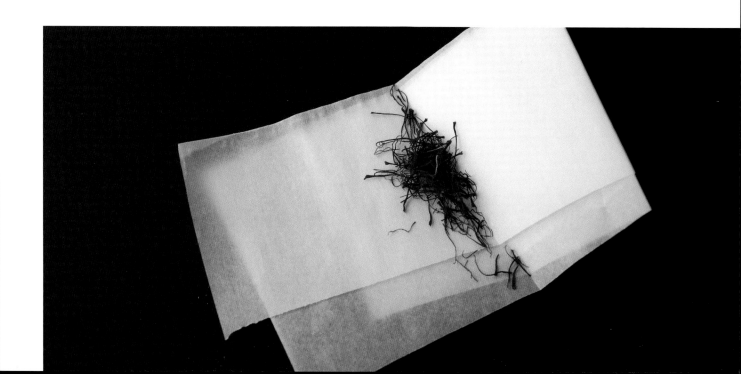

Vanilla Carrots
delicious and distinctive

serves 4

4 carrots

1 spring onion

2 tbsp oil

1 bay leaf

300 ml orange juice

400 ml vegetable stock

150 ml cream

1/2 vanilla pod

80 g butter, diced and chilled

1 – 2 tsp cornflour

a little cayenne pepper

sea salt

1/2 bunch parsley, chopped

mi/on

Peel the carrots and cut diagonally into 5 mm slices. Cut the green part of the spring onion diagonally into fine rings and set aside; finely chop the white part of the onion.

Heat the oil, add the chopped spring onion, bay leaf and sliced carrots and sauté. Pour in the orange juice. Glaze the carrots until the orange juice has reduced completely and the carrots are tender. Remove the carrots and cool. Discard the bay leaf. Add the stock and cream to the reduced juice.

Split the vanilla pod, scoop out the seeds and add to the sauce. Leave to simmer for a few minutes. Whisk in the chilled diced butter. Stir the cornflour into a little water, add to the sauce, stir and bring to the boil. Return the carrots to the sauce and bring up to the boil again. Season to taste with cayenne pepper and salt.

Garnish with the green spring onion rings and the chopped parsley.

Our tip: Serve with whole rice or dill rice with lentils (page 100).

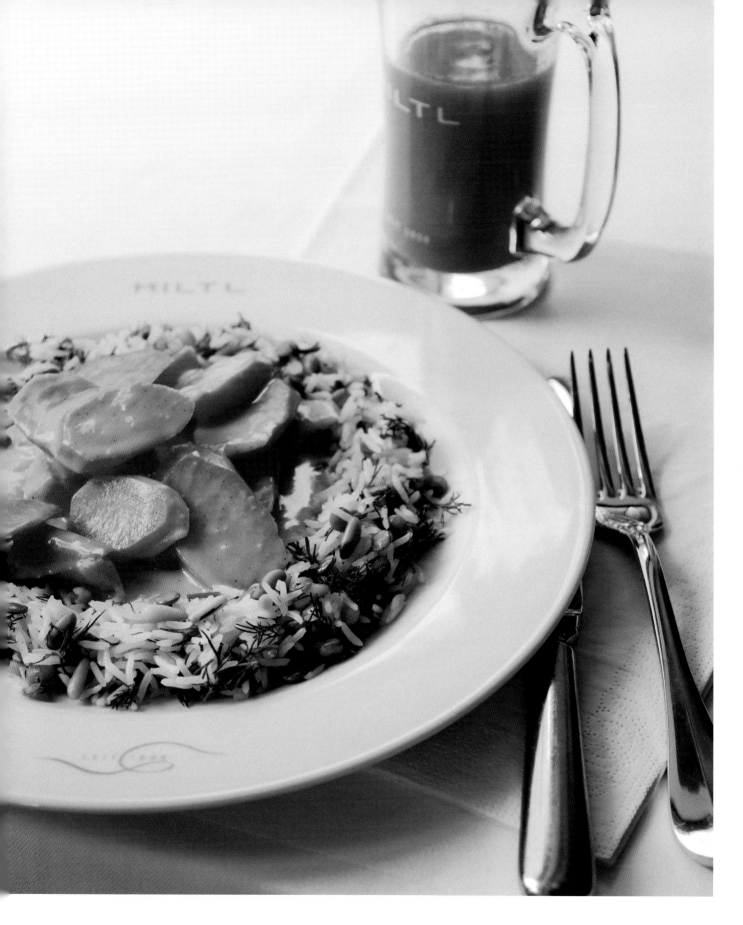

Gorgonzola Courgettes
with freshly diced tomatoes

serves 4

1 tomato

4 courgettes

2 tbsp olive oil

1 onion, chopped

1 bay leaf

1 sprig oregano

1 sprig marjoram

200 ml white wine

300 ml vegetable stock

200 ml cream

1 tsp cornflour

150 g gorgonzola

2 pinches milled white pepper

1 tbsp lemon juice

sea salt, freshly milled pepper

1/2 bunch mixed Italian herbs

ch/mi/on

Snick the top of the tomatoes, plunge them briefly into boiling water, slip off their skins and then cut into 1 cm dice. Cut the courgettes diagonally into 1 cm slices. Heat the olive oil in a frying pan and sauté the onions, bay leaf and herb sprigs until the onion is transparent. Pour in the white wine, stock and cream. Add the gorgonzola, white pepper and lemon juice and bring to the boil.

Discard the bay leaf and herb sprigs, mix briefly and reduce until the sauce has the desired consistency. Season to taste.

Add the courgettes to the sauce and cook until they are al dente. Before serving, chop the mixed herbs and scatter over the courgettes together with the diced tomatoes.

Our tip: Serve with tagliatelle.

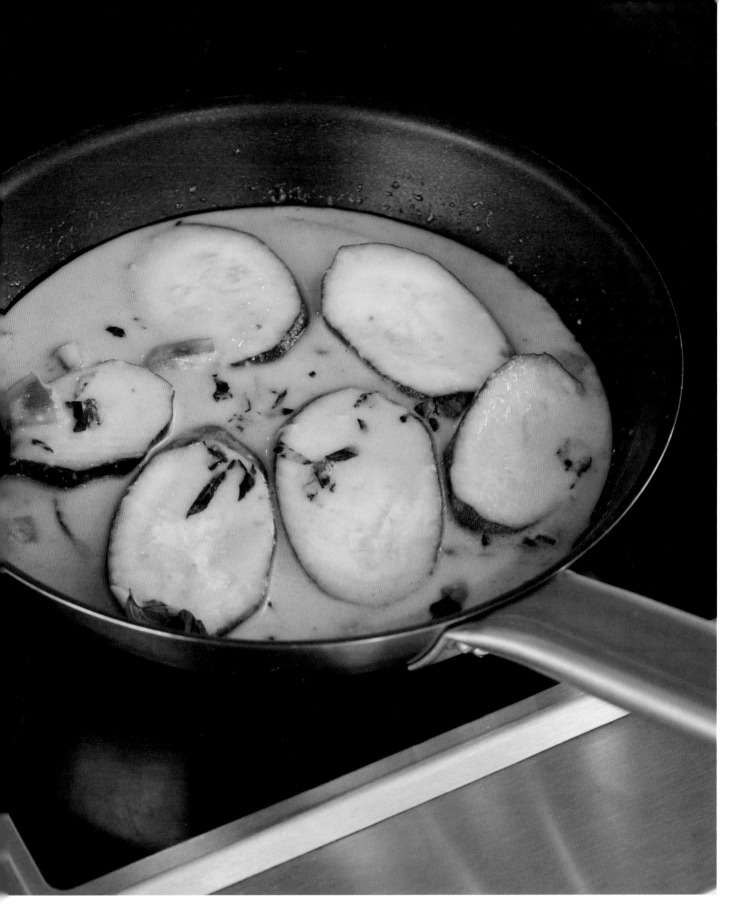

Carrot & Plum Tagine
recipe contributed by Rachid's mother

serves 4

6 carrots, peeled

3 tbsp oil

2 onions, chopped

1 1/2 cloves garlic, crushed

1/2 tsp ground ginger

1 tsp saffron threads

1/2 tsp milled black pepper

1/2 tsp ground cinnamon

1/2 tsp ground coriander

1/2 tsp ground cumin

1 tsp sea salt

1 tbsp honey

1 l vegetable stock

50 g whole almonds, peeled

1 tbsp rose water

150 g prunes, pitted and halved

sea salt, freshly milled pepper

a few whole almonds, peeled

ga/on

Cut the carrots diagonally into 5 mm slices. Heat the oil in a high saucepan, add the onions and sauté till they are transparent. Turn down the heat and add the garlic, spices, salt and honey.

Add the carrots, stir thoroughly, pour in the stock and boil until the carrots are just tender.

Add the almonds, rose water and prunes, bring everything up to the boil again and season to taste with salt and pepper.

Serve with couscous and garnish with whole, peeled almonds.

Our tip: Rose water is available in chemists and Turkish shops. For the couscous recipe see Hiltl. Virtuoso Vegetarian – new revised and updated edition, 2006, page 143.

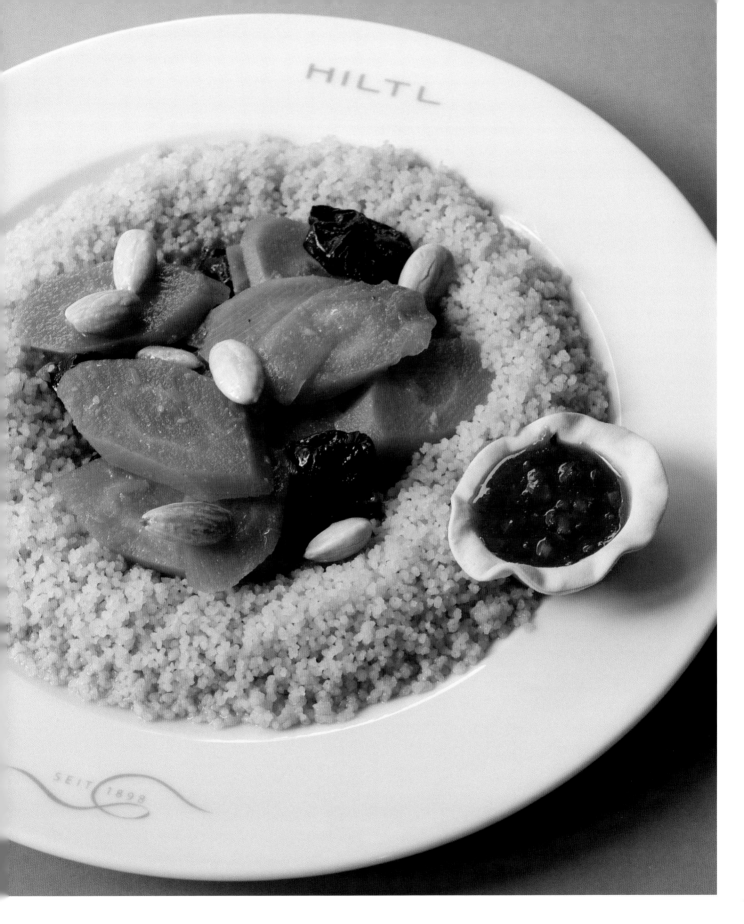

Malaysian Rendang
made in a wok

serves 4

250 g shiitake mushrooms

500 g aubergines

3 courgettes

300 g savoy cabbage

150 ml oil

Sauce:

2 tbsp oil

1 star anise

70 g green Thai curry paste

(page 118)

5 kaffir lime leaves

1 stem lemon grass

1 tbsp tamarind paste

6 tbsp rice vinegar

$1^1/_2$ tsp turmeric

$1^1/_2$ tsp paprika

$1^1/_2$ tsp ground coriander

3 tbsp grated coconut

800 ml coconut milk

$^1/_2$ bunch fresh coriander, chopped

3 tbsp soy sauce

2 tsp Jaffna curry powder

2 tsp sea salt

40 g palm sugar

700 ml water

4 tbsp oil

sea salt, freshly milled pepper

ga/gl/pe/so

Cut off the end of the mushroom stems and, if they are hard, discard the entire stem. Slice the mushrooms. Halve the aubergines lengthwise, cut diagonally into 1 cm slices and sprinkle with salt. Set aside for 30 minutes and then pat dry with kitchen paper. Halve the courgettes lengthwise and cut diagonally into 1 cm slices. Cut the savoy cabbage into 2 cm pieces.

Heat the oil in a wok and fry the aubergines until they are browned. Drain on kitchen paper. Heat 2 tbsp oil in a separate pan, fry the star anise until it smells fragrant. Add all the other ingredients and the water, stir and then simmer for 15 minutes.

For the vegetables, heat 4 tbsp oil in a wok. First fry the mushrooms till they are browned, then add the courgettes and stir-fry for a further 4-5 minutes. Then add the cabbage, lower the heat and cook until the cabbage just starts to wilt.

Add the sauce and the fried aubergine slices and then season to taste with salt and freshly milled pepper.

Our tip: Jaffna curry powder is very hot and has a brown-red colour. It is available in Indian shops; kaffir lime leaves in Thai shops. If you do not have a wok, use a large frying pan. Serve with perfume or basmati rice and rinsed soy bean sprouts.

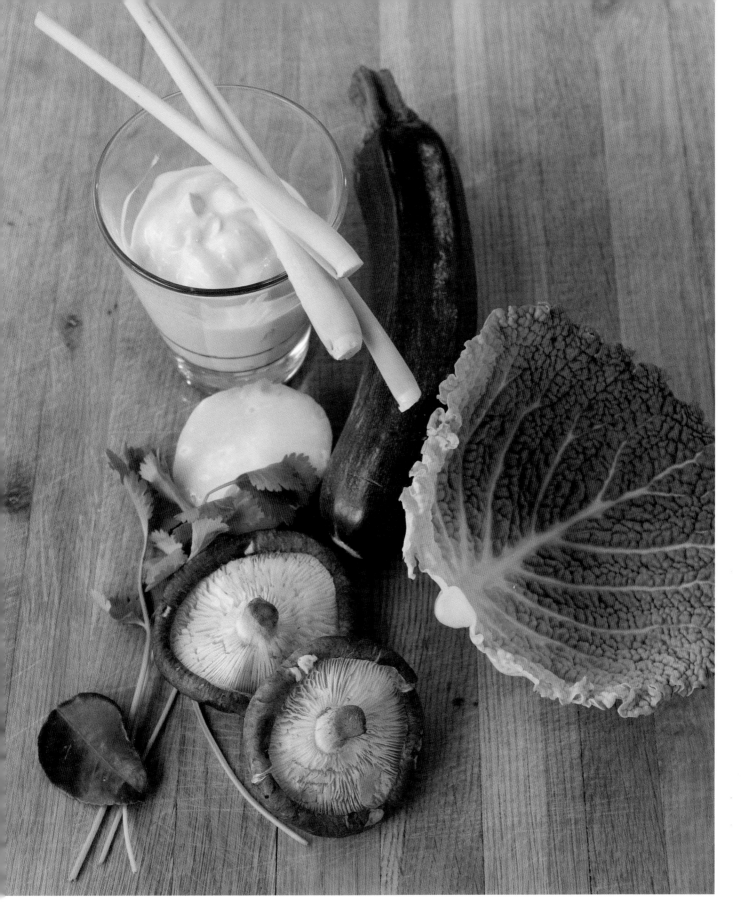

Butternut Squash
in Tomato & Almond Sauce
with Italian herbs

serves 4

500 g butternut squash, peeled and
deseeded
10 cherry tomatoes

3 tbsp olive oil
1 onion, chopped
1 clove garlic, crushed
100 g almond purée
200 ml white wine
100 ml vegetable stock
600 ml tomato juice
1 pinch milled white pepper
1 tsp paprika
1 tsp sea salt
30 g Italian herbs, chopped
sea salt, freshly milled pepper

40 g almond slivers, toasted

ga/on

Cut the butternut squash into 1.5 cm cubes. Halve the cherry tomatoes lengthwise. Heat the olive oil, add the onion and garlic and sauté for 5 minutes. Add the almond purée and mix thoroughly.

Pour in the white wine, stock and tomato juice, and turn the heat down to medium. Add the spices and salt. Blend the sauce and add the chopped herbs.

Add the squash and simmer till tender. Serve garnished with the cherry tomatoes and toasted almond slivers.

Our tip: The butternut squash belongs to the Cucurbita moschata family and a Muscade de Provence pumpkin can be used instead. Serve with long grain rice.

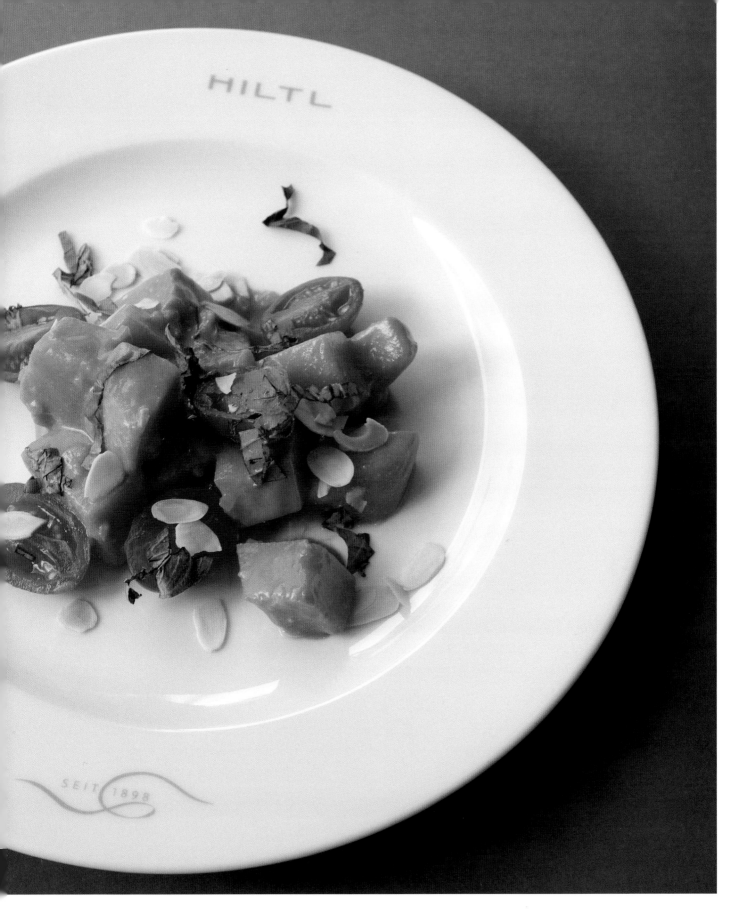

Cauliflower in a Green Pepper Sauce
can also be flambéed

serves 4

1 cauliflower, washed

5 tbsp green peppercorns, pickled

3 tbsp sunflower oil

1 onion, chopped

1 bay leaf

$^1/_2$ tsp nutmeg, grated

$^1/_2$ tsp white pepper, milled

1 tsp sea salt

1 tbsp lemon juice

200 ml white wine

200 ml vegetable stock

400 ml cream

20 g butter

1 tbsp cornflour, if required

sea salt, freshly milled pepper

1 bunch parsley, chopped

mi/on

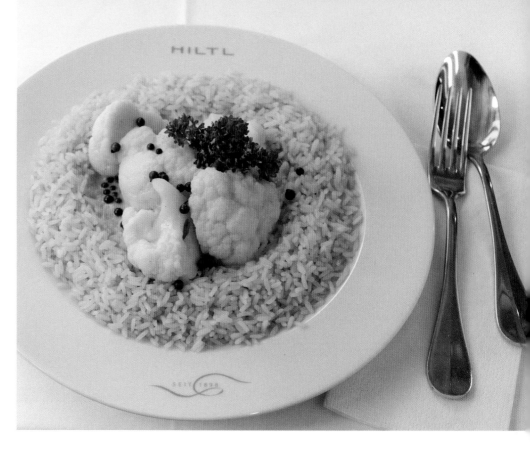

Divide the cauliflower into 4 cm florets, blanch in salted water, refresh in iced water and drain. Crush 1 tbsp of the peppercorns. Heat the oil and briefly sauté the crushed and whole peppercorns. Add the onion and bay leaf and sauté until the onion is transparent. Add the nutmeg, pepper, salt and lemon juice, stir well.

Pour in the white wine and vegetable stock, add the cream and butter, then bring to the boil. Lower the heat to medium, add the cauliflower and simmer until the florets are al dente.

If desired, the sauce may be thickened with a little cornflour. Season to taste with salt and pepper. Serve garnished with chopped parsley.

Our tip: As soon as the peppercorns have been sautéed, add 50 ml cognac and flambé. Draw the pan off the heat till the flame dies down, then replace it and continue as in the recipe above. Prepare this dish in a stainless steel casserole, as such pans are particularly suitable for flambéing. Use an extra long match to set the cognac alight and take care that the flame does not scorch or burn you.

Pepper is won from the fruit of the pepper vine *(Piper nigrum)*. Pepper is native to India, particularly the Malabar Coast. Some 1,000 years ago cultivation of the pepper plant became more widespread, reaching as far as present-day Indonesia and Malaysia. Today, the main pepper producing countries are Vietnam, Indonesia, India, Brazil and Malaysia.

White pepper is fully ripe pepper with the skin of the seed removed. The ripe red pepper berries are soaked in running water for several days (retting) during which the flesh of the fruit decomposes. Any remaining skin and flesh is then removed mechanically and the naked seed dried.

Black pepper is made from the unripe (green) berries of the pepper plant just before they begin to ripen (yellow-orange). They are dried and as the fruit shrinks they become black and wrinkled.

Green pepper is also made from unripe berries harvested early. To ensure that the peppercorns retain their original green colour, the fresh berries are either preserved in brine or dried – either rapid high temperature drying or freeze drying.

Pink pepper is made from ripe red pepper berries and, like green pepper, the peppercorns are generally preserved in either brine or vinegar. However, pickled red pepper is rare, and in its dried form it is very rare indeed. The pink peppercorns readily available are not pepper at all, but the peppery fruits of the Brazilian pepper tree *(Schinus terebinthifolius)*.

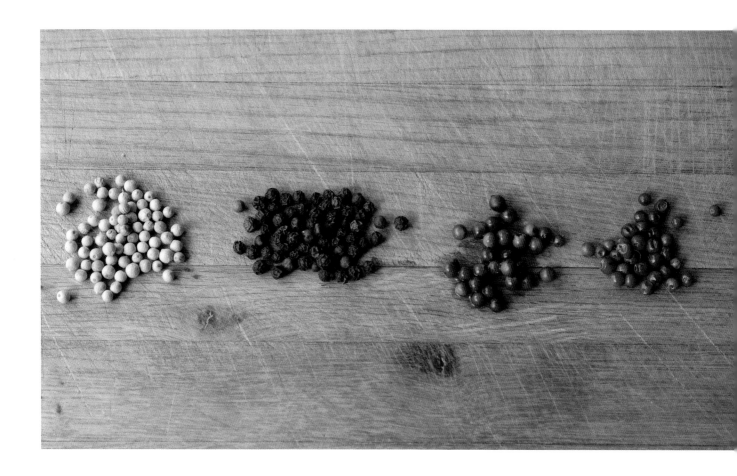

Black Curry from Southern India
with coconut chutney

serves 4

3 aubergines

4 tbsp oil

2 tsp brown mustard seeds

5 tsp fennel seeds

1 1/2 tsp cumin seeds

20 curry leaves

3 onions, sliced into rings

2 tbsp ground coriander

3 1/2 tsp black pepper, crushed

1 tsp cayenne pepper

8 tbsp grated coconut

1 1/2 tbsp tamarind paste

500 g chopped tomatoes (can)

2 cloves garlic, crushed

1 bunch coriander, sliced

1 1/2 tsp sea salt

2.5 l water

500 g potatoes, peeled

5 tbsp oil

sea salt, freshly milled pepper

1/2 bunch fresh coriander, sliced

ga/on

Quarter the aubergines and cut into 2 cm cubes. Sprinkle with salt and set aside for 30 minutes. Then pat dry with kitchen paper.

Heat the oil and sauté the mustard seeds, fennel seeds and cumin seeds until they burst open. Add the curry leaves and sauté briefly, then add the onion rings and sauté until they are transparent.

Now add the spices, grated coconut, tamarind paste, tomatoes, garlic, fresh coriander and salt, and continue sautéing until they form a paste. Add the water, bring to the boil, and reduce the sauce to 1.5 l. Finally blend with a mixing wand.

Cut the potatoes into 2 cm cubes, cook in salt water until tender, drain and add to the sauce.

Heat the oil and brown the aubergines. Add three-quarters of them to the sauce. Season to taste. Serve garnished with fresh sliced coriander and the remaining aubergine cubes.

Our tip: Serve the black curry with lemon rice and coconut chutney (see recipes in Hiltl. Virtuoso Vegetarian – new revised and updated edition, 2006, pages 118 and 158) and papadums.

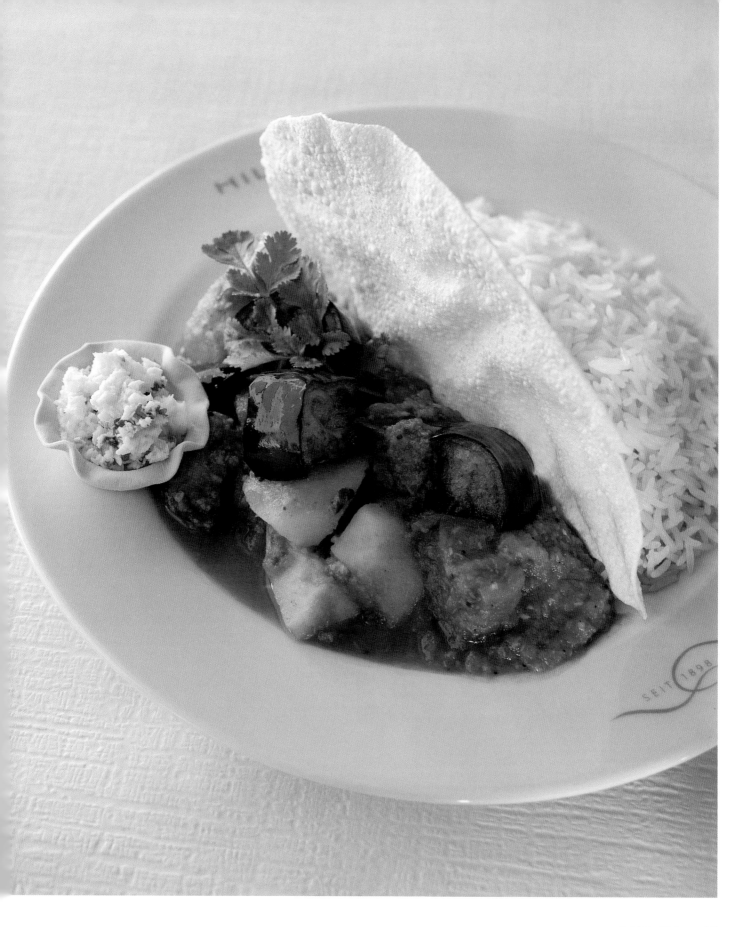

Giant Vegetable Skewer

the vegetarian barbecue special

serves 4

Marinade:

3 tbsp mustard

1 clove garlic crushed

2 tbsp red wine

1 tsp paprika

2 tsp black pepper

200 ml olive oil

Vegetables:

1 red pepper

1 yellow pepper

4 San Marzano tomatoes

2 Spanish onions

2 aubergines

1 tbsp sea salt

2 courgettes

1 tbsp sea salt

8 medium mushrooms

coarse sea salt

Italian herbs

ga/on

For the marinade, mix the mustard, garlic and spices. Then gradually add the olive oil, stirring continuously. Deseed the peppers, cut them lengthwise into strips 3 cm wide, and then halve the strips. Halve the tomatoes horizontally. Peel the Spanish onions and cut into wedges 3 cm wide; discard two inner layers of each wedge so that they will fit better on the skewer.

Cut off the aubergine stalks and slice the aubergines lengthwise into 3 mm slices. Place them on a rack and sprinkle with salt. Leave for 15 minutes and then pat dry with kitchen paper. Roll up the slices.

Cut the courgettes into 2 cm slices and on either side of the green part make a small cut to help guide the skewer. Sprinkle salt on them sparingly and set aside for 15 minutes. Then pat dry with kitchen paper. Cut out the stems of the mushrooms and make a hole on either side to help skewer them.

Thread the vegetables alternately onto long wooden skewers and place them on a flat baking sheet. Brush with marinade on all sides and leave for 30 minutes. During this time brush them again with any marinade that has dripped onto the baking sheet.

Place the skewers on a barbecue over medium heat and grill for about 15 minutes, turning them every now and then. Before serving, sprinkle with a little coarse sea salt and freshly chopped Italian herbs.

Our tip: See page 79

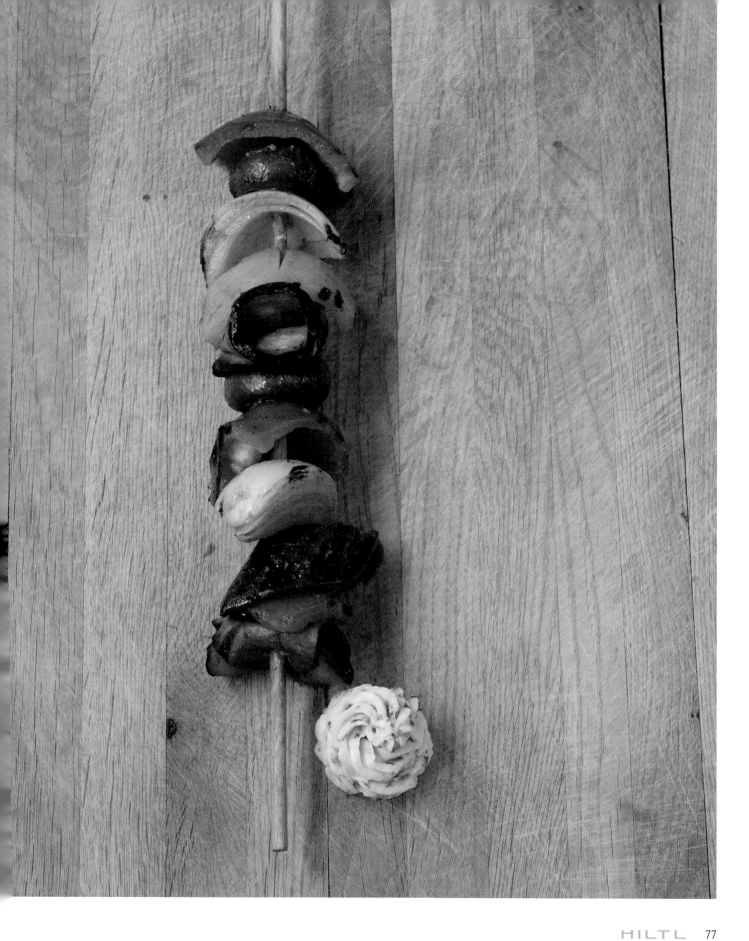

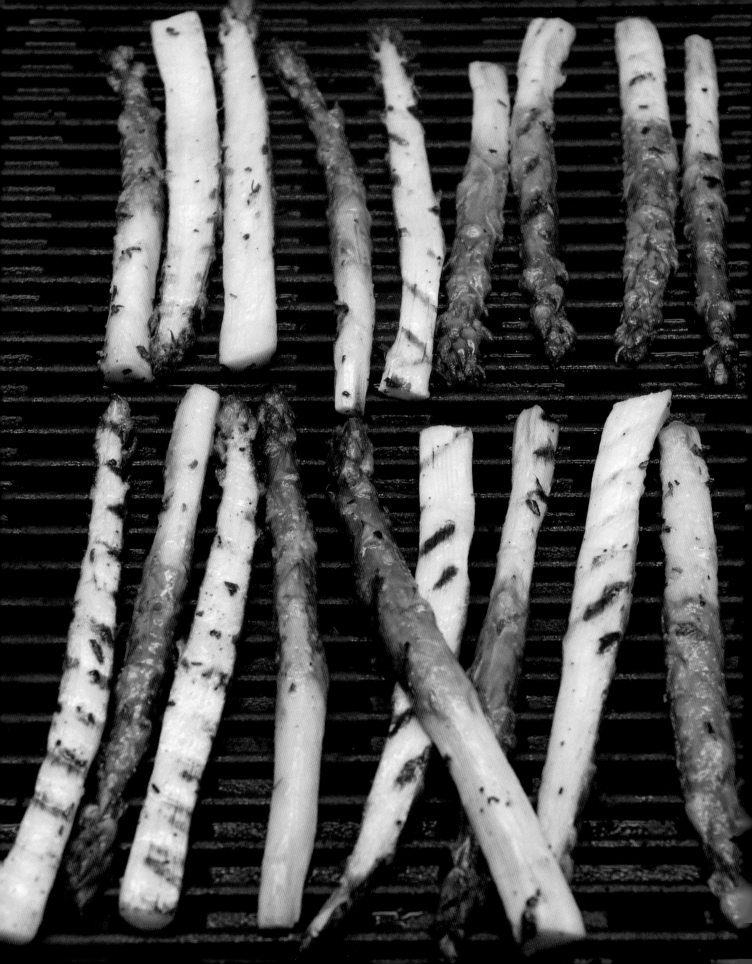

Grilled Vegetables
& Mushrooms

instead of grilled sausages

green asparagus

fennel slices

oyster mushrooms

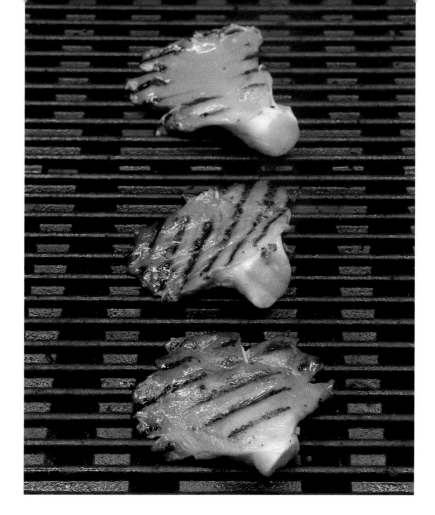

Your guests will be delighted if you don't only concentrate on meat at your barbecue party. You might want to try green asparagus split lengthwise, fennel sliced and blanched, or large oyster mushrooms.

Vary the ingredients for the marinade according to the vegetables or mushrooms used: garlic, ginger, thyme, dill, lemon zests, chopped chillies, black pepper, sesame oil, olive oil, coarse sea salt, Italian herbs, and so on.

The basic marinade recipe is set out on page 76.

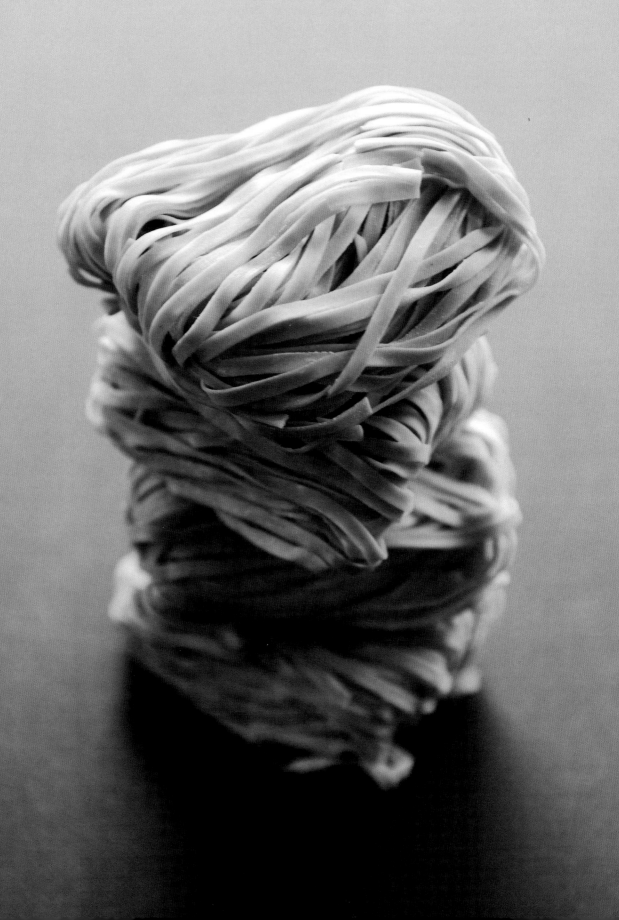

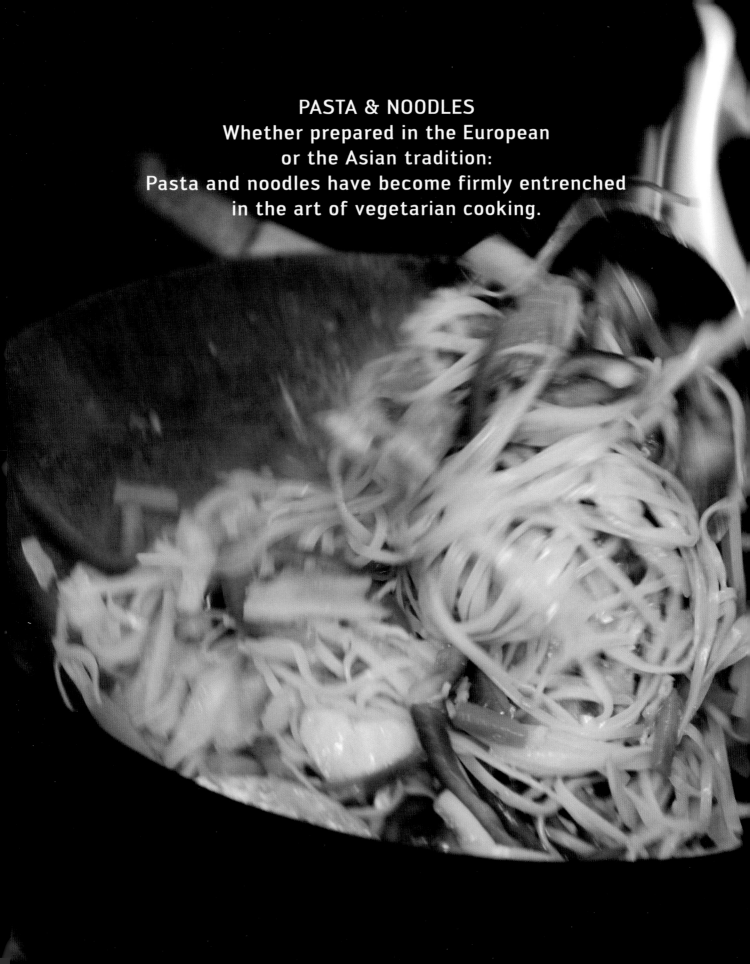

PASTA & NOODLES
Whether prepared in the European
or the Asian tradition:
Pasta and noodles have become firmly entrenched
in the art of vegetarian cooking.

Saffron Noodles
with green asparagus and cherry tomatoes

serves 4

6 thin green asparagus spears
100 g spring onions

15 g butter
250 ml vegetable stock
350 ml cream
220 g mascarpone
1/2 tsp saffron powder
1 tsp sea salt
1 pinch ground white pepper
200 g cherry tomatoes

500 g saffron noodles

saffron threads to garnish

ch/eg/gl/mi/on

Trim the ends of the asparagus spears and peel the lower third. Cut off the tops, halve lengthwise and blanch for 1 minute in boiling salted water. Refresh in iced water and reserve as garnish. Slice the remaining stalks diagonally. Cut the spring onions diagonally into rings.

Heat the butter gently, add the asparagus slices and the spring onions and sauté for 2–3 minutes. Pour in the stock and cream. Add the mascarpone and reduce the sauce until the desired consistency has been reached.

Add the saffron powder and season with salt and pepper. Halve the cherry tomatoes lengthwise and add to the sauce.

Cook the saffron noodles in salted water until al dente, drain, and immediately stir into the sauce. Serve garnished with the asparagus tops and saffron threads if desired.

Our tip: In the winter months, sliced fennel (1 cm wide) makes a good substitute for the asparagus.

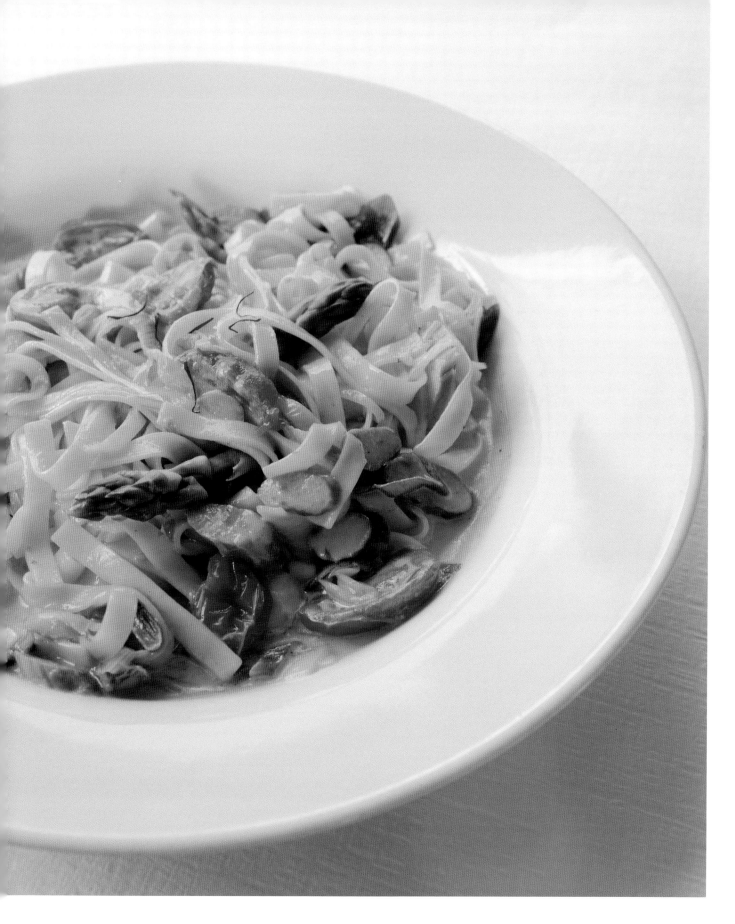

Spaghetti Bolognese
Hiltl style

serves 4

Bolognese:

100 g celeriac, peeled

1 small carrot

5 tbsp oil

200 g soya granules

1 onion, chopped

1 clove garlic, chopped

3 tbsp tomato purée

100 ml red wine

400 g chopped tomatoes (can)

400 ml vegetable stock

1/2 tsp brown sugar

1 pinch ground white pepper

1 pinch ground nutmeg

2 tbsp Italian herbs, chopped

2 sprigs basil, chiffonade cut

sea salt

ce/ga/gl/on/so

Cut the celeriac and carrot into tiny dice (brunoise). Heat the oil, add the soya granules and fry briskly. Add the diced vegetables, onion and garlic and sauté. Add the tomato purée and cook for a further 2 minutes.
Pour in the red wine, add the chopped tomatoes and the stock. Then add the sugar, spices and herbs, stir well and season with salt. Leave the sauce to simmer for 15–30 minutes.

Spaghetti: 500 g spaghetti, 2 tbsp olive oil
Cook the spaghetti in a generous quantity of salted water until al dente. Turn off the heat. Pour off the cooking water and rinse the spaghetti under hot tap water. Return the spaghetti to the saucepan and add the olive oil. Place on the warm hotplate and mix with the sauce.

Our tip: You can also serve the spaghetti in a bowl and pass round the Bolognese sauce separately. The wine we recommend in our restaurant to accompany this dish is Amarone della Valpolicella.

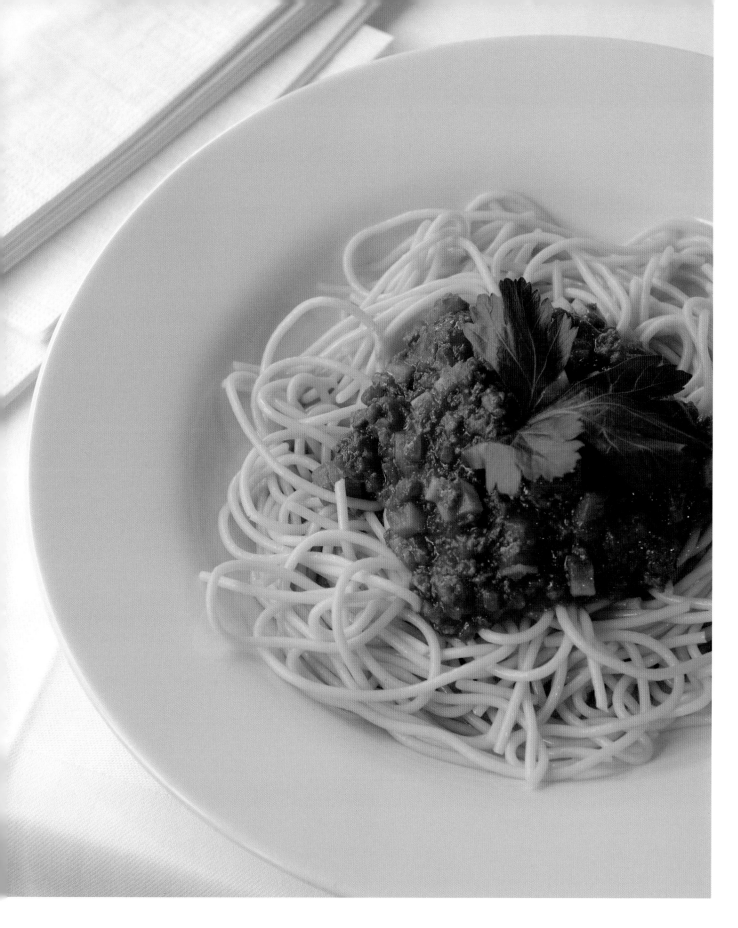

Coconut Noodles from Southern India
with yardlong beans

serves 4

320 g ribbon noodles, 2.5 cm

1 large carrot
1 aubergine
250 g yardlong beans
1 1/2 onions, in rings

3 tbsp oil
1 1/2 tsp black mustard seeds
3 tsp cumin seeds
10 curry leaves, fresh or dried
1 1/2 tsp chilli flakes
1 tsp turmeric
4 tsp mild curry
2 tsp ground cumin
4 tbsp lemon juice
400 ml water
800 ml coconut milk
3 tsp sea salt

3 tbsp oil
200 g green peas, fresh
sea salt, freshly milled pepper
a little fresh coriander, shredded

eg/gl/on

Boil the noodles in salted water until they are al dente, rinse under cold water and drain well. Cut the carrot into julienne sticks. Cut the aubergine into 1.5 cm chunks, place in a colander, sprinkle with salt and leave for 20 minutes. Pat dry with kitchen paper. Cut the beans diagonally into 3 cm slices.

Heat the oil, add the mustard seeds, cumin seeds, curry leaves and chilli flakes, fry until the mustard seeds burst open. Turn down the heat, add the onion rings and ground spices and then stir. Pour in the lemon juice, water and coconut milk, add the salt and simmer for 10 minutes. Blend the sauce with a mixing wand.

Heat the oil in a frying pan and brown the aubergines. Add the carrot juliennes and the sliced beans, turn down the heat and stir fry for a further 5 minutes.

Add the peas, noodles and sauce, mix thoroughly, reheat and season to taste. Serve garnished with fresh coriander.

Our tip: Fresh curry leaves are available from Indian shops. Serve with date chutney (see recipe in Hiltl. Virtuoso Vegetarian – new revised and updated edition, 2006, page 156).

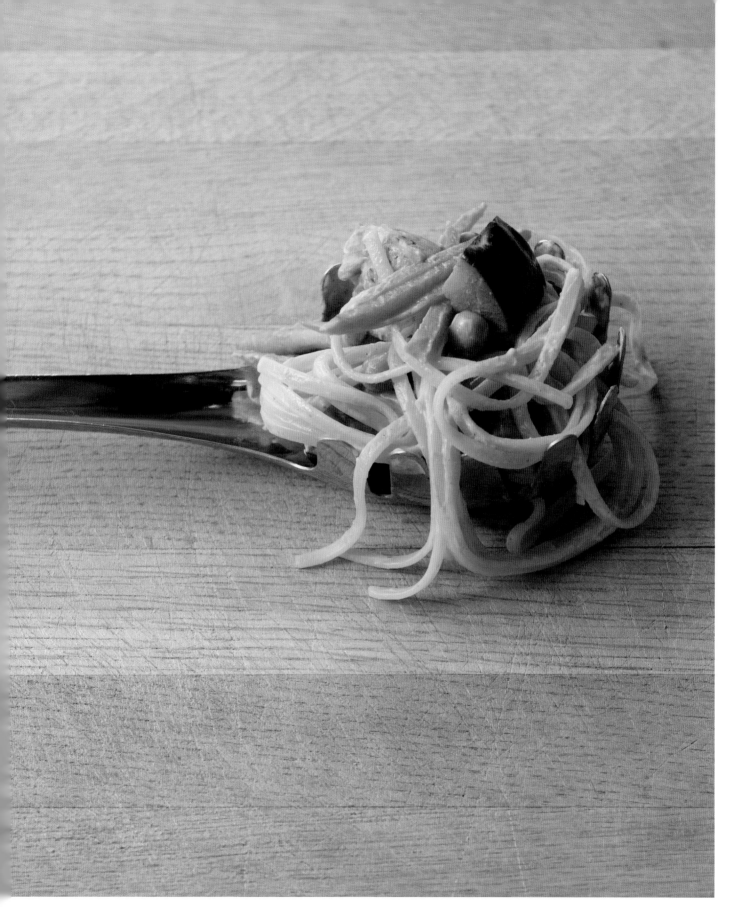

Mee Goreng
with oyster mushrooms and fresh ginger

serves 4

320 g fine Chinese egg noodles

1 carrot

1 green pepper

300 g Chinese cabbage (bok choy)

300 g oyster mushrooms

4 tbsp oil

1/2 onion, chopped

2 walnut-sized chunks fresh ginger

2 cloves garlic

2 small green chillies, chopped

2 tsp mild curry

1 1/2 tsp turmeric

2 tsp brown sugar

1 1/2 tsp sea salt

1 pinch ground white pepper

50 ml light soy sauce

1 tbsp sesame oil

250 ml water

2 tbsp lemon juice

sea salt, freshly milled pepper

1 spring onion, in rings

1 handful bean sprouts, washed

eg/ga/gl/on/so

Place the egg noodles in a bowl, pour boiling water over them and soak until they are al dente. Refresh with cold water and drain thoroughly. Cut the carrot into julienne sticks. Cut the halved, deseeded pepper and the cabbage into narrow slices. Cut the oyster mushrooms into 2 cm strips.

Heat the oil in a frying pan and fry the oyster mushrooms, then add the chopped onion, grated ginger and crushed garlic.

Now add the chopped chillies and the pepper and carrot juliennes and sauté. Finally add the cabbage, sauté for 2 minutes and then add the prepared noodles.

Season with the curry, turmeric, sugar, salt, pepper, soy sauce and sesame oil. Stir well. Pour in the water and lemon juice, stir, reheat and season with salt and pepper to taste. Serve garnished with the spring onion rings and bean sprouts.

Our tip: To give this dish more "bite", fry one third of the noodles till crisp and then add them together with the remaining noodles. Serve with sweet chilli sauce.

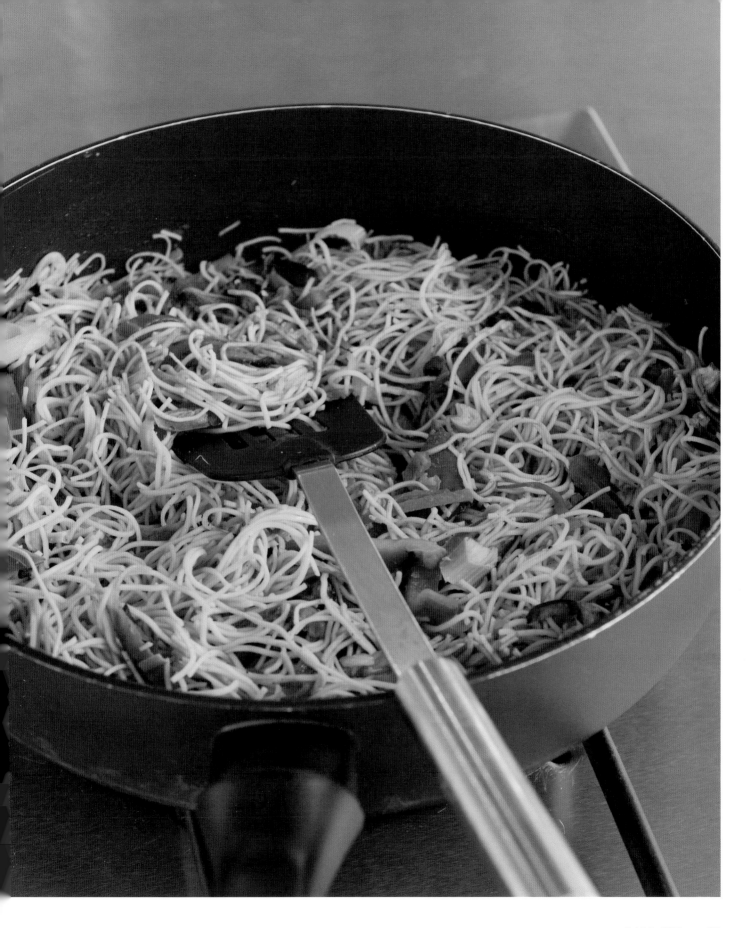

Citrus Noodles
with Sichuan pepper

serves 4

320 g ribbon noodles, 2.5 mm

1 red pepper

1 green pepper

250 g leeks

1 medium courgette

1 tbsp oil

1 clove garlic, crushed

1 lemon, zests

1 orange, zests

1 tsp sambal oelek

250 g peanut butter

1 tbsp sesame oil

1 1/2 tbsp brown sugar

2 1/2 tsp sea salt

1 tsp Sichuan pepper

300 ml orange juice

1 lemon, juice

700 ml water

3 tbsp oil

sea salt, freshly milled pepper

3 tbsp peanuts, toasted

1 tbsp lemon zests

1 spring onion, in rings

eg/ga/gl/on/pe

Boil the noodles in salted water until al dente. Refresh with cold water and drain. Halve both peppers, deseed and cut lengthwise into fine strips. Split the leeks lengthwise, wash, and cut into 6 cm juliennes. Then cut the courgette into juliennes.

Heat the oil in a casserole, turn the heat down, add the garlic, zests and sambal olek and sauté briefly until the aromas are released. Add the peanut butter and allow it to melt. Add the sesame oil, sugar, salt and Sichuan pepper, pour in the orange and lemon juice and then the water. Reduce the sauce for 15 minutes until it binds, then blend with a mixing wand.

Heat 3 tbsp oil in a large frying pan, add the peppers, leeks and courgette and stir-fry until the vegetables are just tender. Add the noodles, mix well and reheat. Add the sauce, mix thoroughly again and season with salt and pepper. Serve garnished with the peanuts, lemon zests and spring onions.

Our tip: We serve this dish with orange pickles (available at Hiltl's takeaway).

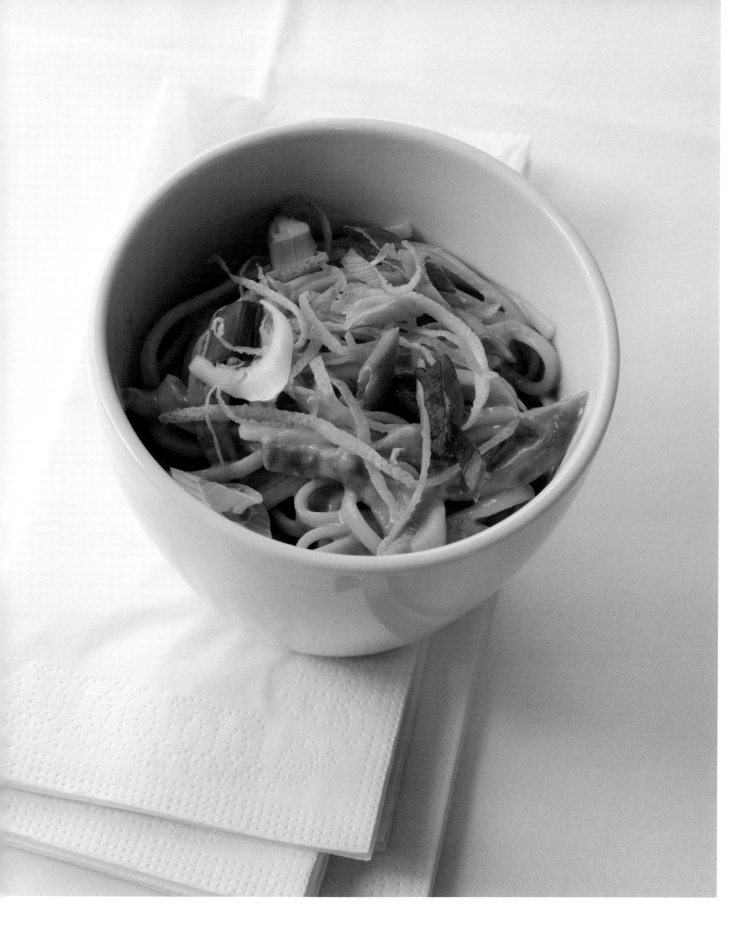

Sam Tam Bamee

with papaya and Thai basil

serves 4

400 g rice vermicelli

400 g celery

300 g white cabbage

125 g soy bean sprouts

2 walnut-sized chunks fresh ginger

1 papaya

280 g oyster mushrooms

5 tbsp oil

3 tbsp oil

1 onion, in rings

1 1/2 cloves garlic, crushed

150 ml light soy sauce

150 ml lemon juice

4 tbsp sweet chilli sauce

sea salt, pepper

2 spring onions, in rings

1 bunch coriander, shredded

1 bunch Thai basil, chiffonade cut

ce/ga/gl/on

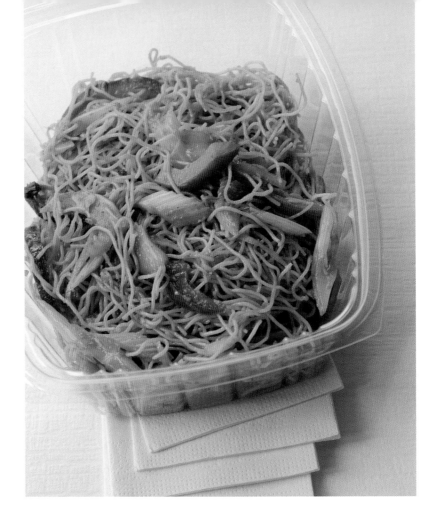

Place the rice vermicelli in a bowl and cover with boiling water, leave for 5 minutes and then drain. Wash the celery and cut diagonally into slices. Halve the cabbage, remove the hard core, and cut into fine strips. Wash the bean sprouts and finely chop the ginger. Peel and deseed the papaya and cut into julienne sticks. Cut the oyster mushrooms into fine strips. Heat 5 tbsp oil in a frying pan and fry the mushrooms until well done, drain on kitchen paper.

Heat 3 tbsp oil in a wok, add the onion rings and garlic and sauté. Add the celery, cabbage, bean sprouts and ginger, and stir-fry till they release their aromas.

Add the soy sauce, lemon juice and sweet chilli sauce, and mix well. Add the papaya julienne, together with the noodles and the mushrooms, stir and reheat. Serve garnished with spring onions, coriander and basil.

Our tip: Serve with sweet chilli sauce.

Ginger

Ginger *(Zingiber officinale)* is a reed-like perennial within the Zingiberaceae or ginger family, which can reach a height of up to 2 metres. The plant's tuberous rhizomes are used in cooking and medicine. China and Nigeria are the main suppliers, but today ginger is cultivated in almost all tropical countries such as India and Jamaica. Ginger has a pungent bouquet and a fiery, pungent flavour.

Ginger was probably brought to Europe during Christ's lifetime. Ginger is said to relieve morning and motion sickness, nausea, digestion problems, side effects from chemotherapy, headaches, colds and fevers, and to improve blood circulation. However, it is no longer of much importance in the medical industry. Ginger is still used in the production of spirits and confectionery, and also in the cosmetics industry.

Pieces of ginger can be planted in a container, left in a warm place and watered generously – though they must not actually stand in water. Less water should be given in winter, and the plants taken indoors.

The tender side rhizomes are generally used for both dried and fresh ginger; the thicker middle pieces are often marketed as crystallized or candied ginger. Stem ginger is made of fresh young roots preserved in a heavy syrup. Paper-thin, tender slices of pickled ginger *(gari)* are served with sushi. The pale pink colour comes from the addition of a very little food colouring. To make whole dried pieces, the peeled ginger is first dipped into chalk water so that it turns almost white and then dried. Unpeeled dried ginger from Africa is ground to make the buff-coloured spice, ground ginger.

Ground ginger is one of the ingredients commonly found in the various curry mixtures. It is used fresh or in its powdered form in gingerbread, biscuits and cakes, in meat, poultry and fish dishes, in fruit salads, compotes, sauces, pastes, ice cream, liqueurs, beer and soft drinks. Fresh ginger root contains zingibain, an enzyme that breaks down protein. Consequently, meat marinated or cooked with ginger becomes very tender.

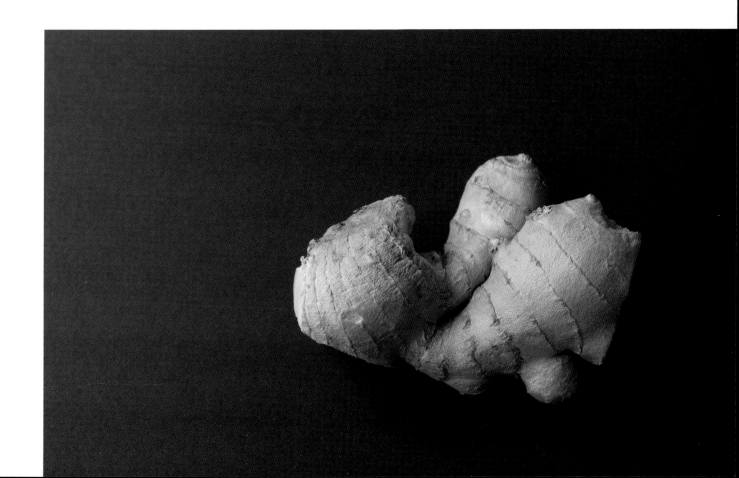

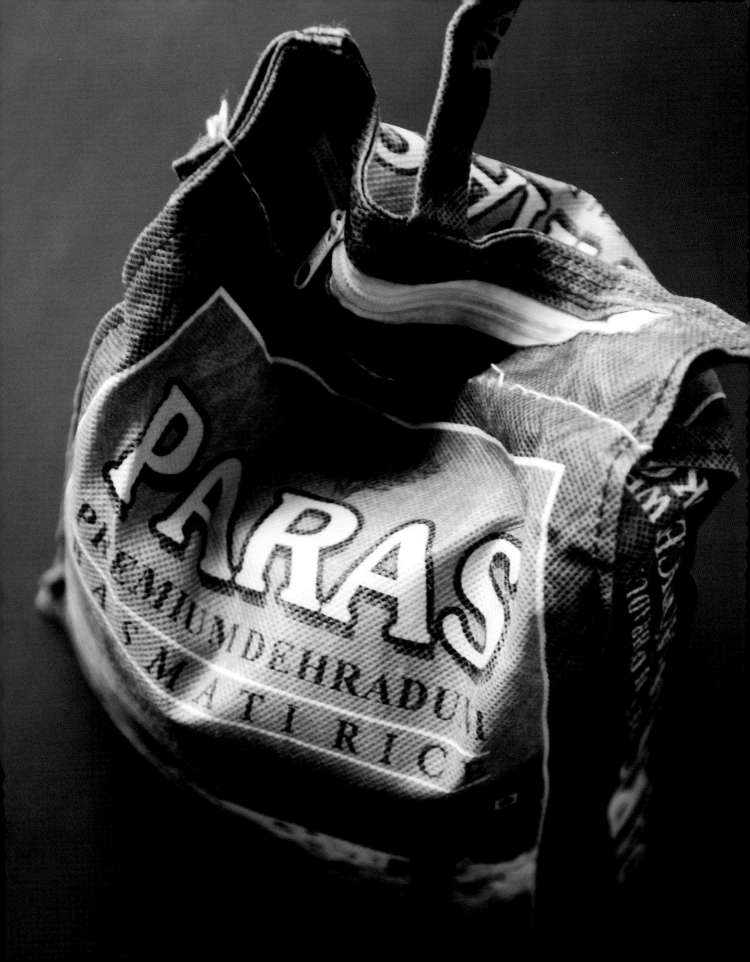

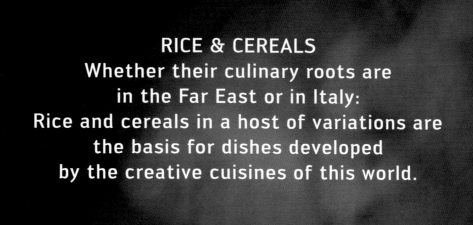

RICE & CEREALS
Whether their culinary roots are
in the Far East or in Italy:
Rice and cereals in a host of variations are
the basis for dishes developed
by the creative cuisines of this world.

Vegetable Paella
with jalapeños

serves 4

150 g cauliflower

1/2 red pepper

100 g mushrooms

140 g artichoke bottoms, deep frozen

100 g french beans

100 g peas

Garnish:

1 small aubergine

sea salt

8 jalapeños

500 ml oil

4 tbsp olive oil

1/2 onion, chopped

1/2 tsp paprika

1/2 tsp saffron powder

200 g long grain rice, parboiled

100 g chopped tomatoes (can)

400 ml vegetable stock

sea salt, freshly milled pepper

1 lemon, wedges

on

Divide the cauliflower into small florets. Deseed the pepper and cut into 2 cm pieces. Slice the mushrooms finely. Cut the artichoke bottoms into four or six pieces. Blanch the beans until the are just tender and refresh in ice water. In the same hot water briefly blanch the peas and also refresh in ice water.

Cut the aubergine for the garnish into 5 mm slices, sprinkle salt over them and set aside for 30 minutes. Pat dry with kitchen paper.

Heat 4 tbsp olive oil and sauté the onions until the are transparent, turn down the heat. Add the cauliflower florets and artichoke pieces and sauté. Dust with paprika and saffron powder, add the rice and sauté until it glistens.

Add the chopped tomatoes and cover with the stock. The rice must be stirred continuously while it is cooking. Just before the rice is ready, add the sliced mushrooms and the pepper pieces. Season to taste with salt and pepper.

To finish the garnish, heat 5 ml oil in a separate pan and brown the aubergine slices. Drain on kitchen paper. Briefly fry the jalapeños and also drain on kitchen paper.

When the paella rice is ready, mix in the blanched peas and beans. Arrange on plates and garnish with the jalapeños, aubergine slices and lemon wedges.

Our tip: To make this vegetable paella look like the "real thing", onion rings can be deep-fried in batter so that they look like vegetarian fried calamari (squid rings).

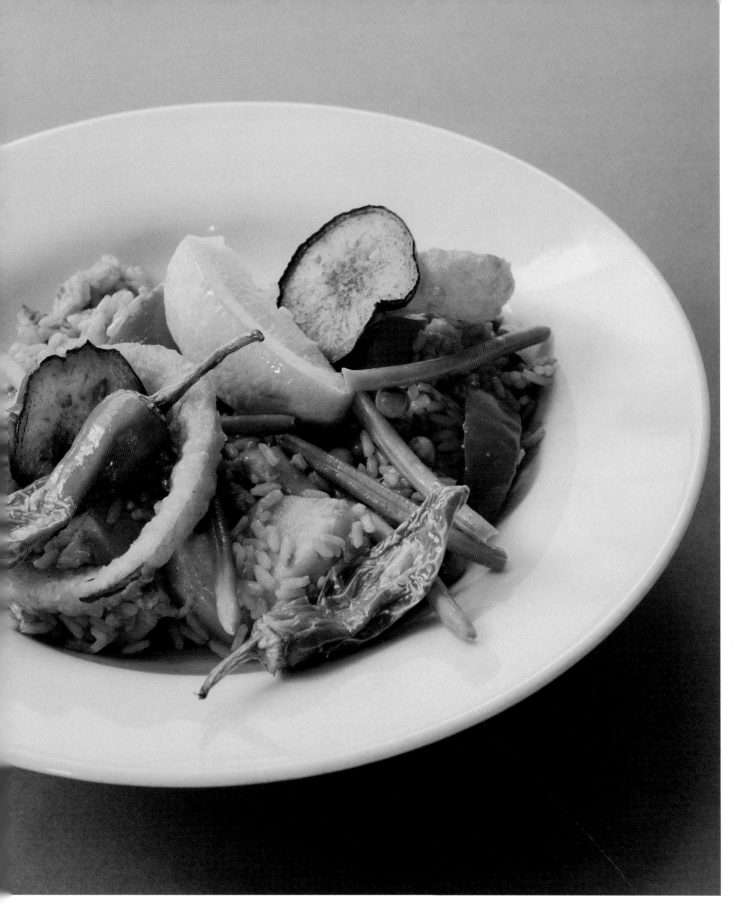

Pumpkin Risotto
with honey and fresh rosemary

serves 4

300 g diced pumpkin (1.5 cm)

3 tbsp oil

2 sprigs fresh rosemary, chopped

2 tbsp olive oil

1 onion, chopped

1 clove garlic, crushed

500 g risotto rice (Vialone)

1 bay leaf

150 ml white wine

800 ml vegetable stock

1 – 2 tbsp honey

20 g pumpkin seeds, toasted

2 tbsp mascarpone

15 g parmesan, grated

50 ml white wine

sea salt, freshly milled pepper

rosemary sprigs, tips

ch/ga/mi/on

In a non-stick frying pan, brown the diced pumpkin in a little oil, add salt, pepper and rosemary, then set aside. Heat the olive oil and sauté the onions and garlic. Add the risotto rice and bay leaf and sauté a little longer.

Add the white wine and then half of the stock – the liquid should be about 2 cm over the rice; if not, add a little water. Simmer for 45 minutes, stirring continuously. During this time keep adding some of the remaining stock.

Then add the honey, pumpkin seeds and browned pumpkin to the risotto and simmer until the rice is al dente. Fold in the mascarpone and parmesan and add the remaining white wine. When the rice is ready, season with salt and pepper to taste and serve garnished with the rosemary.

Our tip: We recommend Sauvignon blanc from the Zurich region (such as Lattenberger) for cooking the risotto as well as to accompany the meal.

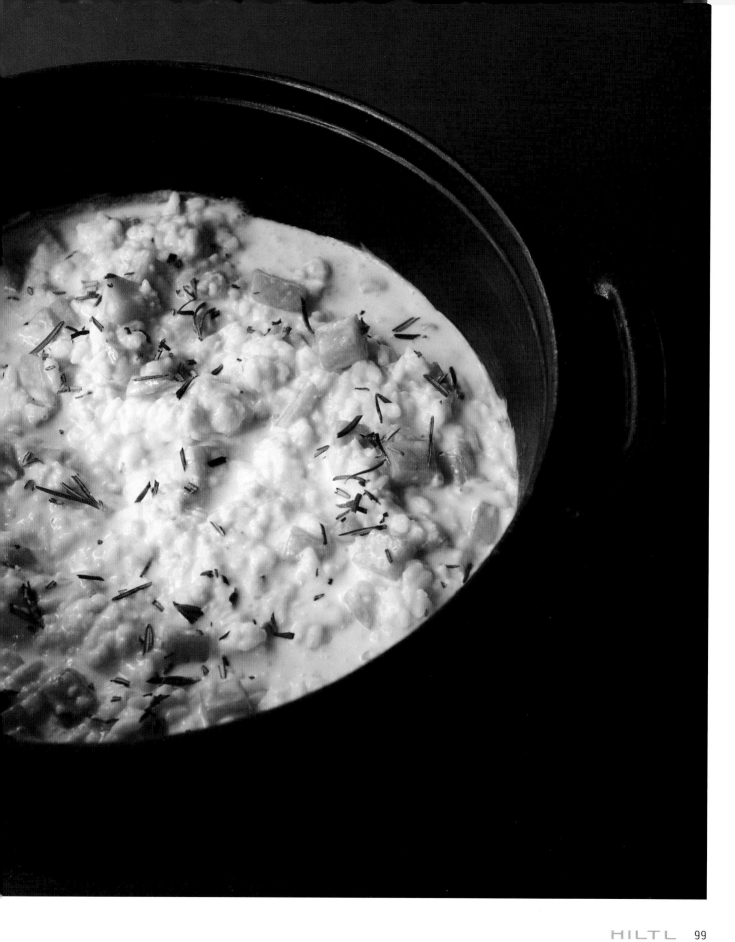

Dill Rice with Lentils
and pine nuts

serves 4

320 g basmati rice

1 bay leaf

1 level tsp sea salt

600 ml water

50 g brown lentils

$1/2$ tsp sea salt

1 bunch fresh dill, chopped

1 tbsp oil

50 g pine nuts, toasted

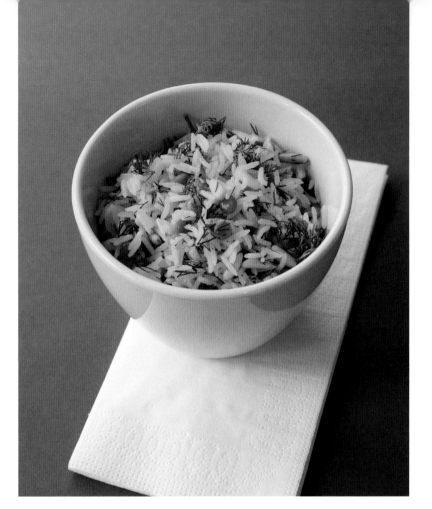

Place the rice in a sieve and rinse with cold water. Transfer the rice to a saucepan, add the bay leaf, salt, pepper and water and bring to the boil. Cook until small craters form on the surface. Turn off the heat, cover the rice and leave it on the cooker for 20 minutes to absorb the water.

Pick over the lentils, rinse them and, in another saucepan, cook them in salted water until just tender. Drain.

Discard the bay leaf and add the chopped dill, cooked lentils and oil to the rice. Mix with a fork. Serve garnished with pine nuts.

Our tip: Serve as a side dish with vanilla carrots (page 62).

Barberry Pilaff

Ana's recipe from Persia

serves 4

320 g basmati rice

600 ml water

1 level tsp sea salt

2 tbsp oil

2 tbsp oil

1 onion, chopped

1/4 tsp ground cardamom

20 g barberries, washed

4 tbsp brown sugar

4 tbsp peeled pistachios, unsalted

1/2 tsp saffron powder

4 tbsp hot water

1 tbsp rose water

on

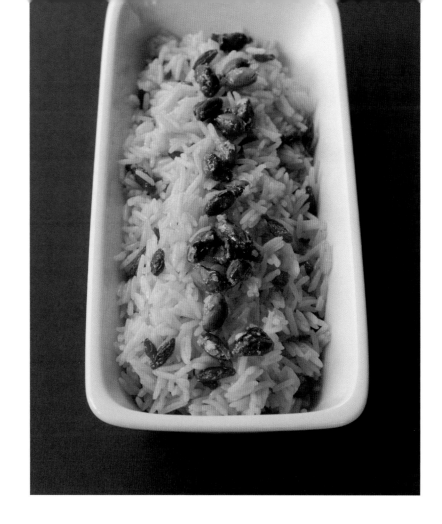

Place the basmati rice in a sieve and rinse with cold water. Transfer the rice to a saucepan, add water, salt and oil, and bring to the boil. Cover and leave to simmer over a low heat for 15 minutes. Stir the rice twice with a fork.

Heat the oil, sauté the onions until they are transparent, add the cardamom and stir. Turn down the heat, add the barberries and sugar, and fry briefly. Take care not to burn the barberries. Add the pistachios and mix thoroughly.

Add the barberry mixture to the rice and mix well. Stir the saffron into the hot water and pour it over the rice together with the rose water. Turn off the heat. Leave the rice to stand on the hotplate for a further 10 minutes to absorb the liquids.

Our tip: The berries of the European barberry are rich in vitamin C and have a sharp flavour. They can be bought dried. They are popular in Persian and Chinese cooking.

Helmut's Caesar Dumplings
original recipe from Austria

serves 4

1/2 bunch chives

1 stalk lovage

2 sprigs marjoram

1 large onion

25 g butter

75 g butter, soft

1 tsp sea salt

1/4 tsp ground black pepper

1 pinch nutmeg, grated

280 g breadcrumbs

6 eggs

2 l vegetable stock

eg/gl/mi/on

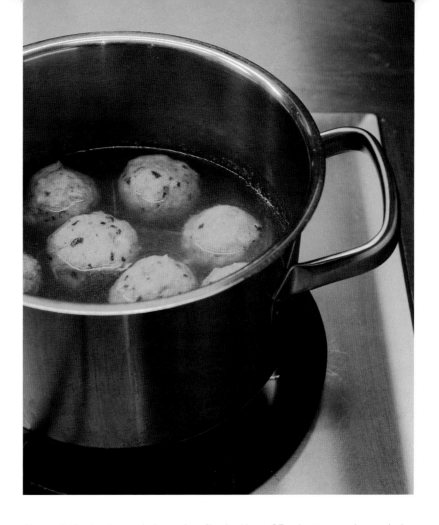

Chop all the herbs and the onion finely. Heat 25 g butter and sauté the onion until transparent. Take off the heat and cool. Add the remaining butter and whisk till foamy. Add the salt, spices and chopped herbs. Mix well. Add the breadcrumbs, and then the eggs, one by one. Mix gently to form a smooth dough.

Please note: Only mix briefly, otherwise the dumplings will be hard. Cover and leave to rest in the fridge overnight.

Bring the vegetable stock to the boil and, using your hands, form dumplings of about 50 g each and let them glide gently into the hot stock. Bring the stock up to simmering point, cover, and poach the dumplings for about 30 minutes. Lift the cooked dumplings out of the stock with a slotted spoon and serve.

Our tip: Serve with fresh chanterelles (page 58).

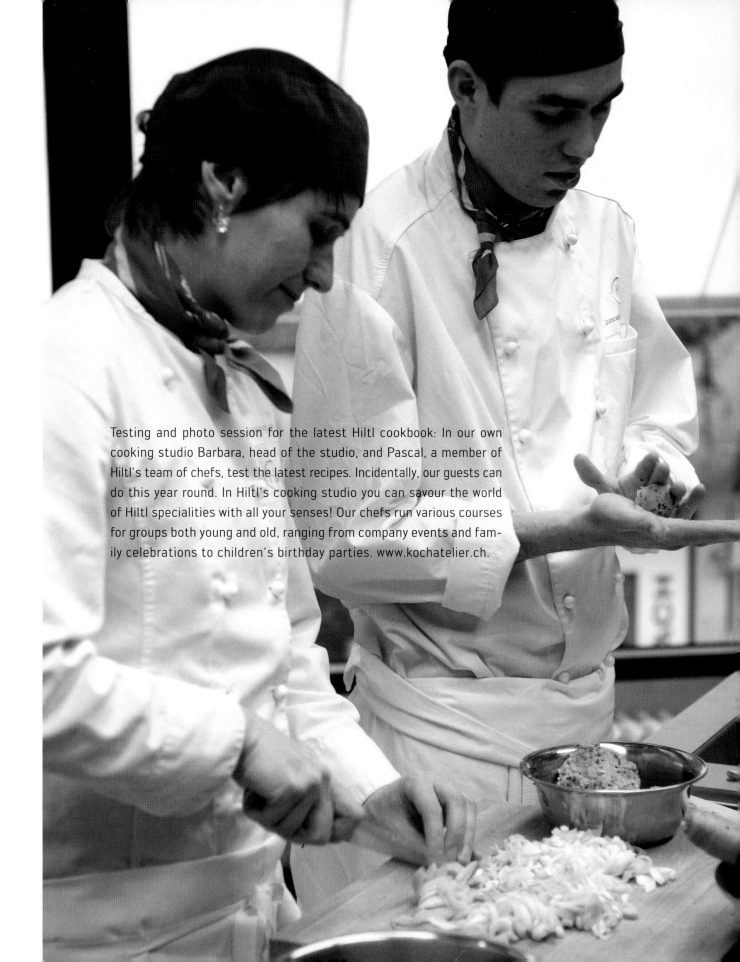

Testing and photo session for the latest Hiltl cookbook: In our own cooking studio Barbara, head of the studio, and Pascal, a member of Hiltl's team of chefs, test the latest recipes. Incidentally, our guests can do this year round. In Hiltl's cooking studio you can savour the world of Hiltl specialities with all your senses! Our chefs run various courses for groups both young and old, ranging from company events and family celebrations to children's birthday parties. www.kochatelier.ch.

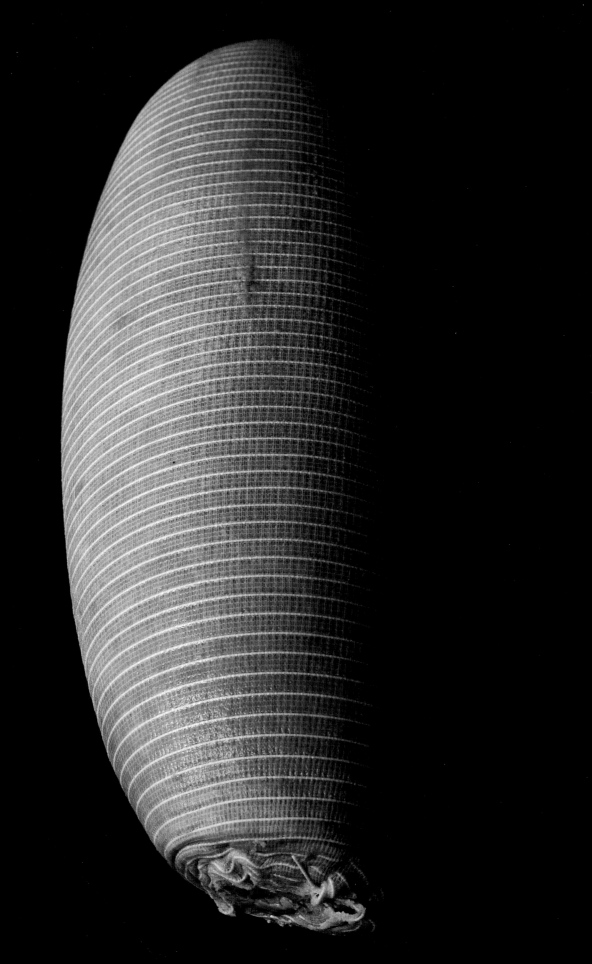

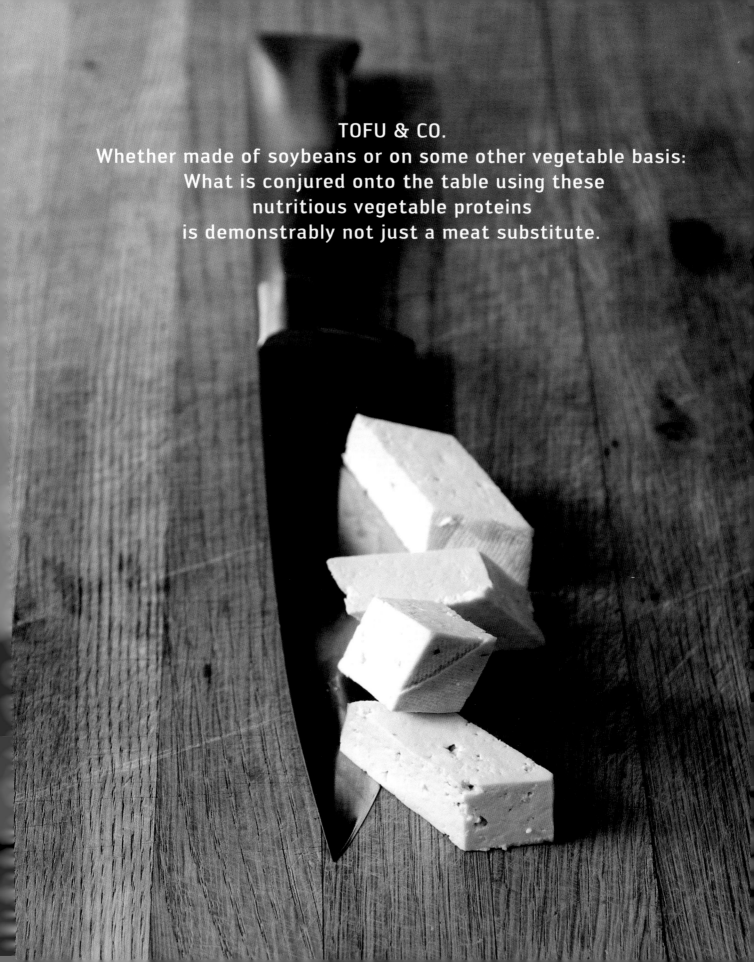

TOFU & CO.
Whether made of soybeans or on some other vegetable basis:
What is conjured onto the table using these
nutritious vegetable proteins
is demonstrably not just a meat substitute.

Tofu Mirsang
with fresh spinach

serves 4:

750 g tofu

Marinade:
1 lemon, juice
2 cloves garlic, crushed
1 tbsp ginger, grated
1 1/2 tsp turmeric
2 pinches cayenne pepper
1 tsp ground coriander
1 tsp ground cumin
1/2 tsp ground white pepper
1 tsp sea salt
100 ml light soy sauce

1 large red pepper
1 onion
1 medium potato, peeled
3 tbsp oil
2 pinches ground cardamom
2 pinches ground cloves
1 tbsp paprika
1 tsp fennel seeds, crushed
1 tbsp fenugreek leaves
1 l vegetable stock
3 tbsp oil
600 g plain yoghurt
600 g fresh spinach leaves
sea salt, freshly milled pepper

ga/gl/mi/on/so

Cut the tofu into 2 cm cubes. Mix all the ingredients for the marinade, add the tofu and leave to marinate overnight. Deseed the pepper and cut into squares. Slice the onion into rings and cut the potatoes into chunks. Heat the oil, sauté the onion rings and the pepper until the onion is transparent. Add the spices, sauté briefly and then add the stock.

Add the potatoes and simmer gently for 30 – 45 minutes. Blend with a mixing wand.

Lift the tofu cubes out of the marinade with a slotted spoon and drain thoroughly. Add the marinade to the pepper sauce.

Heat the oil in a frying pan and brown the tofu on all sides. Add to the sauce and reheat.

Whisk the yoghurt using an electric hand whisk and add to the sauce. Do not bring to the boil again. Add the spinach leaves and season to taste with salt and pepper.

Our tip: If you like your food hot, you can use chopped red chillies instead of cayenne pepper. Serve with basmati rice and coconut chutney (see recipe in Hiltl. Virtuoso Vegetarian – new revised and updated edition, 2006, pages 116 and 158).

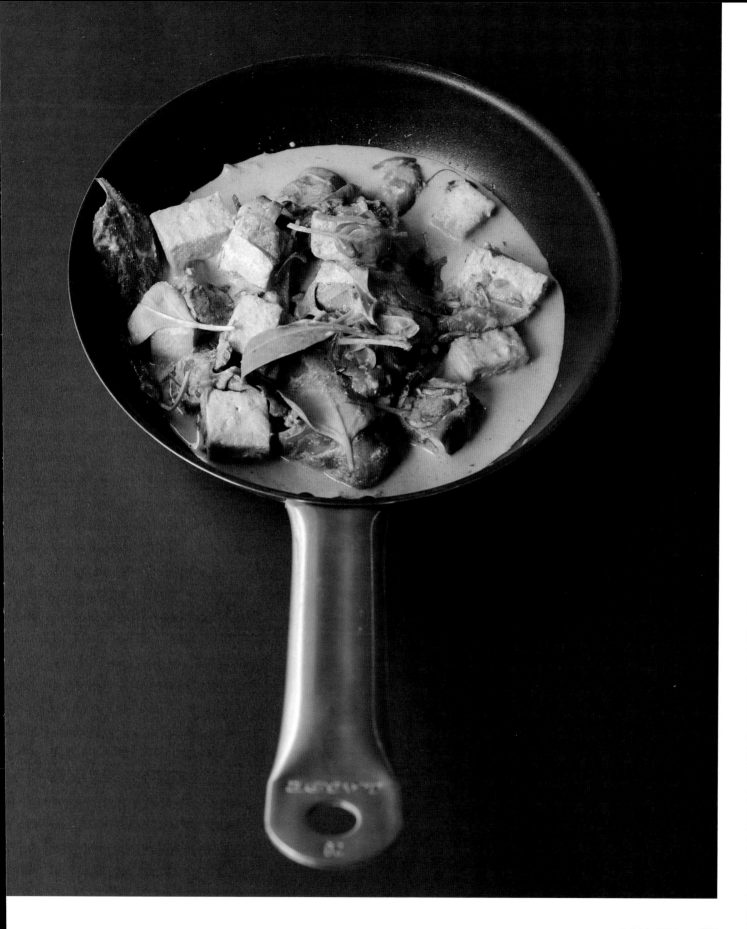

Seitan & Vegetable Fricassee

with red wine sauce

serves 4

Sauce:

200 g carrots

100 g celeriac

4 tbsp olive oil

1 onion, chopped

50 g tomato purée

1 sprig marjoram

1 sprig oregano

1 sprig thyme

1 sprig rosemary

2 cloves

3 bay leaves

1 tsp black peppercorns

2 tsp brown sugar

1 l red wine

1 l vegetable stock

2 – 3 tbsp cornflour

Seitan and vegetables:

600 g seitan (wheat gluten)

120 g mushrooms

3 tbsp cooking butter

sea salt, freshly milled pepper

1 carrot, peeled

120 g celeriac, peeled

sea salt, freshly milled pepper

ga/gl/mi/on/se

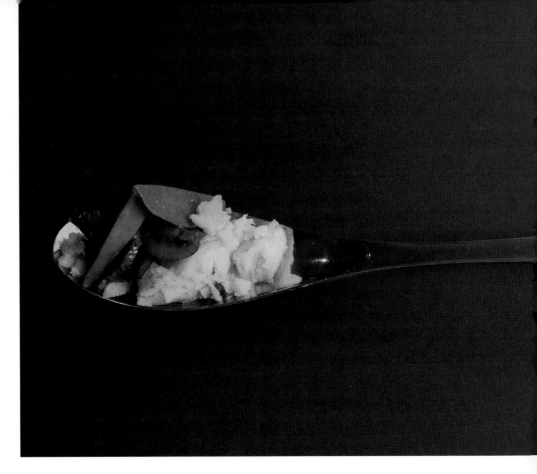

For the sauce, peel and dice the carrots and celeriac. Heat the olive oil and fry the onion and vegetables briskly. The vegetables and onion may be browned lightly. Add the tomato purée, all the herbs and spices, and the sugar and again fry briskly. Add the red wine and reduce to 500 ml, strain. Add the stock and reduce to 900 ml. Stir the cornflour into a little wine, add to the sauce and bring to the boil.

Using a vegetable slicer or large knife, cut the wheat gluten into very thin slices, then cut these into pieces measuring roughly 2 x 3 cm. Slice the mushrooms.

Heat the cooking butter and fry the seitan and mushrooms separately in small portions until they are golden brown. Season with salt and pepper and set aside. For the vegetables, halve the carrot lengthwise and slice diagonally. Cut the celeriac into 1.5 cm sticks and also slice diagonally. Blanch both vegetables until they are just tender, drain and add to the sauce together with the seitan and mushrooms. Season to taste with salt and pepper.

Our tip: Serve this dish with mashed potatoes or cornmeal gnocchi.

Seitan More than one thousand years ago Zen Buddhists in China and Japan discovered wheat gluten as a meat substitute for their cuisine, and developed various methods of preparation. Wheat gluten prepared as seitan is most widespread in Chinese cuisine, although this name is a modern term introduced by the Japanese-born founder of the macrobiotic diet. Seitan contains purely vegetable proteins and has a very high nutritional value. It is made from wheat flour, usually won from hard winter wheat as this has a higher gluten content than soft winter wheat or spring wheat. The procedure for making seitan is to wash the starch out of the wheat flour, leaving the insoluble gluten as an elastic mass. This dough is then boiled in a mixture of soy sauce, kombu seaweed and spices. The seitan is then left to soak in its cooking liquid for a further two days or so. The most commonly used form of wheat gluten in Japan is *fu,* for which the gluten pieces are steamed. This makes them much softer than poached seitan. Seitan is available shrink wrapped, pasteurized, or in one piece for 2 – 4 helpings. 1 kg portions are also available.

The nutritional value of 100g seitan is roughly: water 75 g, protein 21 g, carbohydrate 2g, fat 1 g, minerals 1 g. Energy value 438 kJ / 103 kcal. In Japan today many products are made of a mixture of wheat gluten and soybean protein and marketed as "gluten meat".

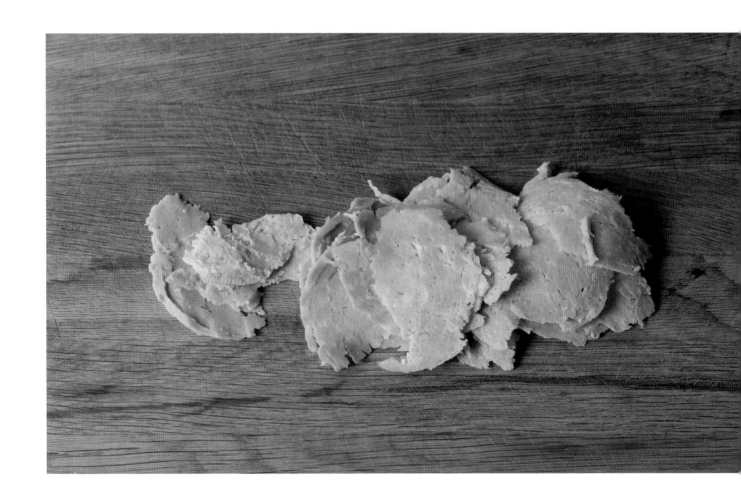

Kung Pao
out of the wok

serves 4

10 g dried mu-err mushrooms
500 g Quorn or seitan
2 tbsp rice flour or cornflour
180 g yardlong beans
1 medium pepper

Sauce:
60 ml light soy sauce
2 tbsp dark sweet soy sauce
50 ml rice wine
70 ml water
120 g brown sugar
2 limes, juice
3 pinches cayenne pepper

5 tbsp oil
sea salt, freshly milled pepper

a few soybean sprouts

eg/gl/mi/so

Soak the mu-err mushrooms in lukewarm water overnight.
Cut the Quorn diagonally into 1 cm slices and mix with the rice flour or cornflour. Cut the beans into 6 cm lengths, the deseeded pepper and the soaked mu-err mushrooms into juliennes. Mix all the ingredients for the sauce thoroughly.
Heat the oil in the wok and brown the Quorn. Add the vegetables and mushrooms and continue frying briefly. Pour in the sauce, reheat and season to taste.
Rinse the soybean sprouts, drain, and scatter over each serving. Serve with jasmine rice.

Our tip: Kung pao can also be made with tofu. In this case, marinate the tofu in the sauce overnight. The next day, drain off the sauce and reserve. Cook the dish as above and add the reserved sauce / marinade.

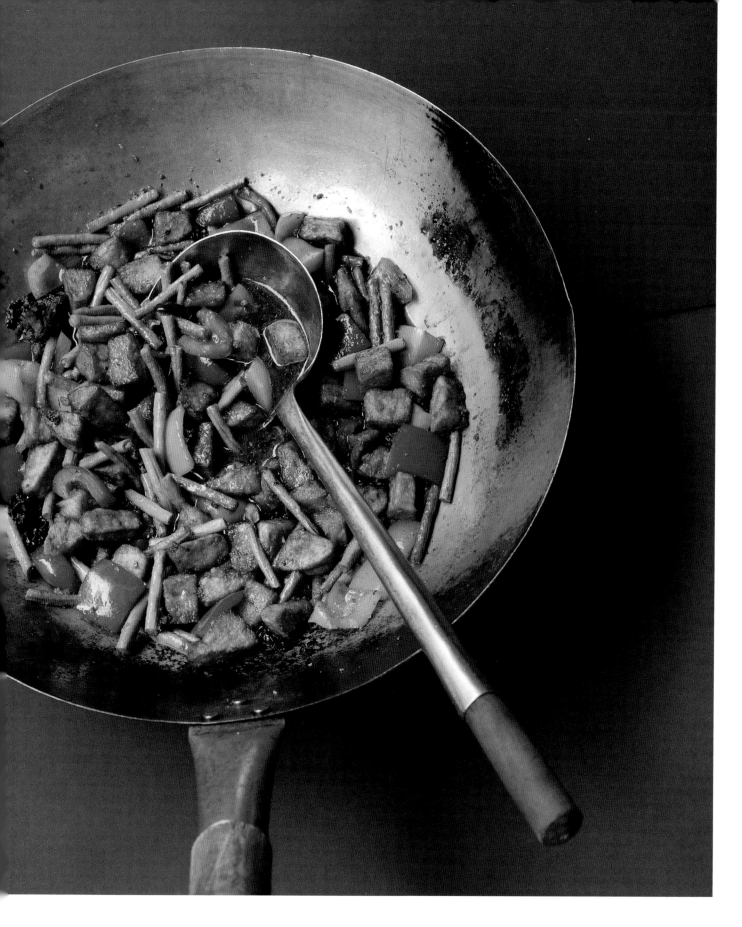

Vindaloo
from Western India

an old recipe from Goa

serves 4

100 g silverskin onions

350 g potatoes

250 g Quorn

200 g fresh pineapple, peeled

2 tomatoes

250 g onions

3 tbsp sunflower oil

1 cinnamon stick

2 whole cloves

1 tbsp cumin seeds

3 small green chillies, chopped

3 cm fresh ginger, peeled

1 tbsp tomato purée

4 tbsp paprika

1 tsp cayenne pepper

2 pinches turmeric

3/4 tbsp ground cumin

1 pinch ground white pepper

1 tbsp tamarind paste

1 tbsp mild mustard

2 tbsp cider vinegar

1 tbsp brown sugar

2 tsp sea salt

500 ml water

3 tbsp oil

eg/mi/on

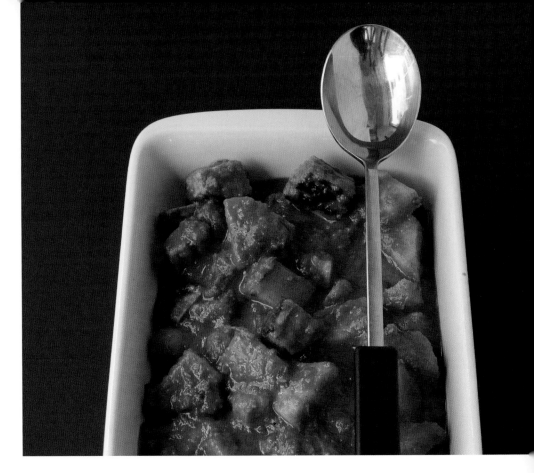

Rinse the silverskin onions in cold water. Peel the potatoes. Cut the potatoes, Quorn and pineapple into 2 cm chunks, and set aside separately. Dice the tomatoes and slice the onions into rings. Heat the oil and sauté the whole spices until they release their aromas. Add the onion rings and sauté gently until they are transparent. Add the chillies and ginger and sauté for 5 minutes over medium heat. Add the diced tomatoes and tomato purée, stir well.

Add the ground spices, tamarind paste, mustard, cider vinegar, sugar and salt, stir, and add the water. Leave the sauce to simmer gently for 20 minutes. Discard the cinnamon stick. Blend the sauce with a wand mixer. Add the potatoes to the sauce and cook for about 30 minutes until they are just tender. Heat the oil in a frying pan and stir-fry the Quorn until it is browned on all sides.

Before serving add the pineapple, silverskin onions and fried Quorn to the potatoes. Season to taste with sea salt and pepper.

Our tip: Goa was a Portuguese colony from 1510 to 1961. The name of this dish comes from *carne em vinha de alhos*, which means meat marinated in wine and garlic. Other sources suggest that the name comes from vingar (vinegar) and aloo (potatoes). Serve with basmati rice and date chutney (see recipe in Hiltl. Virtuoso Vegetarian – new revised and updated edition, 2006, pages 116 and 156).

Cayenne Pepper and Paprika

Cayenne pepper *(Capsicum annuum)* is made from finely ground dried chillies. Like paprika and bell peppers, the cayenne fruits belong to the nightshade family. The indigenous peoples of Latin America were already cultivating chillies thousands of years ago. Even today, many Amerindian dishes call for *aji;* though *aji* is not strictly cayenne pepper but Peruvian hot pepper *(Capsicum baccatum),* the term is now widely used in Latin America to designate chilli or cayenne pepper.

Cayenne pepper gets its hotness from the high capsaicin content, some 20 percent higher than that of paprika. Cayenne pepper is a main ingredient in many spice mixtures such as curry and chilli powder, and is also used in the production of Tabasco and chilli sauces. The hotness and the brownish red colour of cayenne pepper come from grinding the seeds together with the hot peppers.

First of all, the **fresh fruits** in their entirety are dried. They are then roasted whole and cooked in the sauces.

Flaked cayenne peppers together with their seeds are also marketed. However, cayenne pepper is most commonly available in its **powdered** form, for which the dried cayenne peppers are finely ground together with their seeds.

Paprika is made of different (milder) peppers. Only the best fruits are used for delicate paprika, and their seeds removed (mild paprika). Some of the seeds are ground for noble sweet paprika. The entire fruit is processed for rose and hot paprika.

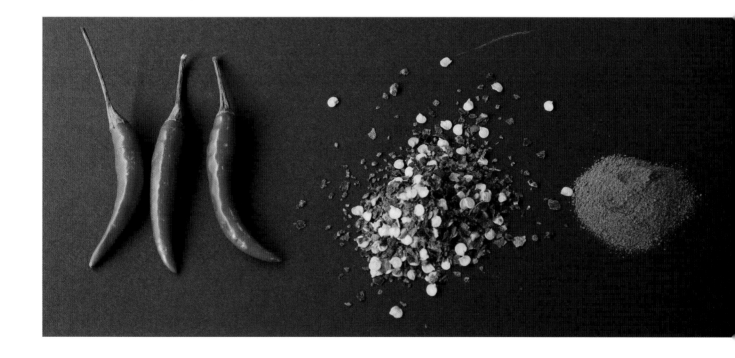

Karhai Paneer
with fenugreek leaves

serves 4

350 g tomatoes

350 g potatoes

350 g paneer (Indian cream cheese)

1 onion, chopped

2 tbsp cooking butter

3 tbsp tomato purée

2 cm ginger, chopped

3 tsp ground cumin

1/2 tsp cayenne pepper

1 tsp turmeric

2 tsp ground coriander

1/2 bunch fresh coriander, chopped

1 tsp channa masala

1/2 tsp asafoetida

2 whole cloves

1 tsp fennel seeds

1 tbsp fenugreek leaves

2 tbsp lemon juice

100 ml cream

50 g cashew nuts, chopped

1 tsp sea salt

500 ml water

2 tbsp cooking butter

sea salt, freshly milled pepper

1/2 bunch coriander, chopped

ch/mi/on

Snick the top of the tomatoes, plunge them briefly into boiling water, slip off their skins and then dice. Peel the potatoes and cut into 2 cm chunks. Cut the paneer into 2 cm cubes. Slice the onion into 8 wedges. Heat the cooking butter and gently sauté the tomato purée, onion wedges and ginger. Add all the spices and the diced tomatoes, and sauté a little longer.

Add the lemon juice, cream, cashew nuts and salt, stir thoroughly and pour in the water. Add the potatoes and cook in the sauce until just tender.

Heat a little cooking butter in a non-stick frying pan and briefly stir-fry the paneer until lightly browned. Add the paneer to the potatoes and season the sauce to taste. Serve garnished with chopped coriander. Basmati rice makes a good accompaniment.

Our tip: In Switzerland paneer is available by the kilo from Käserei in Zezikon, canton Thurgau. You can, of course, make your own paneer (for paneer and basmati rice recipes see Hiltl. Virtuoso Vegetarian – new revised and updated edition, 2006, pages 130 and 116).

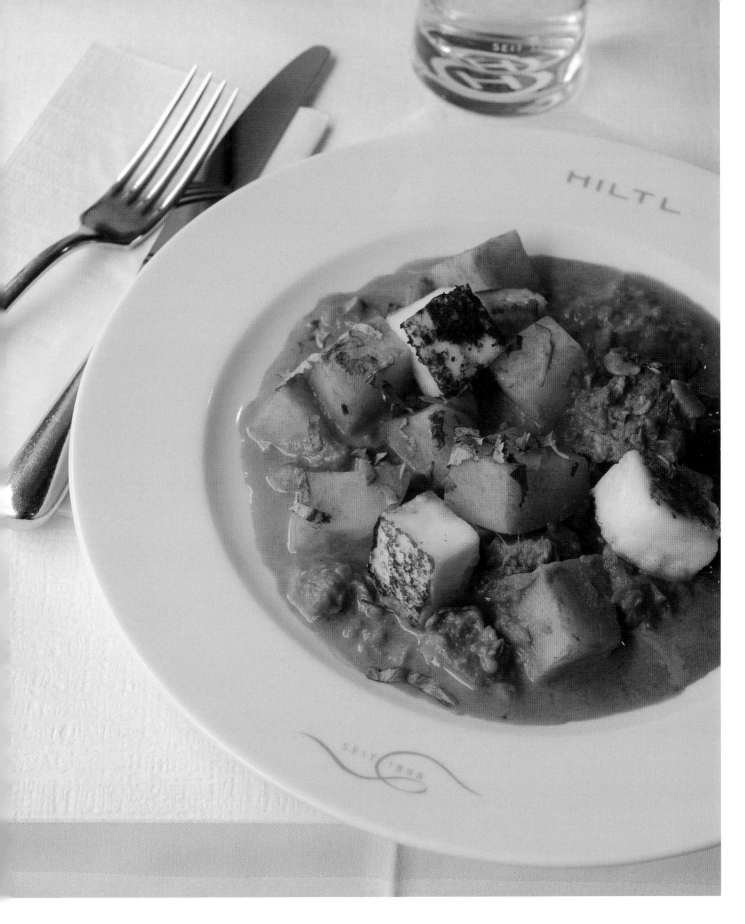

Green Thai Curry
Even an out-and-out "carnivore" will enjoy this dish

serves 4

1 small aubergine
50 ml sunflower oil

3 tbsp sunflower oil
1/2 onion, chopped
1 tbsp fresh ginger, chopped
2 stalks lemon grass
25 g Thai curry paste
(see page 118)
1/2 lime, quartered
1 tsp turmeric
1 tsp sea salt
1 tbsp brown sugar
600 ml coconut milk
600 ml vegetable stock

1 tbsp cornflour
2 tbsp water
200 g fresh mini corn cobs

200 g yardlong beans
250 g Quorn
2 tbsp sunflower oil
sea salt, freshly milled pepper

1/2 bunch coriander
1 lime

eg/ga/mi/on/pe

Cut the aubergine into 1.5 cm chunks, sprinkle with salt and leave for 30 minutes. Pat dry with kitchen paper. Heat 3 tbsp oil and gently sauté the onion and ginger. Add the lemon grass, curry paste and lime quarters and sauté briefly. Add the turmeric, salt and sugar, stir and pour in the coconut milk. Let the sauce simmer for 5 minutes.

Add the stock, bring back to the boil and simmer for a further 10 minutes. Discard the lemon grass and lime quarters and then blend the sauce. Mix the cornflour with the water and stir into the sauce, add the mini corn cobs, reheat and simmer over a low heat for 10 minutes until tender.

Cut the beans into 6 cm lengths, blanch for 3 minutes and refresh in iced water. Heat 50 ml sunflower oil and thoroughly brown the aubergine chunks; drain on kitchen paper.

Cut the Quorn into 1.5 cm slices. Heat 2 tbsp oil and fry the Quorn until well browned.

Add the Quorn and beans to the sauce, reheat and season to taste. Scatter the aubergine chunks over each serving and garnish with lime wedges and coriander. Serve with jasmine rice.

Our tip: Tofu can be used instead of Quorn.

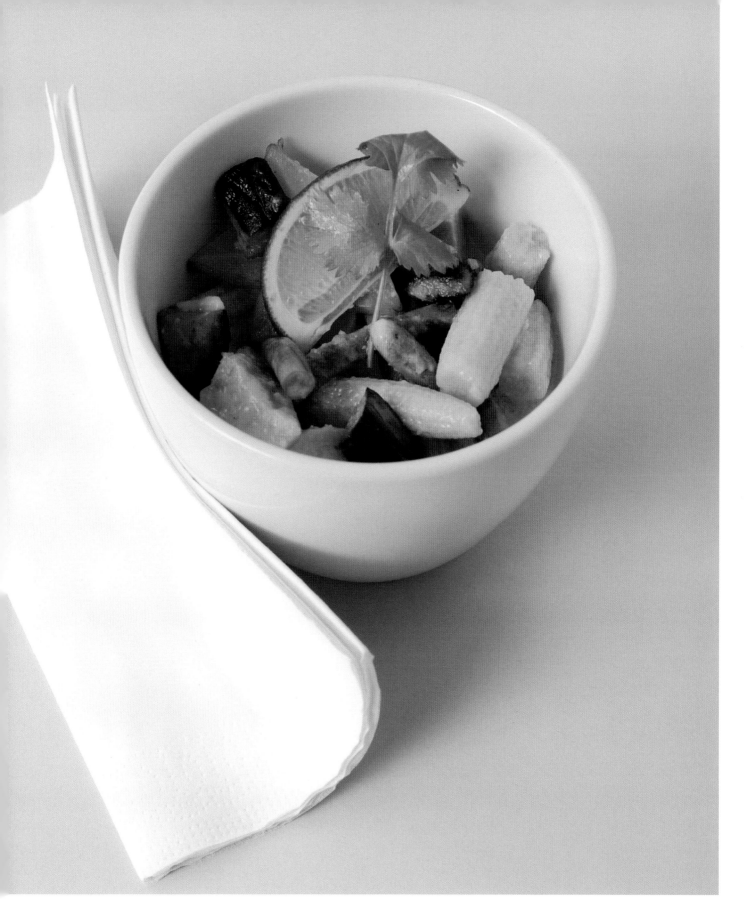

Green Thai Curry Paste
fresh and vegetarian

makes 280 grams

1 shallot

50 g garlic cloves

80 g green chillies, destalked

10 kaffir lime leaves

2 limes

1 $^{1}/_{2}$ tsp ground coriander

$^{1}/_{2}$ tsp ground cumin

25 g galangal

$^{1}/_{2}$ tsp black pepper, crushed

$^{3}/_{4}$ tsp turmeric

1 $^{3}/_{4}$ tbsp sea salt

120 ml groundnut oil

ga/on/pe

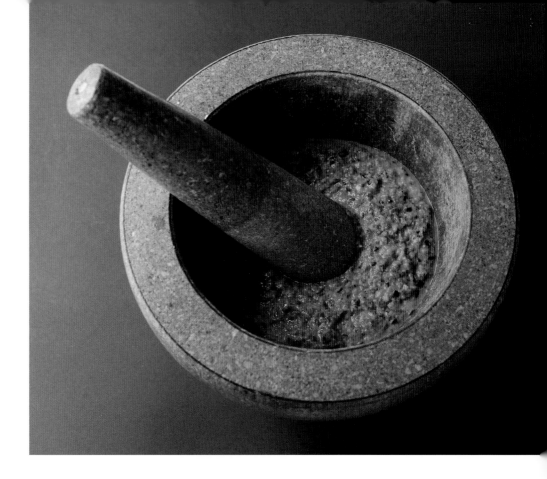

Chop the shallot, garlic and chillies coarsely. Remove the central rib of the lime leaves and chop the leaves as finely as possible. Wash the limes in hot water, dry carefully, and grate the peel.

Using a wand mixer or a mortar and pestle, blend the chopped ingredients together with the grated lime peel until you have a fine paste. Remove the paste and mix in the oil.

Fill the paste into a screw top glass, smooth the top and cover completely with oil. Treated in this way the paste can be stored for up to 4 weeks in the fridge.

Our tip: Galangal is sometimes marketed as galanga or blue ginger. It belongs to the ginger family (Zingiberaceae).

Indian Curry Curry is the Tamil name for a kind of ragout or stew of meat, fish or vegetables served with rice or with various breads such as chapati, naan or puri. In India or Britain the term curry is still used to describe a dish of this kind, whereas in Germany, for example, curry is used to designate a mixture of Indian spices – what the British call curry powder. These curry powders are not used in India, though they are produced there for export.

Indians call their spice mixtures masalas. The combination of spices used differs from region to region, from place to place, and even from household to household, ranging from sweet or spicy to extremely hot. Masalas in Southern India tend to be hotter than in other parts of the country.

Turmeric *(Curcuma longa)* is often a main ingredient. Many curries reflect its typical flavour and rich yellow colour. Other spices often found in curry powders are pepper, chilli, cardamom, coriander seeds, ginger, cumin, nutmeg, fenugreek, pimento, cloves, mace and curry leaves. The spices are generally toasted and then ground in a mortar or spice mill.

Thai Curry In Europe we use the term curry for some dishes known as *gaeng* in Thailand. They are similar to Indian curries, served as a very liquid stew or as soup. Chilli is a main spice in all *gaeng* dishes. Our name for *gaeng phet,* for example, which means spicy soup, is red curry. The spices for these dishes are used in the form of a paste: Roots, fresh leaves and fresh chillies are ground in a mortar with shrimp paste until a homogenous, paste-like mass has formed. To make the chillies milder, the paste is often mixed with coconut milk. Apart from red Thai curry, the green and yellow Thai curries are also popular in Europe.

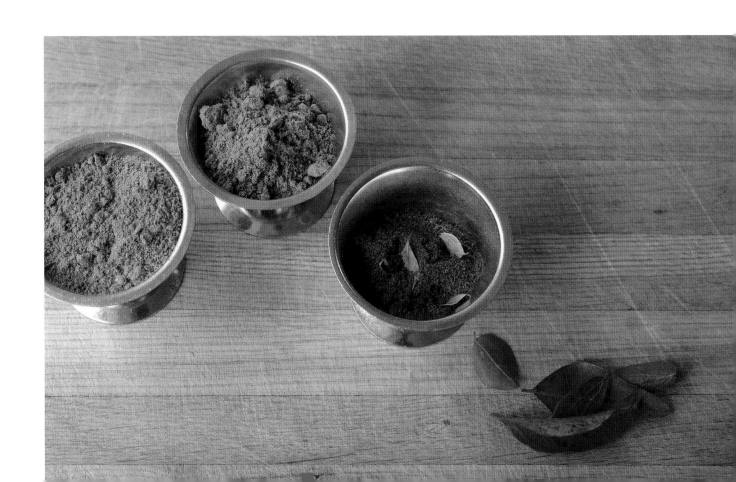

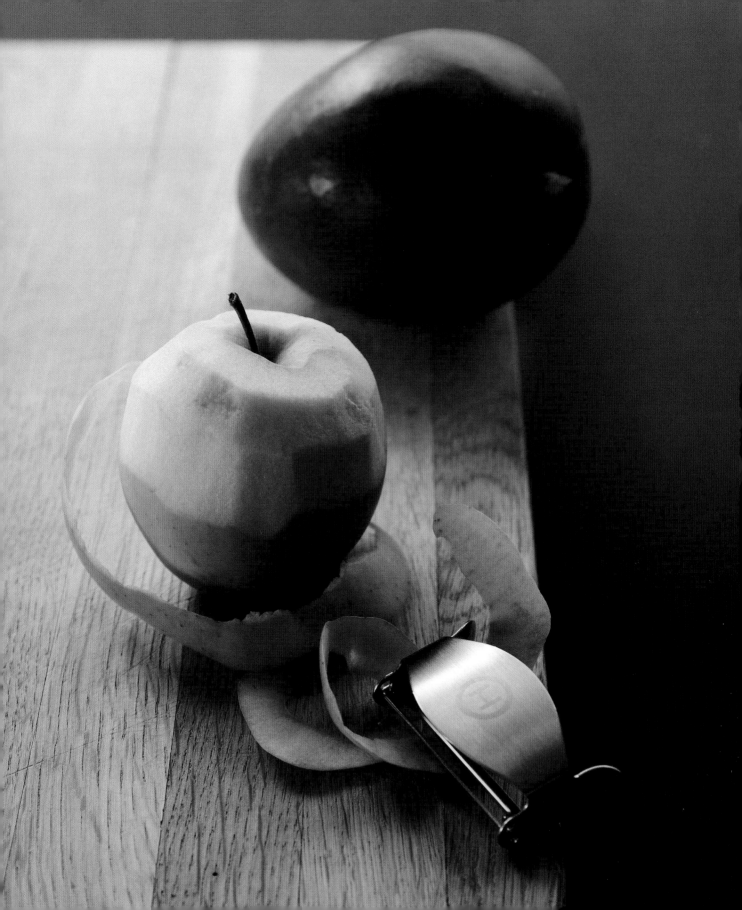

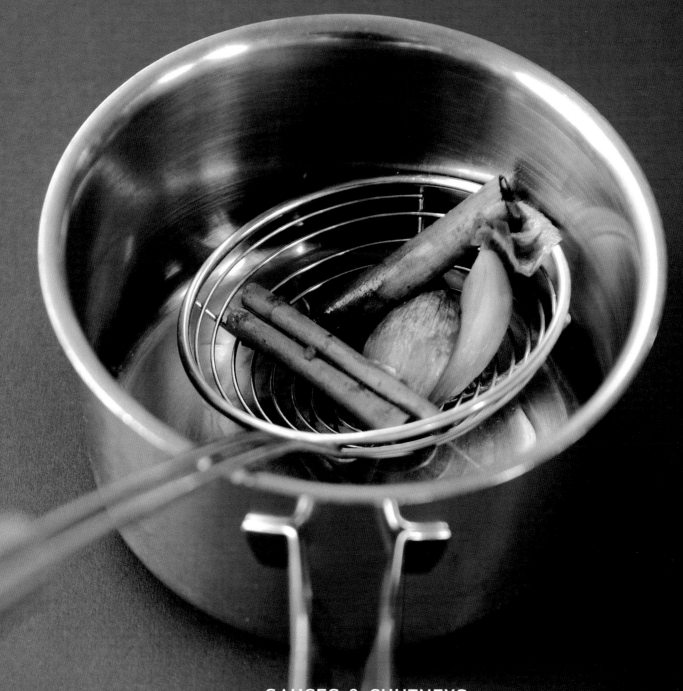

SAUCES & CHUTNEYS
Whether to round off the meal or as a counterpoint:
The contrast between sweet and sour,
mild and hot, local and exotic is what good dining is all about –
dipped and savoured to the very last morsel.

Mango & Apple Chutney

Hiltl's most popular chutney

makes 450 grams

250 g apples, peeled

100 ml cloudy apple juice

50 ml cider vinegar

1 stick cinnamon

$^1/_2$ tsp ground coriander

2 pinches turmeric

1 pinch cayenne pepper

$^1/_2$ tbsp sugar

$^1/_2$ tsp sea salt

1 level tsp ground ginger

180 g mango pulp

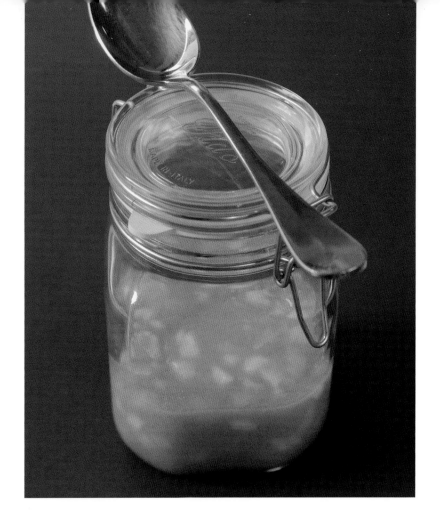

Core the apples and cut into 1 cm dice. Add the spices and cider vinegar to the apple juice and bring to the boil. Then add the diced apples and cook until tender.
Add the mango pulp and leave to cool. In a closed jar the chutney can be stored for at least a week in the fridge.

Our tips: Golden delicious are the best apples for this chutney, with the right balance of acidity and sweetness; they also cook well. Mango pulp is available from Indian stores. Ripe alphonso mangos, puréed with a little water, can be used instead. This chutney tastes best if left in the fridge for about four days. Mango & apple chutney goes well with Indian dishes.

Cranberry & Apple Sauce

with cardamom

makes 300 ml

250 ml cloudy apple juice

150 cranberry juice

150 ml orange juice

1 stick cinnamon

1 tsp ground cardamom

1 walnut-sized piece fresh ginger

1 shallot, halved

2 tbsp brown sugar

1 – 2 tbsp cornflour

3 tbsp red wine

on

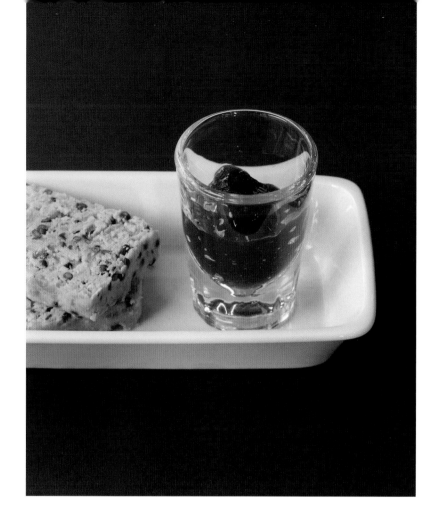

Pour the fruit juices into a saucepan, add the spices and sugar, bring to the boil and reduce by half. Mix the cornflour with the red wine, stir into the sauce and boil for 2 minutes until it binds.
The sauce goes well with our lentil terrine (page 52). In a closed container it will keep in the fridge for 2 weeks.

Our tips: Use pure cranberry juice with no sugar added. This sauce goes well with spicy pies and terrines. Serve with stilton as a starter or with a selection of cheeses at the end of the meal.

Cinnamon Harissa

with fresh coriander

makes 200 grams

140 g sambal oelek

2 tbsp tomato purée

1 tbsp fresh coriander, chopped

2 tbsp parsley, chopped

1/2 onion, chopped

1 1/2 tbsp lemon juice

1/2 tsp sea salt

1/2 tsp ground cinnamon

100 ml water

3/4 tbsp brown sugar

1/2 tsp ground cumin

on

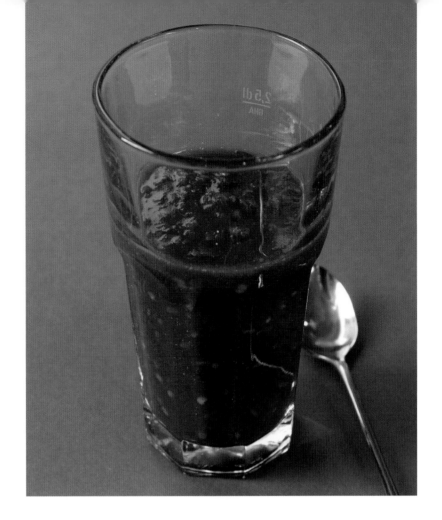

Place the sambal oelek and the tomato purée in a bowl. Add the chopped herbs, onion, lemon juice and all the spices and stir thoroughly. Stored in a closed container this harissa will keep in the fridge for 1 week.

Our tips: Cinnamon harissa goes well with carrot & plum tagine (page 66) or can be used in sauces instead of fresh red chillies to give them a very special flavour. Traditionally, cinnamon harissa is served with couscous dishes (for recipe see Hiltl. Virtuoso Vegetarian – new revised and updated edition, 2006, page 144).

Cinnamon

Cinnamon (left below) is the dried bark of the cinnamon tree, more specifically of the true cinnamon tree native to Sri Lanka (*Cinnamomum verum* or *C. zeylanicum*). It belongs to the laurel family. For the production of cinnamon only the thin inner bark is used which, when the woody outer bark is removed, curls into rolls as it dries. These fine inner barks are packed in layers one inside the other to form layered rolls called "quills". They are then left to dry. The thinner the individual barks, the more aroma the finished quill has. Cinnamon sticks keep well because they give off their aroma very slowly. Cinnamon oil is made from the smaller branches and the leaves of the cinnamon tree.

Cinnamon is one of the oldest spices known, and was probably used as early as 3000 B.C. by the Chinese. Vasco da Gama, the Portuguese explorer, brought true cinnamon from Sri Lanka (Ceylon) to Europe around 1503. From the 16th to the 18th century, cinnamon was a very expensive and very valuable spice in Europe. The Sri Lankan quality grading system divides the cinnamon quills into four main groups on the basis of their diameter. The groups are then sub-divided into specific grades depending on quill diameter and number of quills per kilogram. The cinnamon mainly available in Europe is the fourth quality group known as "Hamburg", and is considered to have the poorest quality quills. Once ground, however, the flavour is the same as ground cinnamon from the other groups.

In Europe we tend to use cinnamon together with sugar for desserts, cakes, tea and mulled claret rather than for savoury or spicy food or with meat dishes as they do in Northern India, for example. Cinnamon oil is used to flavour liqueurs and as a fragrance in the perfume industry. In certain regions cinnamon leaves are used just as we use bay leaves.

Cassia Cinnamon

Cassia Cinnamon (right below) True (Sri Lankan) cinnamon is often confused with the cheaper cassia cinnamon (also called Chinese cinnamon). Cassia cinnamon is made from a related cinnamon tree species, and has a stronger, harsher flavour than true cinnamon. Its bark is thicker and coarser and, unlike the bark from the Sri Lankan plant, only curls to one side. Before drying, the outer parts of the bark are only scraped off superficially. The quality of cassia cinnamon can be enhanced by peeling the bark to remove lichen and tannin. This process improves the flavour, because the harshness comes from the amount of tannin in the bark.

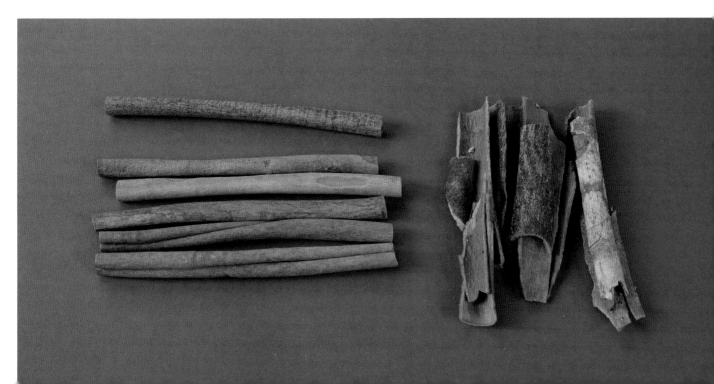

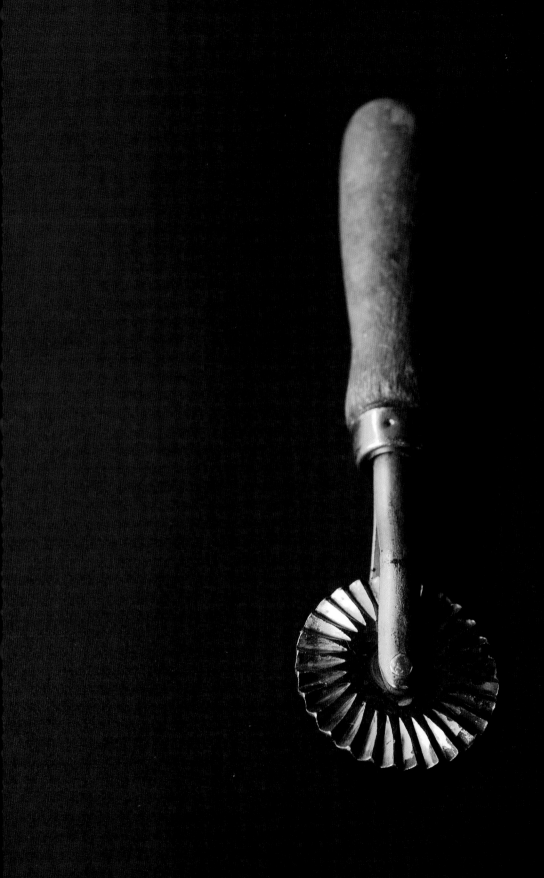

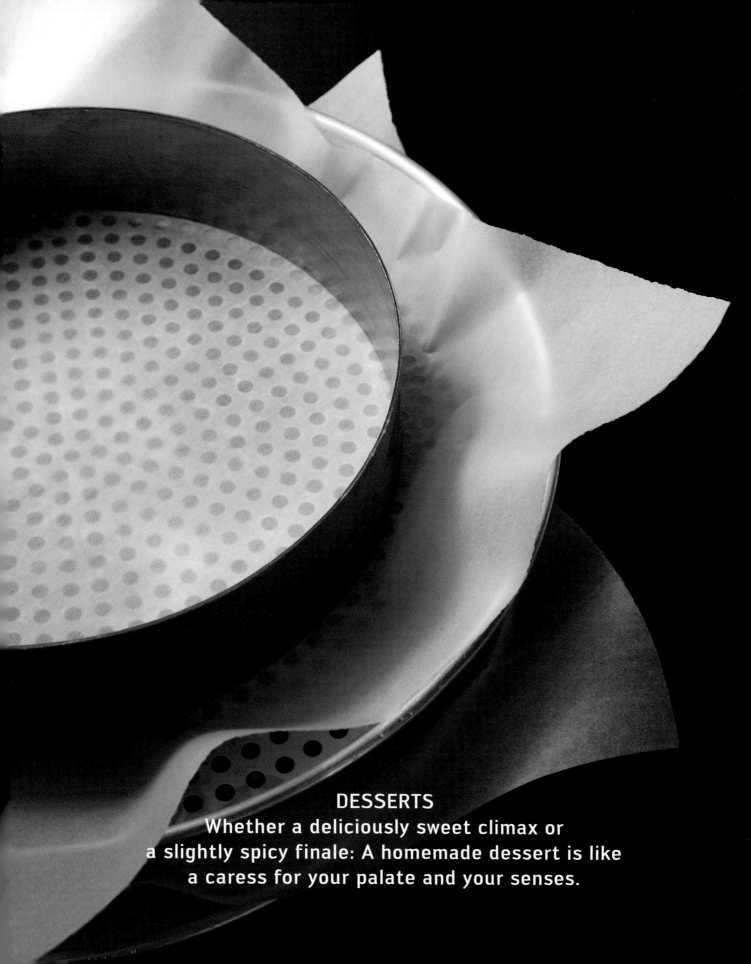

DESSERTS
Whether a deliciously sweet climax or
a slightly spicy finale: A homemade dessert is like
a caress for your palate and your senses.

Crème Brûlée
one of our most popular desserts

serves 4

200 g brown sugar
50 ml water
1 tsp lemon juice
750 ml milk

3 tbsp milk
3 tbsp cornflour

3 eggs
2 1/2 tbsp brown sugar

200 ml whipping cream, whipped
4 tbsp brown sugar

eg/mi

Caramelise the sugar with the water and lemon juice until golden brown. Pour in the milk and bring to the boil to liquefy the caramel. Stir the cornflour into 3 tablespoons of milk, add to the caramel milk and bring up to the boil again.

Beat the eggs and sugar, stir in a little of the hot caramel milk and then pour everything into the remaining caramel milk. Bring up to simmering point: The crème must not boil because then it would burn and the eggs curdle. Strain the crème and leave to cool.

Fold the whipped cream into the cooled crème. Fill the crème into ramekins and refrigerate. Just before serving, sprinkle the crèmes with the brown sugar and caramelise with a chef's blowtorch. Serve immediately.

Our tip: An open flame will immediately caramelise the sugar before it collects any moisture. The crème should be served cold with a hot crust.

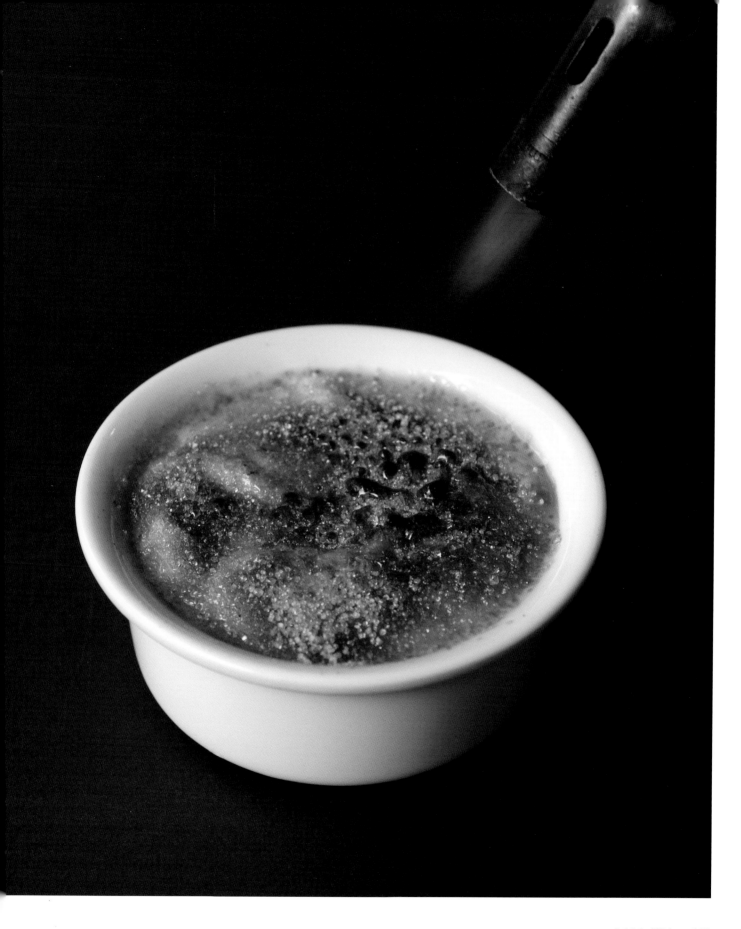

Cheesecake
a Hiltl recipe since 1970

for a 24 cm springform cake tin

100 g butter, cold

200 g flour

100 g brown sugar

2 pinches sea salt

1 egg

2 eggs

80 g sugar

$^1/_2$ lemon, grated rind

2 $^1/_2$ tbsp cornflour

200 ml milk

200 g double cream cheese

400 g low fat curd cheese

60 g raisins

ch/eg/gl/mi

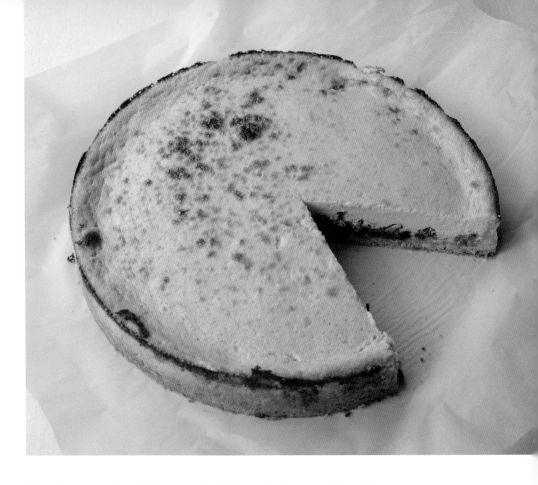

Cut the butter into flakes and rub into the flour until you have very fine crumbs. Mix in the sugar and salt. Using a dough scraper, incorporate the egg into the pastry. Bring the pastry together and leave to rest in the fridge for 30 minutes. Whisk the eggs, sugar and grated lemon rind until foamy.

Whisk up the milk and cornflour and stir into egg mixture. Add the cream cheese and curd cheese and whisk again. Then stir in the raisins. Roll out the pastry about 3 mm thick and 2 cm wider than the diameter of the springform. Butter the cake tin, dust with flour and lift the pastry into the tin, turning up the edges.

Preheat the oven to 170 °C.

Pour the filling onto the pastry and immediately place the cheesecake on the middle shelf of the oven and bake for 45 – 50 minutes. The cheese mixture should be a golden yellow colour with a few flecks of golden brown here and there.

To test if the cheesecake is cooked: Stick a wooden toothpick into the filling; if it comes out clean, the cheesecake is done.

Our tip: Instead of raisins use fresh berries according to season from May to September. The original cheesecake was baked in a rectangular tin and cut into squares.

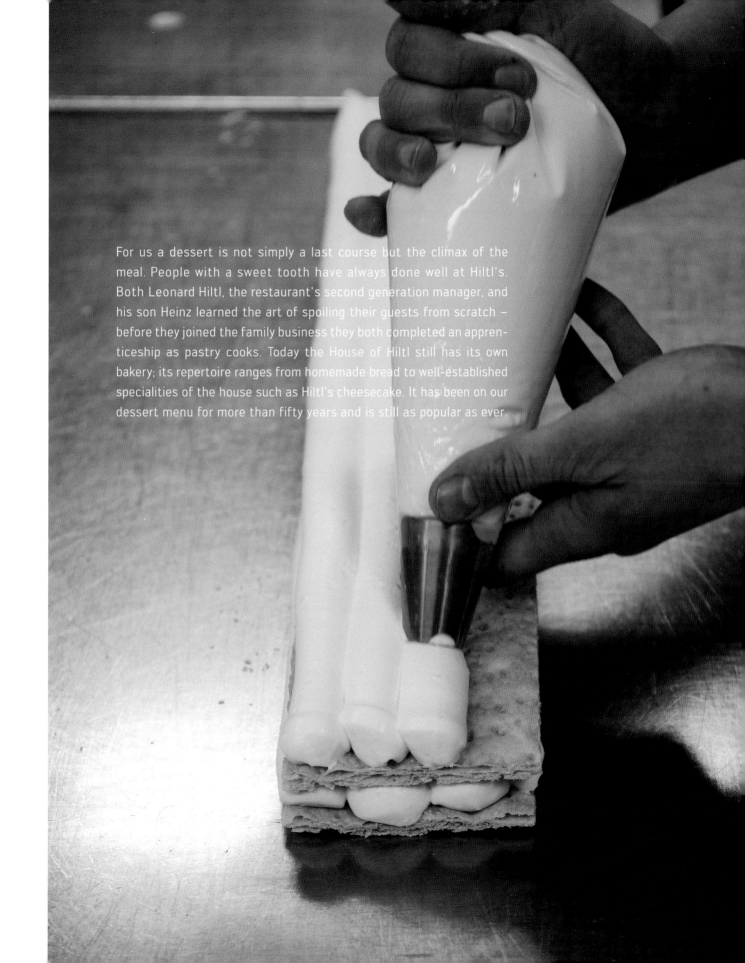

For us a dessert is not simply a last course but the climax of the meal. People with a sweet tooth have always done well at Hiltl's. Both Leonard Hiltl, the restaurant's second generation manager, and his son Heinz learned the art of spoiling their guests from scratch – before they joined the family business they both completed an apprenticeship as pastry cooks. Today the House of Hiltl still has its own bakery; its repertoire ranges from homemade bread to well-established specialities of the house such as Hiltl's cheesecake. It has been on our dessert menu for more than fifty years and is still as popular as ever.

Linzertorte
a classic from Austria

for a 24 cm springform cake tin

175 g butter, cold
175 g blanched almonds, ground
175 g flour
175 g white sugar
1 egg
1 – 2 tbsp water

350 g raspberry jam

1 egg yolk
1 tbsp water

eg/gl/mi

Cut the butter into flakes and rub into the flour and ground almonds until you have very fine crumbs. Mix in the sugar. Using a dough scraper, incorporate the egg and water into the pastry. Bring the pastry together and leave to rest in the fridge for 30 minutes.

Roll out the pastry about 4 mm thick and 2 cm wider than the diameter of the springform. Butter the tin, dust with flour and lift the pastry into the tin, turning up the edges. Preheat the oven to 180 °C.

Spread the jam evenly over the pastry.

Roll out the remaining pastry to about 24 x 24 cm and 3 mm thick and, using a pastry wheel, cut it into strips 1.5 cm wide. Place the strips diagonally over the jam to form a lattice pattern. Fold the edges of the pastry over the filling and the ends of the pastry strips.

Mix the egg yolk and water and brush over the pastry to glaze. Bake in the middle of the over for 30 – 45 minutes until golden brown.

Our tip: You can use ground hazelnuts instead of ground almonds.

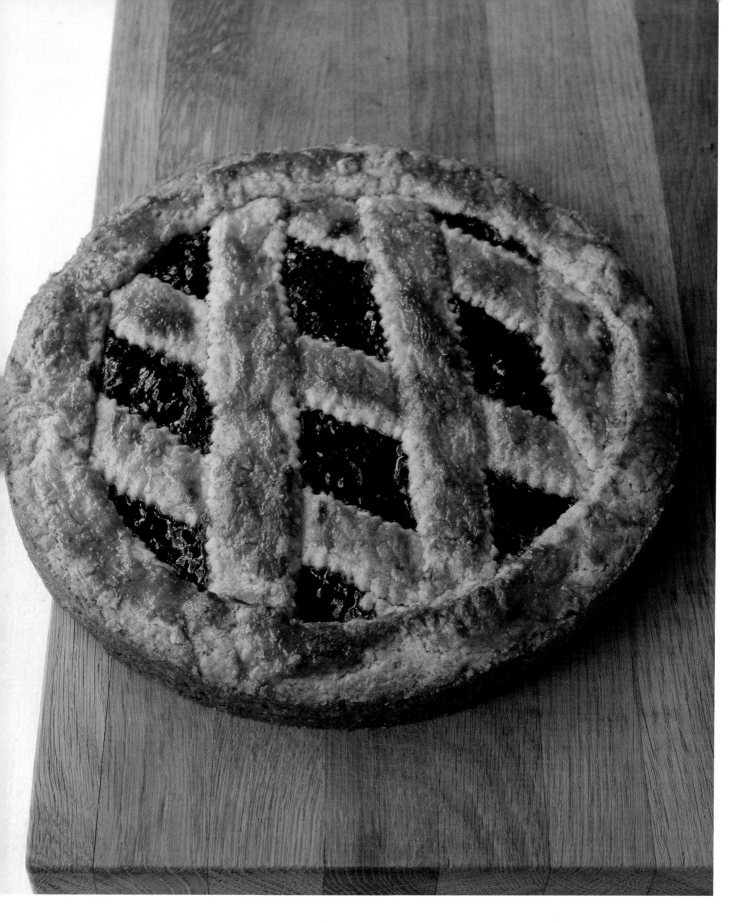

Hiltl's
Chocolate Mousse
with bitter chocolate

serves 4

400 ml cream

120 g bittersweet couverture
120 g grand-cru couverture 72 %
2 tbsp milk

70 g egg yolk
2 tbsp white sugar

eg/mi

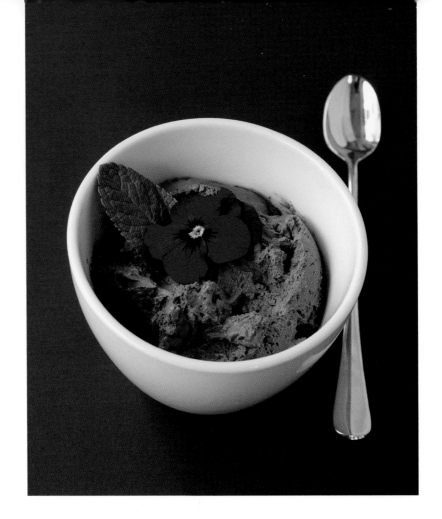

Whip the cream. Melt the couvertures with the milk in a bain marie.
Beat the egg yolks and sugar until you have a light, very foamy mass
and mix with the liquid couverture.
Fold the whipped cream into the chocolate and egg mixture and refrigerate for 4 hours.

Our tip: The chocolate mousse will be even firmer if you cool it for an entire day. Use pasteurised egg yolk.

Edible flowers

Many flowers found in gardens and meadows are edible and can add a touch of colour and flavour to your favourite recipes. Flowers can be used just like herbs and spices, or as edible decoration. Large funnel-shaped flowers like courgette blooms can be deep-fried in batter, or filled with vegetables, cheese or meat. Small flowers like daisies, borage and pansies are simply scattered over the dish before serving, whereas larger flowers can be carefully divided. With flowers from the Asteraceae family (pot marigold, chrysanthemum, sunflower) only the tender outer petals are used. The number of flowers used depends on the intensity of their aroma. Small flowers and petals frozen in ice cubes or ice bowls can be used in many ways. Candied flowers are commonly used for desserts and pastries, especially rose petals and violets. Rose petals are also popular for a "love feast", for example in risotto. Orange blossom and roses are used to make orange blossom water and rosewater. In Europe they often figure among the ingredients for special cakes and pastries at Christmastime. In the cuisines of North Africa, the Middle East and India they are used for festive meals, even in meat dishes.

Edible flowers for use in the kitchen must come from plants that have not been sprayed with toxic pesticides. A word of warning: Many poisonous plants have extremely attractive flowers. In Switzerland, specialised nurseries grow edible flowers so that quality and availability are guaranteed. They are sold in delicatessen stores and in certain supermarkets.

Here's a list of some of the best-known edible flowers: Yarrow, chives, ramsons (wild garlic), dill, fuchsia, daisy, borage, pot marigold, elderflower, cornflower, chrysanthemum, sunflower, hyssop, lavender, peony, sage, dandelion, nasturtium, violet, rose, phlox, marigold, brown knapweed, oxeye daisy, cowslip, day lily, phalaenopsis, bergamot, carnation, jasmine, orange blossom, courgette.

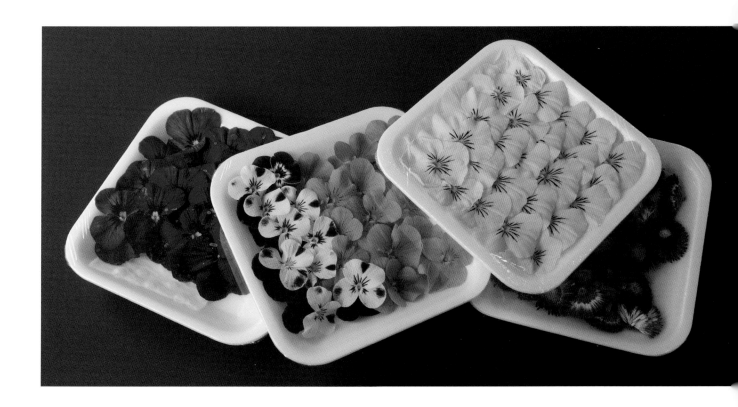

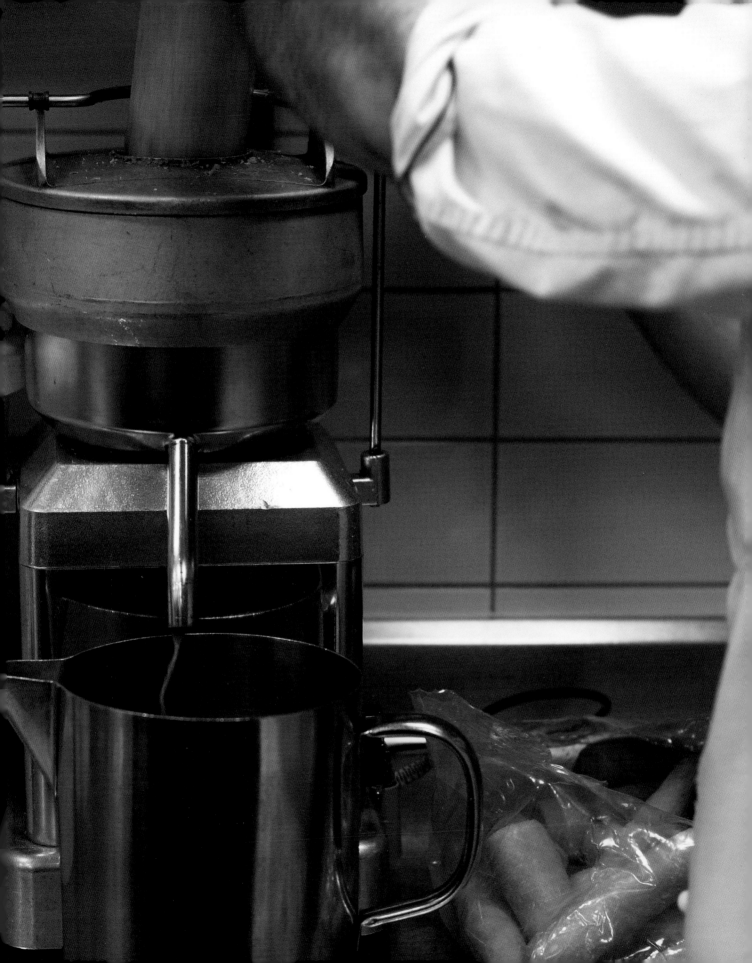

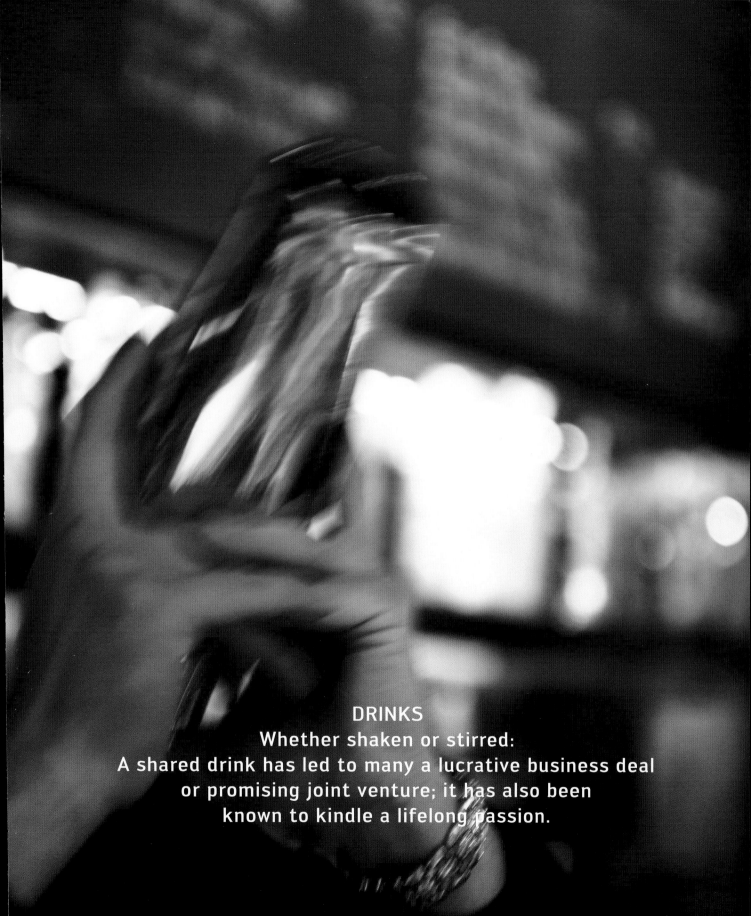

DRINKS
Whether shaken or stirred:
A shared drink has led to many a lucrative business deal
or promising joint venture; it has also been
known to kindle a lifelong passion.

Tutti-Frutti Juice

top among our freshly squeezed juices

makes 1.2 l (6 drinks)

6–7 oranges

1 banana, peeled

20 g sea-buckthorn syrup

2 golden delicious apples, peeled

2 pears, peeled

1 kiwi, peeled

200 ml water

Halve the oranges and use a citrus press to squeeze out the juice, there should be about 600 ml. Slice the banana finely directly into the juice, add the sea-buckthorn syrup.
Core the apples and pears, dice and immediately add to the orange juice. Add the water and blend thoroughly with a mixing wand. Pass through a sieve.

Our tip: The water makes the juice flow better.

Litchi & Mandarin Juice

exotic vitamin bomb for winter

makes 1.2 l (6 drinks)

7–8 mandarin oranges

4–5 oranges

900 g fresh litchis

130 g fresh pineapple, peeled

(approx. 1/4 pineapple)

Halve the mandarins and oranges and squeeze separately: this should give 400 ml mandarin juice and 250 ml orange juice. Peel the litchis and pit them, this juice calls for 400 g litchi flesh.
Dice the pineapple and litchis and add to the juices. Pour into a mixing jug , blend thoroughly and pass through a sieve.

Our tip: In summer when litchis are not in season, this drink can be made with well drained, canned litchis.

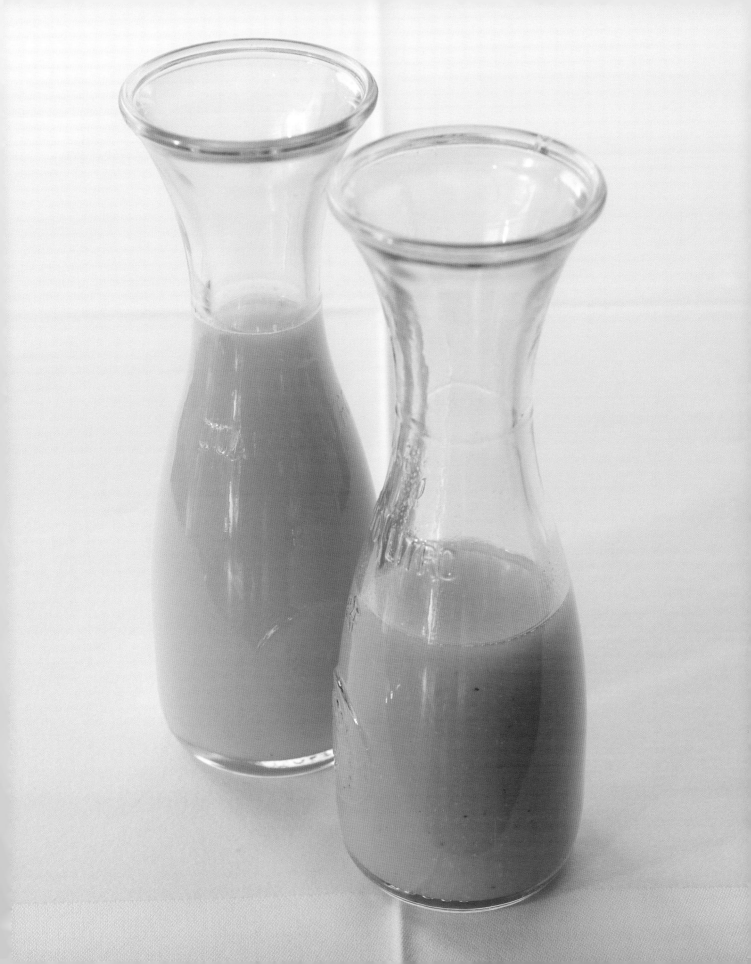

Green Jelly Baby
with fresh pineapple juice

1 drink

20 ml amaretto

20 ml Soho litchi

10 ml blue curaçao

pineapple juice

1 sprig mint

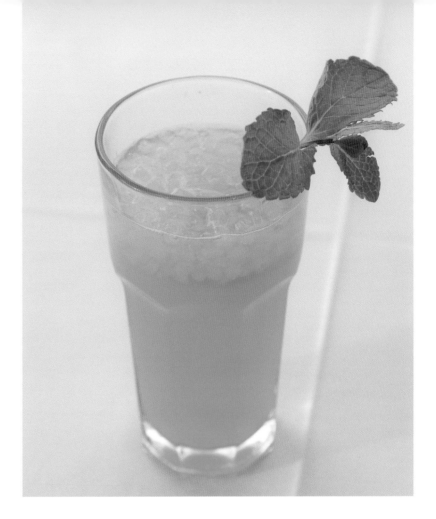

Fill a cocktail shaker with ice cubes. Add all the ingredients except the pineapple juice. Cover and shake well. Pour the drink into a long-drink glass and top up with pineapple juice. Decorate with a sprig of mint and serve with a drinking straw.

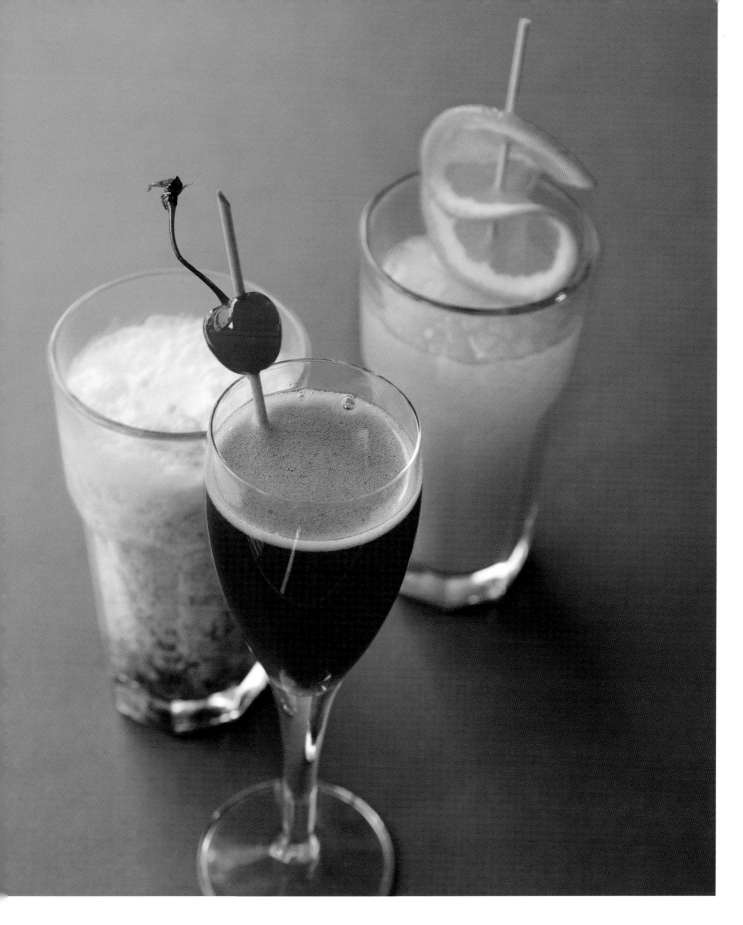

1 drink

20 ml Absolut vodka
10 ml Batida de Coco
10 ml cassis liqueur
1 single serve coffee creamer
pineapple juice
cassis liqueur

mi

Purple Rain (photo page 141, left)

Fill the cocktail shaker with ice cubes. Add all the ingredients and the pineapple juice. Cover and shake well. Pour the contents into a long-drink glass and serve immediately with a drinking straw.

Our tip: Use fresh pineapple juice

1 drink

10 ml Absolut raspberry
10 ml raspberry concentrate
prosecco
1 cocktail cherry

Nancini (photo page 141, centre)

Fill a prosecco glass with crushed ice. Add Absolut raspberry and raspberry concentrate, then stir with a bar spoon. Fill up with prosecco and stir again. Garnish with a cocktail cherry and serve with a drinking straw.

1 drink

20 ml Absolut madarin
10 ml peach concentrate
orange juice
orange slice

Spring Breeze (photo page 141, right)

Fill a cocktail shaker with ice cubes. Add all the ingredients, cover and shake well. Pour into a long-drink glass. Garnish with a slice of orange and serve with a drinking straw.

Honeymoon

1 drink

20 ml Galliano
20 ml Bailey's
1 scoop vanilla ice
1 double espresso
1 single serve coffee creamer

whipped cream,
chocolate covered coffee beans

eg/mi

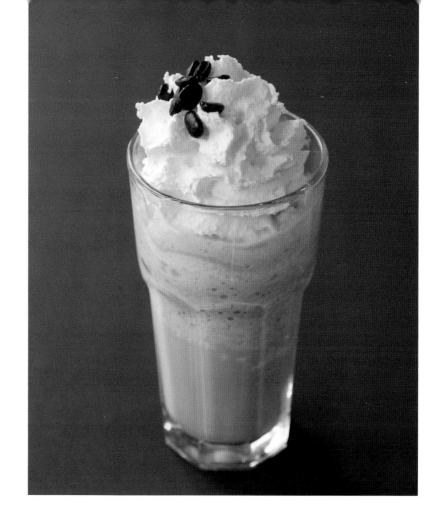

For this drink you need a blender. Put all the ingredients together with half a long-drink glass of crushed ice into the blender and blend thoroughly. Pour the drink into a long-drink glass, top with whipped cream and garnish with chocolate covered coffee beans. Serve with a drinking straw.

Our tip: Our honeymoon drink also makes a good dessert.

Orange Syrup
with orange blossoms

makes 1l

1 orange

150 g fruit sugar

2.5 g orange blossoms

400 ml water

850 ml orange juice

Wash the oranges with hot water, dry carefully, and finely grate the rind. Place the fruit sugar, orange blossoms and grated orange rind in a jug. Bring the water to the boil, pour over the orange blossoms and leave to infuse for 3 minutes. Strain.

Reduce the orange juice to 400 ml, add to the orange blossom infusion and mix thoroughly. In a sealed bottle the syrup will keep for at least 1 week in the fridge.

Orange Lemonade:
Fill a 250 ml glass one-quarter full with crushed ice, add 100 ml sparkling mineral water, 80 ml orange syrup and 40 ml orange juice. Garnish with a slice of orange and serve with a drinking straw.

Our tip: Orange blossoms are sold in specialised tea shops. Always try and use freshly squeezed orange juice.

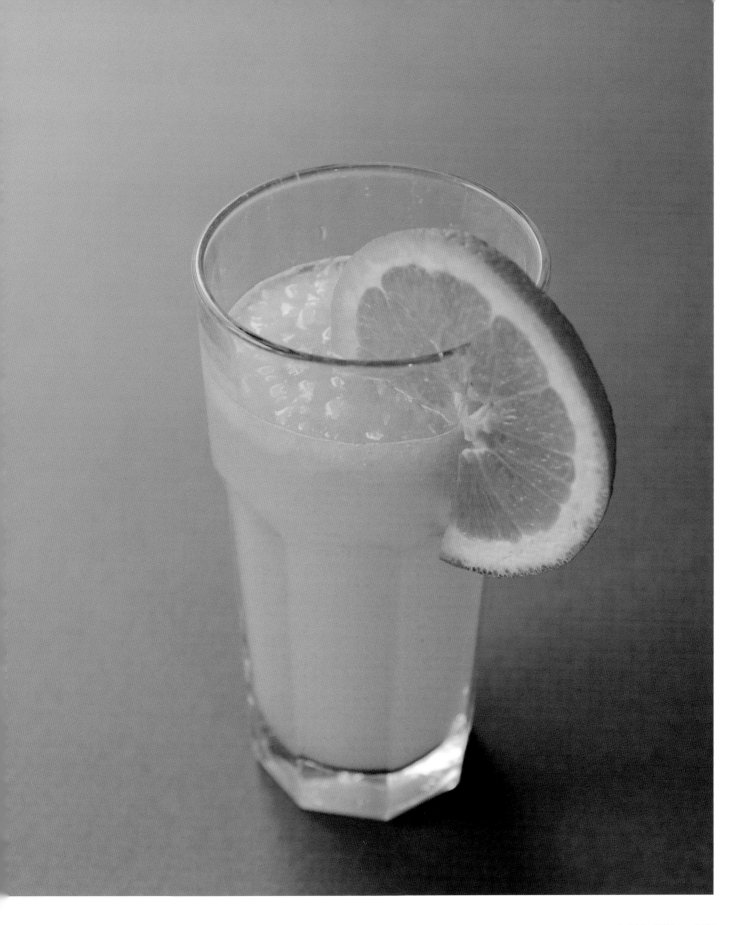

Iced Rooibos Tea
with fresh mint

makes 1.5 l

800 ml water

2 sprigs fresh mint

5 teabags Rooibos tea

30 g fruit sugar

250 ml orange juice

600 ml water

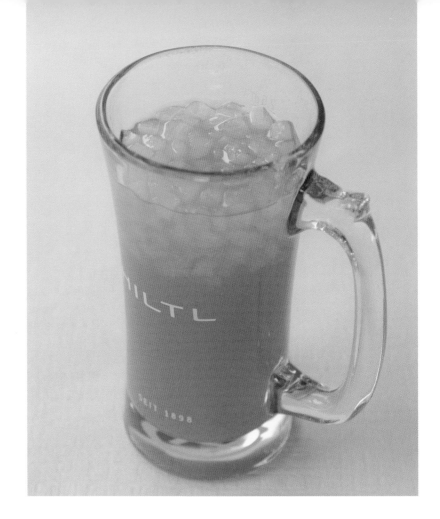

Place the mint and the teabags in a large jug. Bring the water to the boil and pour over the teabags, leave to infuse for 15 minutes. Remove the mint and teabags and squeeze out any remaining liquid.
Add the fruit sugar and stir thoroughly. Pour in the orange juice and water. Serve the iced tea with crushed ice.

Our tip: Use freshly squeezed orange juice, as we do at Hiltl. This tea is suitable for children as it does not contain any black tea.

Rooibos (Afrikaans: rooi = red; bos = bush) comes from South Africa and is a member of the legume family of plants. Here in Switzerland, rooibos or red tea has been a popular alternative for black tea since the 1990s. Rooibos is only grown in a small area in the Cederberg region of the Western Cape province. In South Africa, rooibos is also used for cooking and baking, in the production of cosmetics and as a hair colorant. It is not known when the rooibos plant arrived in South Africa nor how long ago people started making use of it. In 1772 it was described by the botanist Carl Thunberg as a plant with healing properties. In the wild the plant grows to a height of about one metre. The rooibos bush has a number of strong offshoots with delicate side branches. Its leaves are green, thin and long – rather like pine needles except that they are very soft. A bush has to be about 18 months old before its leaves can be harvested.

In the 1930s methods were developed together with the local farmers to lay out rooibos plantations. These experiments led to Clanwilliam in the Cedar Mountains becoming the centre for the cultivation of the rooibos plant. Today there are numerous varieties.

After cutting, the branches are bundled and taken to the processing yard. There they are chopped, bruised and dampened with water. In the warm climate they are then left to oxidise and ferment for 8 – 24 hours. During this process certain compounds are broken down and some new ones formed. This is how rooibos tea gets its amber colour and fruity flavour. Once it has been dried it is sieved to cleanse it and then pasteurised using water vapour. Green rooibos tea is unfermented and has a much more delicate flavour.

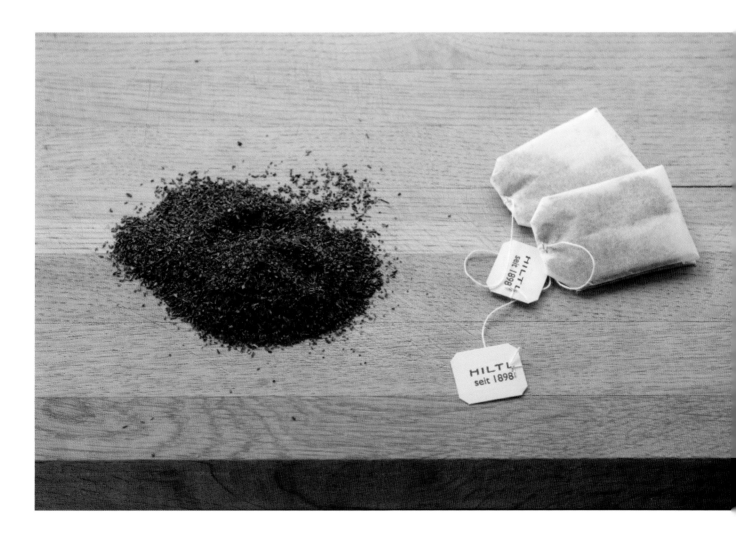

Glossary

Absinthe: Absinthe is an alcoholic beverage. It was originally produced in Val de Travers, Neuchâtel, using wormwood, aniseed, fennel and a selection of herbs that vary according to the distillery.

Agar agar is a vegetarian gelling product made of red seaweed. Not all agar agar products gel equally strongly, hence the amount stated in the recipe may have to be increased or reduced. Agar agar is only suitable for food that is prepared hot, and it sets after 6 hours of cooling. After more than 48 hours it loses its gelling properties.

Asafoetida is also marketed as hing or asant. Where unavailable, garlic can be used instead.

Aubergines are also called egg plants. As they are members of the nightshade family of plants, aubergines are related to tomatoes and potatoes. To ensure that they will taste good and become tender when cooked, they should always be sprinkled with sea salt after slicing and set aside for about 20 minutes. Before cooking, the slices should be drained on kitchen paper.

Brunoise are very finely diced vegetables (2 – 3 mm).

Cambozola: As its portmanteau name suggests, Cambozola is a combination of the white rind mould of Camembert outside and the blue veined Gorgonzola inside. It is a German mild and subtle full-fat cheese.

Canned tomatoes: If no fresh, very ripe tomatoes are available it is advisable to use canned chopped tomatoes.

Channa masala is a spice mixture for chickpeas available in Indian specialty stores. It is also the name of a popular chickpea and tomato dish in Indian cuisine.

Chef's blowtorch is used for turning sugar into caramel. Available in kitchen shops and the household departments of larger stores.

Chestnuts: Edible chestnuts, sometimes called sweet chestnuts, should not be confused with horse or conker chestnuts. Edible and horse chestnuts are easy to tell apart – the edible ones are not round like conkers but have a distinct point at the top.

Chiffonade: Tightly rolled herb or salad leaves cut into fine strips.

Coriander is called cilantro in the United States and dhani in India. Although all parts of the plant are edible, in Europe mainly the leaves and seeds are used. Seeds are available whole or in powdered form. Coriander roots are commonly used in Thai cuisine.

Cornflour: cornstarch

Courgette also known as zucchini or baby marrow is a popular summer squash. Its flowers can be stuffed or deep-fried.

Couverture is chocolate with a higher percentage of cocoa butter. It is used by professionals for dipping, coating, moulding and garnishing.

It can be melted and re-melted through warming and is easier to handle than cooking chocolate. The cocoa solids in couverture and other chocolates are shown in percent. There are special grand cru couvertures made of only one type of cocoa bean and their place of origin can be traced back.

Cumin is also marketed as jeera.

Fenugreek is also marketed as methi.

Feta is a white, brined curd cheese made of sheep's and / or goat's milk. It is produced on the Greek mainland and the island of Lesbos. It is crumbly and has a spicy, slightly sour taste.

Five spice powder is a classical Chinese spice mixture made of star anise, cassia cinnamon, cloves, fennel seeds and Sichuan pepper.

Garam masala is an Indian spice mixture.

Jalapeños are green, medium-hot peppers about 3 inches (7 cm) long. They are often stuffed and deep-fried, but can also used to add an extra "kick" to certain dishes.

Juliennes are very finely sliced vegetables (strips 2 – 3 mm wide).

Kaffir lime: The kaffir lime is a citrus plant. It has fragrant, bumpy fruits smaller and less sour than limes or lemons. Its pungent leaves are commonly used in Southeast Asian and Thai cooking and are an essential ingredient in Thai green curry paste.

Mu-err mushrooms are also known as Chinese morels, Judas's ear or jelly ear fungus. They grow on various deciduous trees more or less worldwide and are commonly used in Asian cuisine, particularly in China. They are mostly sold dried.

Paneer is an Indian fresh cheese made of cow's milk.

Peppers are also called bell peppers.

Quorn: Quorn is a registered brand for a meat substitute product made from edible fungus (mycoprotein) mixed with chicken egg albumen, onions, spices, manioc flour and the gelling agent pectin.

Radicchio rosso: Red radicchio can be used like other salad leaves. It has a small firm head of dark red, white veined leaves and a slightly bitter taste. It is excellent in a mixed leaf salad.

Sea salt: Hand-harvested fleur de sel is considered the best salt in the world.

Seitan: A pure wheat gluten product available in health stores.

Star fruit is also known as carambole.

Stock is often called bouillon in the United States. In the recipes we used our homemade vegetable stock. Gluten-free or glutamate-free stock (bouillon) cubes or granules make a good substitute.

Tamarind paste is a concentrate of the fruit pulp of the tamarind tree (Indian date tree). It is available from Indian stores.

Tofu is a very high protein product made of soaked and then ground soybeans. These are brought to the boil and the resulting milky liquid is coagulated using nigari (magnesium chloride), citric acid or calcium sulphate (gypsum). Subsequently, the coagulants are separated through heating, skimming or filtering. The soy curds are then pressed to form blocks. The process is very similar to cheese making.

Turmeric may be sold as haldi in Indian stores.

Vermicelli are very fine noodles. The vermicelli used in our recipes are made with rice flour.

Wakame is a brown seaweed rich in iodine. It is often used in Japanese and Korean cuisine.

Yardlong beans are about 16 inches (40 cm) long and are sold by the bunch. They are also known as snake beans, asparagus beans and, in the UK, as Chinese long beans.

Hiltl's guiding principles for product buying:

- extra virgin olive oil
- no genetically manipulated foods
- no animal-based gelatine
- no food additives and no glutamate
- where possible domestic products or products from neighbouring European countries
- $1/3$ of the products seasonal (neighbouring European countries)
- organic quality for milk, various cheeses, vegetables and cereals, Swiss organic free-range eggs

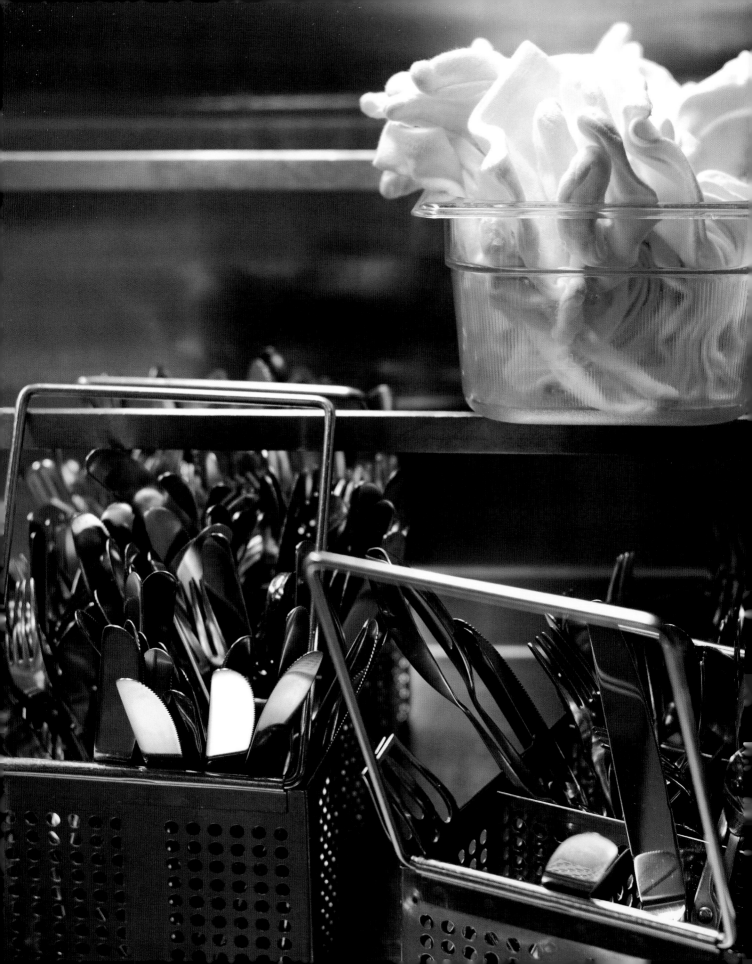

Notes to the Recipes

Quantities: We always state the number of servings or the quantity made for each recipe.

Measurements:

Tbsp = 1 level tablespoon ≈ 15 ml (US), 18 ml (UK)

16 tbsp = 1 cup = 240 ml = 225 g

Tsp = 1 level teaspoon ≈ 5 ml (US), 6 ml (UK)

l = litre, 1 l = 1000 ml

g = gram, 100 g = 3.5 ounces (oz)

kg = kilogram, 1 kg = 2.205 pounds (lb)

Oven temperatures:

°C	°F	Gas Mark
140	275	1
170	325	3
190	375	5
220	425	7

Declaration of ingredients:

All ingredients in the recipes in this cookbook and the dishes available in the House of Hiltl are precisely declared. Our guests with allergies, food intolerance or simply dislike of certain flavours greatly appreciate this service.

ce = celery / celeriac

ch = cheese

eg = eggs

ga = garlic

gl = gluten

mi = milk

nu = nuts

on = onions

pe = peanuts

so = soybeans

vegan = without ch/eg/mi

Season to taste: Seasoning with salt and pepper is according to individual taste and therefore no amounts are given.

Salt: In the House of Hiltl and for the recipes we use sea salt. The most exquisite sea salt is called fleur de sel.

Sugar: In the House of Hiltl we mostly use brown sugar. If white sugar should be used for reasons of colour or flavour, this is stated in the recipe. In some recipes sugar is used to regulate acidity (e.g. of tomatoes or vinegar). In such cases adding sugar is optional.

Vegetarianism: The Vegetarian Society, founded in 1847, claims to "have created the word vegetarian from the Latin 'vegetus' meaning lively" (which is how these early vegetarians said their diet made them feel). Vegetarianism is used to describe a stimulating way of life with a diet in which, apart from vegetables, only food derived from living animals may be eaten (eggs, milk, honey). Various types of vegetarians reject some or all animal-based food.

Various vegetarian diets:

Ovo vegetarians: no meat, fish, milk

Lacto vegetarians: no meat, fish, eggs

Lacto-ovo vegetarians: no meat, fish

Vegans: no animal-based foodstuffs (meat, fish, milk, eggs, honey).

Vegans use a pear concentrate instead of honey.

All foods include the products made from them.

Positive aspects of vegetarianism

▥ high intake of vitamins, minerals, fibres, carbohydrates

▥ low risk of heart disease, diabetes, high blood pressure, overweight, high cholesterol level

▥ many secondary plant products (in fresh vegetables and fruit) have anticarcinogenic, antioxidant or antithrombotic properties

Please note:

▥ The supply of vitamin D and B12 can be critical, as these are only found in animal-based foods. Vitamin D is also formed in the body through light, so that enough time should be spent outdoors to avoid insufficiency.

▥ Low iron levels are frequently observed, but not a lack of red blood corpuscles.

▥ Supplementary minerals are recommended for risk groups (children, young people, pregnant women, active sportspersons).

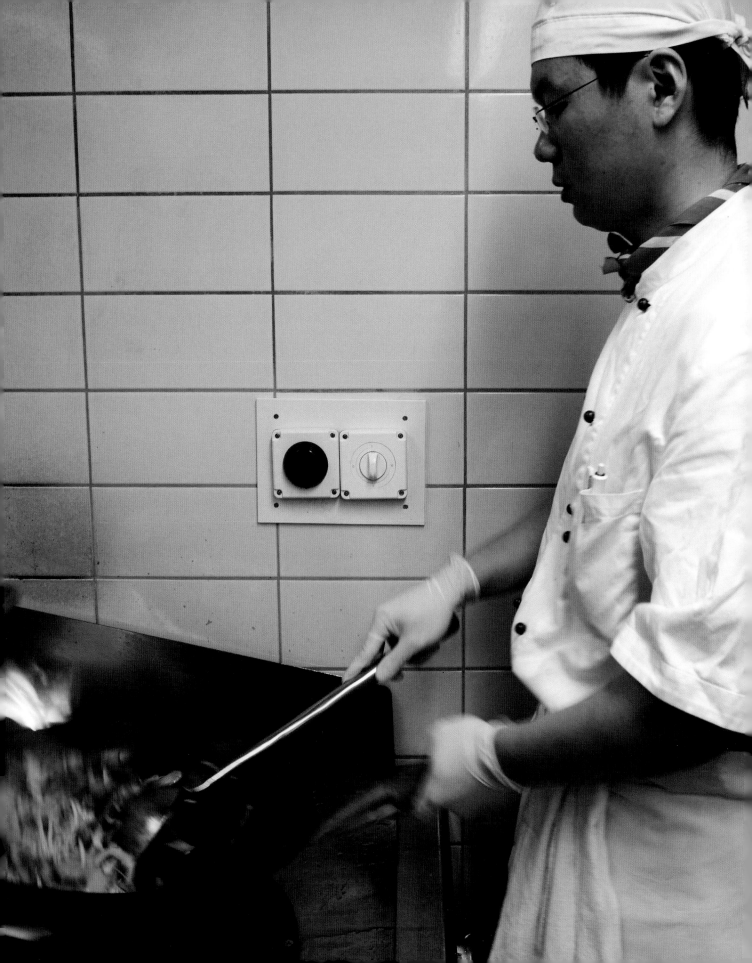

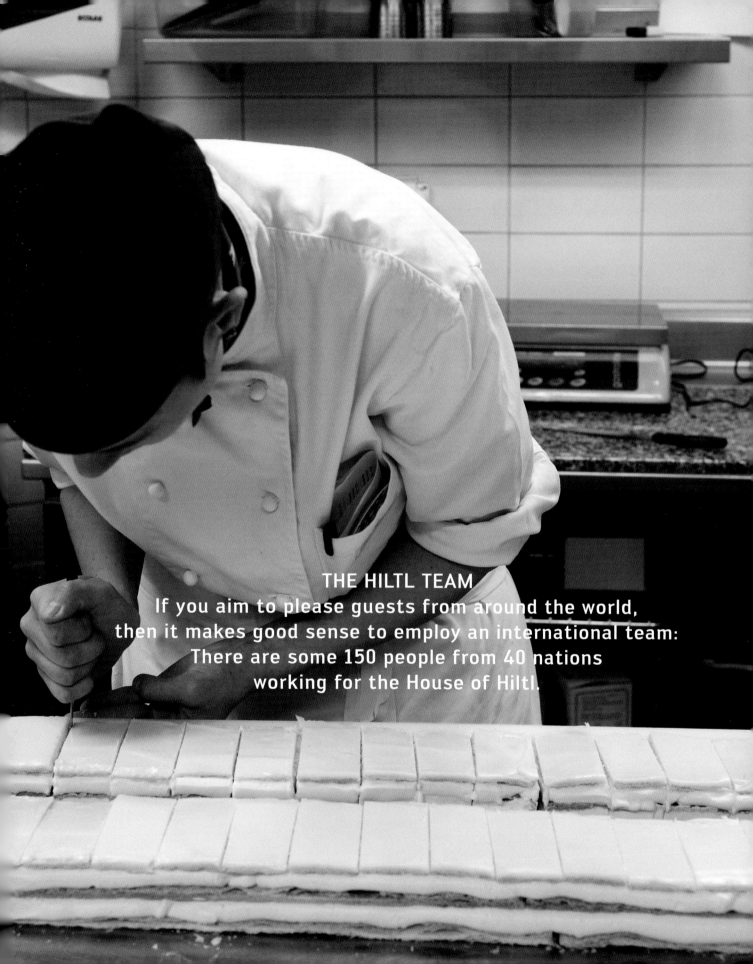

THE HILTL TEAM
If you aim to please guests from around the world,
then it makes good sense to employ an international team:
There are some 150 people from 40 nations
working for the House of Hiltl.

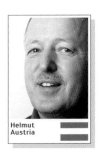
Helmut
Austria

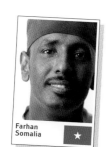
Farhan
Somalia

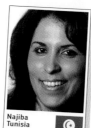
Najiba
Tunisia

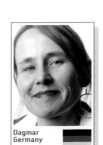
Dagmar
Germany

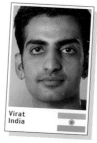
Virat
India

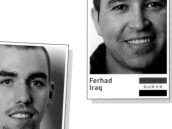
Pascal
Switzerland

Ferhad
Iraq

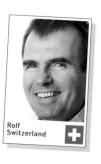
Rolf
Switzerland

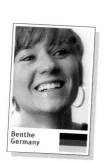
Benthe
Germany

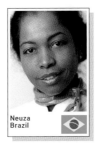
Neuza
Brazil

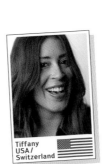
Tiffany
USA /
Switzerland

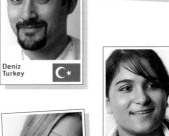
Deniz
Turkey

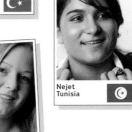
Nejet
Tunisia

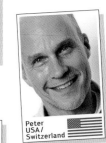
Khalid
Iraq

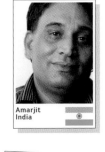
Amarjit
India

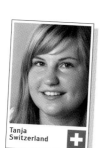
Tanja
Switzerland

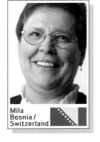
Mila
Bosnia /
Switzerland

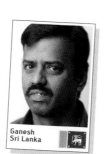
Ganesh
Sri Lanka

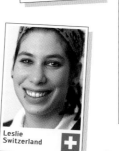
Claudia
Switzerland

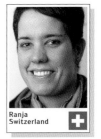
Leslie
Switzerland

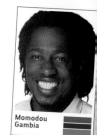
Ranja
Switzerland

Peter
USA /
Switzerland

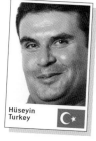
Hüseyin
Turkey

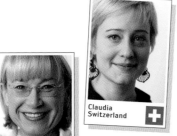
Mirjana
Croatia

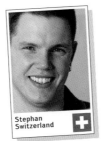
Claudia
Switzerland

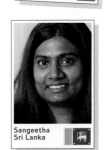
Stephan
Switzerland

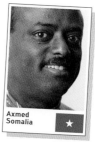
Sangeetha
Sri Lanka

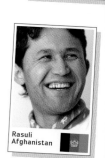
Axmed
Somalia

Momodou
Gambia

Rasuli
Afghanistan

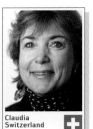
Claudia
Switzerland

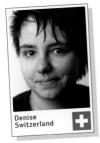
Denise
Switzerland

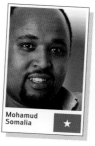
Mohamud
Somalia

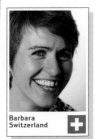
Barbara
Switzerland

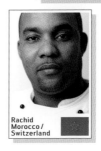
Rachid
Morocco /
Switzerland

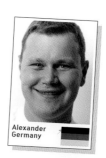
Alexander
Germany

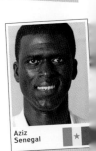
Aziz
Senegal

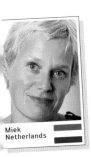
Miek
Netherlands

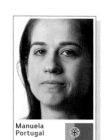
Manuela
Portugal

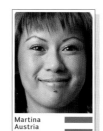
Martina
Austria

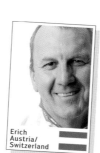
Erich
Austria/
Switzerland

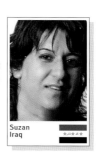
Suzan
Iraq

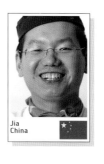
Jia
China

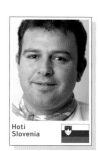
Hoti
Slovenia

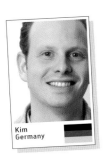
Kim
Germany

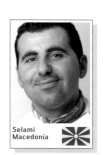
Selami
Macedonia

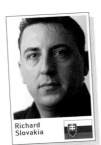
Richard
Slovakia

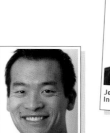
Tingfeng
China/
Switzerland

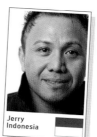
Jerry
Indonesia

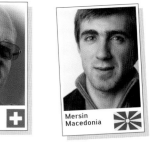
Karl
Switzerland

Mersin
Macedonia

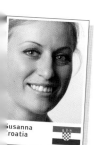
Susanna
Croatia

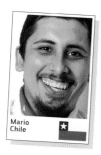
Mario
Chile

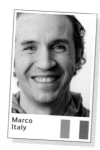
Marco
Italy

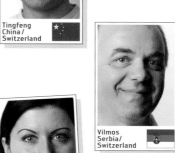
Vilmos
Serbia/
Switzerland

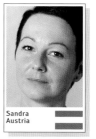
Sandra
Austria

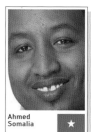
Ahmed
Somalia

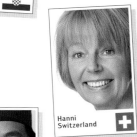
Hanni
Switzerland

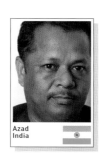
Azad
India

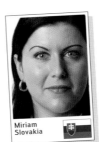
Miriam
Slovakia

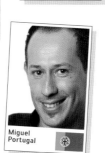
Miguel
Portugal

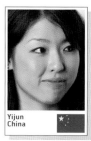
Yijun
China

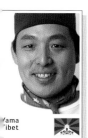
Yama
Tibet

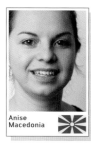
Anise
Macedonia

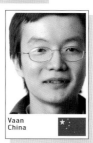
Vaan
China

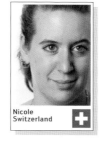
Nicole
Switzerland

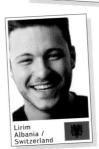
Lirim
Albania/
Switzerland

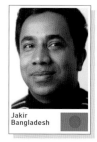
Jakir
Bangladesh

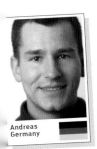
Andreas
Germany

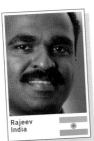
Rajeev
India

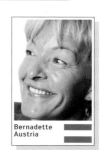
Bernadette
Austria

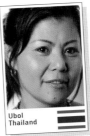
Ubol
Thailand

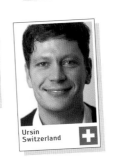
Ursin
Switzerland

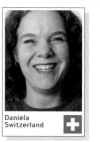
Daniela
Switzerland

HILTL 155

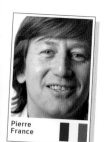
Pierre
France

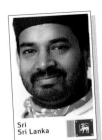
Sri
Sri Lanka

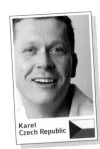
Karel
Czech Republic

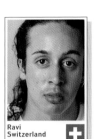
Ravi
Switzerland

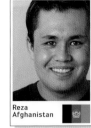
Reza
Afghanistan

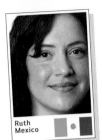
Ruth
Mexico

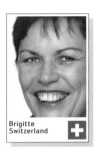
Brigitte
Switzerland

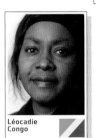
Léocadie
Congo

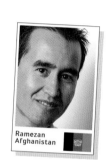
Ramezan
Afghanistan

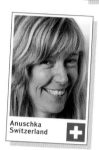
Anuschka
Switzerland

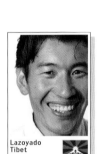
Lazoyado
Tibet

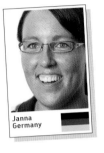
Janna
Germany

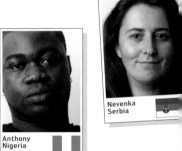
Anthony
Nigeria

Nevenka
Serbia

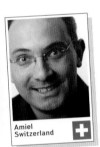
Amiel
Switzerland

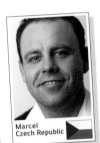
Marcel
Czech Republic

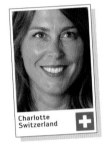
Charlotte
Switzerland

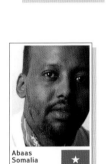
Abaas
Somalia

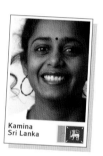
Kamina
Sri Lanka

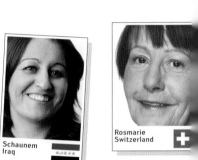
Schaunem
Iraq

Rosmarie
Switzerland

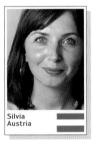
Silvia
Austria

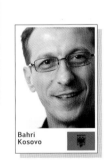
Bahri
Kosovo

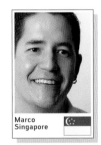
Marco
Singapore

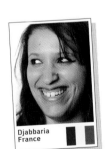
Djabbaria
France

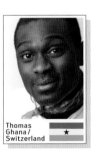
Thomas
Ghana /
Switzerland

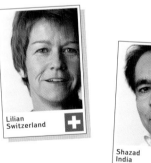
Lilian
Switzerland

Shazad
India

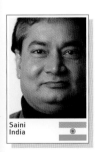
Saini
India

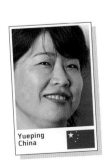
Yueping
China

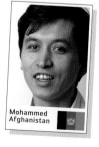
Mohammed
Afghanistan

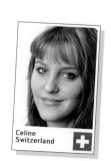
Celine
Switzerland

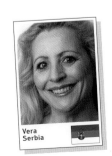
Vera
Serbia

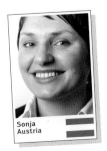
Sonja
Austria

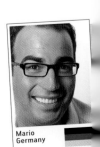
Mario
Germany

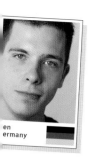
...en
...ermany

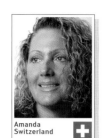
Amanda
Switzerland

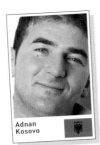
Adnan
Kosovo

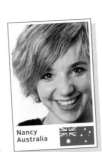
Nancy
Australia

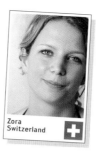
Zora
Switzerland

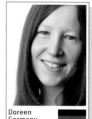
Doreen
Germany

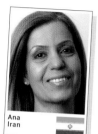
Ana
Iran

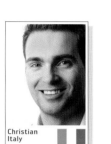
Christian
Italy

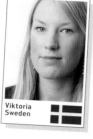
Viktoria
Sweden

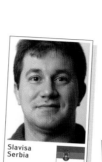
Slavisa
Serbia

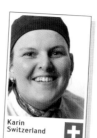
Karin
Switzerland

Miriam
Switzerland

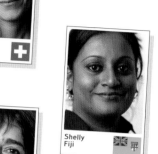
Desirée
Switzerland

Shelly
Fiji

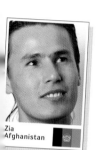
Zia
Afghanistan

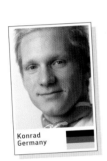
Konrad
Germany

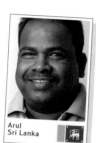
Arul
Sri Lanka

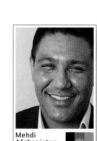
Mehdi
Afghanistan

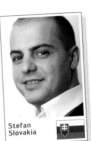
Stefan
Slovakia

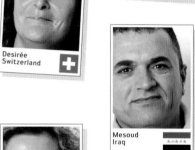
Marielle
France

Mesoud
Iraq

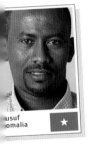
...usuf
...omalia

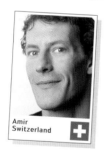
Zorica
Serbia

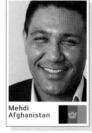
Amir
Switzerland

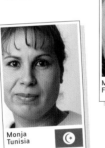
Monja
Tunisia

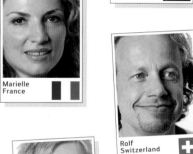
Rolf
Switzerland

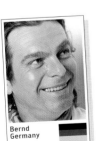
Bernd
Germany

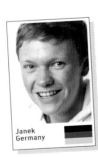
Janek
Germany

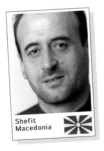
Shefit
Macedonia

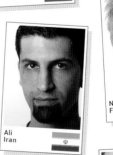
Ali
Iran

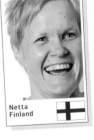
Netta
Finland

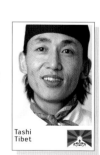
Tashi
Tibet

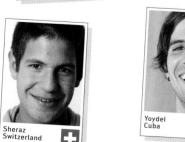
Sheraz
Switzerland

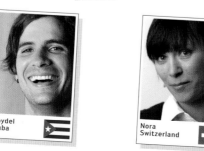
Yoydel
Cuba

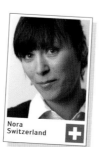
Nora
Switzerland

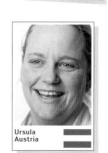
Ursula
Austria

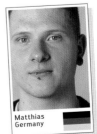
Matthias
Germany

HILTL 157

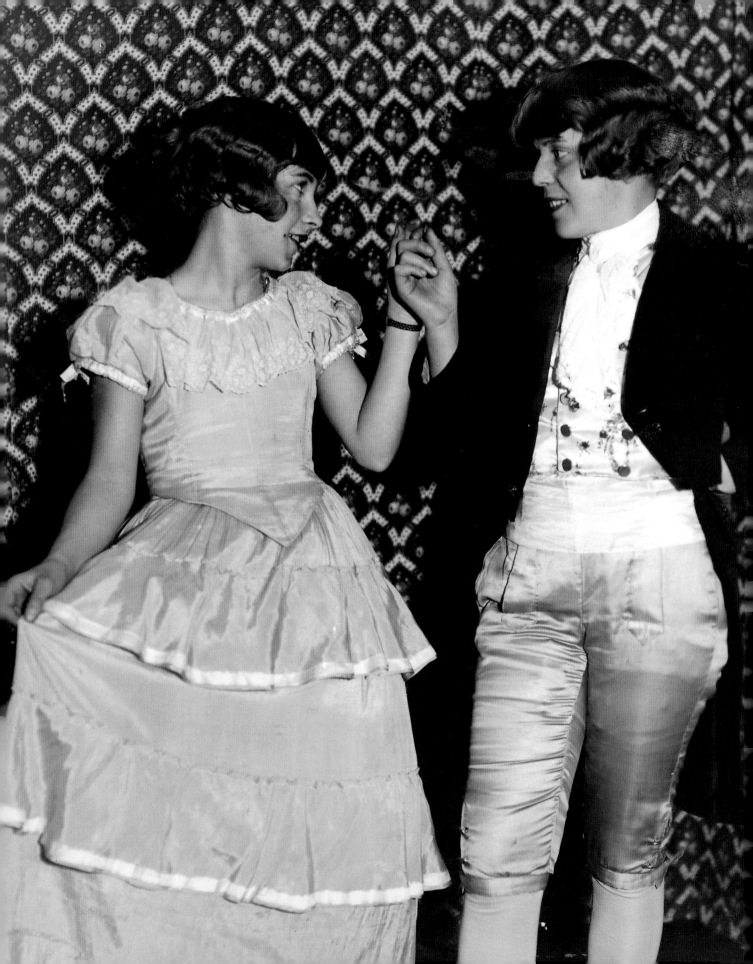

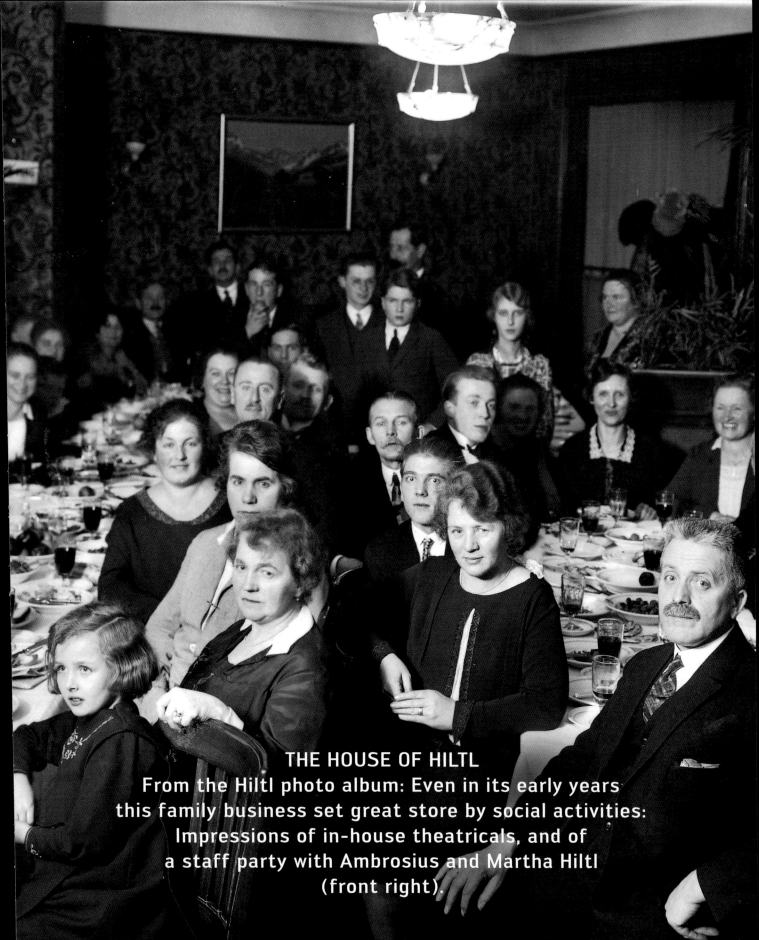

THE HOUSE OF HILTL
From the Hiltl photo album: Even in its early years
this family business set great store by social activities:
Impressions of in-house theatricals, and of
a staff party with Ambrosius and Martha Hiltl
(front right).

True to their roots for four generations

This is the story of the oldest vegetarian restaurant in Europe, of a family business steeped in tradition, which has repeatedly reinvented itself and yet remained true to its roots. Let's flash back to the last few years of the 19th century and focus on Ambrosius Hiltl, a twenty-year-old journeyman-tailor from Bavaria, who settled in Zurich after his travels. Ten years later, not only was he no longer a foreigner, he had acquired his own restaurant and become a citizen of Zurich.

Actually, Ambrosius Hiltl had expected to earn his living with needle and thread, but a severe illness changed the direction of his life: He developed rheumatoid arthritis, which meant he had to give up the tailoring trade he had only just learnt and, moreover, to stop eating meat. The latter was the real catalyst for change: His health improved and his new vegetarian diet brought him in contact with a rundown vegetarians' home and teetotal café, which had been founded by other German immigrants in 1898 and shortly after that relocated to Zurich's Sihlstrasse. In 1903 he took over as head of the ailing restaurant and, just twelve months later, he was appointed manager of the entire business. Finally, during this time he met and married Martha Gneupel from Saxony, the vegetarian cook and general assistant at the vegetarians' home. Her recipes shaped the nature of the business for decades, and some still do to this very day.

Ambrosius Hiltl took over the vegetarians' home in the same year that Max Bircher-Benner, an early advocate of a meat-free diet, opened his sanatorium in the Dolder area of Zurich. The growing popularity of his ideas on healthy nutrition were later to impact positively on the vegetarians' home, though it did not really begin to flourish until the 1930s. The decades up to then meant extremely hard work for the Hiltls, and their daily turnover of about 35 francs did not stretch very far. But Ambrosius did not give up hope. He was known as a man of considerable strength, of calmness and dependability together with an exceptional sense of purpose – qualities that make pioneers.

Over the years, the number of detractors dwindled, and those who had initially dubbed Zurich's teetotal restaurant "root cellar" and openly ridiculed its "grass-eating" vegetarian guests grew noticeably quieter. With increasing success the Hiltls toyed with the idea of expanding to Berlin, Paris or other major cities. But Ambrosius, who claimed that moderation is all things was the secret of a ripe old age, resisted this temptation – just as his descendants were to do in the years to come. He managed the business until 1955, actively supported in his later years by his sons: Leonhard, a trained pastry cook, and Walter, who subsequently served as chef de cuisine for forty years. Ambrosius remained mentally and physically active. Even in his nineties he still travelled across half the world, and when he was at home, he worked every day in his Zurichberg allotment.

The spirit of innovation lives on

Ambrosius Hiltl's spirit of innovation and his tenacity were passed on from generation to generation. In the 1930s, his son Leonhard Hiltl installed the first fully-electric restaurant kitchen, which aroused considerable comment in the trade. In the 1950s, his wife Margrith Hiltl won out over all the sceptics and introduced recipes and elements from Indian cuisine. At first mainly Indian guests were enthusiastic, but gradually many local guests also began to appreciate this innovation. The art of Indian cooking is still a major element in the Hiltl programme.

When Leonhard died, aged only 53, Margrith Hiltl took over the management of the business and her son Heinz, a recently qualified pastry cook and graduate of the hotel management college in Lausanne, joined the business at the age of 22. Three years later he married Hanni Döhla, whom he had met at the college. In the following years he never tired of advocating the advantages of eating well-prepared fresh fruit, vegetables and whole foods. In 1969, in a text he contributed to the *Aktion Gesundes Volk* (movement for a healthy population), he called on restaurateurs to rethink their approach. However much people like meat, its preparation could not be the sole yardstick to measure the skills of a restaurant's cooks. Surely the quality of a so-called side dish was just as decisive. Indeed, he suggested that they turn the tables and begin to regard meat as a side dish.

This family business was a bastion of calm in the surge of discussions about healthy food – and with its cuisine based on fresh foods, it became a trendsetter and a yardstick for others. The restaurant had been renamed "Hiltl's Vegi", and apart from its café and tea room, it now also included the term "diet restaurant" in its name. And it is true that from the very beginning the restaurant prepared low-salt and low-fat meals on request, since no one else catered for guests with such needs. Moreover, at the end of the 1960s, a special low-cal menu was introduced for weight watchers. However, Heinz Hiltl was well aware that for many people diet food was what you ate when you were ill or convalescent. To counteract this prejudice he decided to freshen up the restaurant's image – a move that the next generation was to take a few steps further twenty years later. Despite his mother's protests, he remodelled the restaurant in 1973. This was when the legendary salad buffet was first introduced, a pioneering act in Zurich. More extensive refurbishments were undertaken in 1892 and 1993, with Heinz's son Rolf playing a major part in the second refurbishment. It was Rolf who broke with a tradition dating back to Hiltl's beginnings: From 1993 onwards alcoholic beverages were served. But of course there was no change with regard to confining the menu to vegetarian food, after all, in this respect Hiltl had become a synonym for top quality, innovative cuisine.

In the 1990s, too, Hiltl lived up to its reputation as an innovator in matters of technology. One example is the introduction of ordering via keystrokes – orders were typed into a small box and beamed directly to the kitchen. At the time, many people regarded this as a kind of science fiction gimmick, ten years later it has become almost commonplace.

Change as a matter of principle

In 1998, with the restaurant's 100th anniversary, the fourth generation took over. Management was put into the hands of Rolf Hiltl, born in 1965, who had already been working closely with his father for some years. After training as a cook in the five-star Grand Hotel Dolder in Zurich and attending the hotel management college in Lausanne, he – unlike his father – found the time to work abroad for some years. His travels took him to San Francisco, where he worked as a bartender; to Acapulco, where he helped to ensure the wellbeing of the guests at the top hotel Las Brisas; and to Paris, where for twelve months he was active in community catering. With this wealth of experience in his backpack he joined the family business. Although the great-grandson of the founder, he did not see his job as merely managing his inheritance. Instead, he took up the challenge of grooming the business for the future. He and his wife Marielle, a Parisienne whose maiden name Maître already suggests an affinity with the hospitality industry, managed a rare balancing act: With their judicious refurbishment they attracted many more young people without, however, betraying the restaurant's traditions or driving away the old-established regular guests. Their successful move helped to establish the House of Hiltl as an international top venue in a city which, since the beginning of the 21st century, has enjoyed a new lease of life and now figures among the world's most desirable places to live, work, and play. A survey Rolf Hiltl had commissioned at the beginning of the 1990s underscored his belief that the growing number of occasional vegetarians could best be reached by focusing on the pleasurable aspects of eating. He himself is certainly not dogmatic, says he is a part-time vegetarian, and markets the advantages of a temporary meat-free diet in a light-hearted, witty, sometimes mischievous way. Some of the provocative Hiltl advertising over the past few years may well have irritated the more conservative somewhat, but it should be taken as a reflection of the new spirit of freshness and light-heartedness. The prospects for vegetarian cuisine have never looked so rosy, not just because of BSE and other meat scandals

at the turn of the 21st century but because there is a general trend towards a healthier, more balanced diet. Hiltl can rightly claim that it sets the standards in terms of culinary quality and variety that make meat-free dining an unqualified pleasure. Given this reputation Hiltl can afford to offer vegetarian dishes on its menu named after standard meat-based favourites such as spaghetti Bolognese; they may taste different, but they are just as good. And with its careful declaration on the menu of the ingredients and substances used in each dish, the restaurant offers a service that all the guests appreciate, whether vegetarians, vegans, people suffering from allergies or those with a food intolerance. Another new venture tailored to today's lifestyle is the Tibits restaurant launched together with the Frei brothers in the year 2000 in Zurich's Seefeld area. This new label, which uses many Hiltl recipes, was an immediate success and is now established in four Swiss cities and even in London. Thus the well-known Hiltl buffet (or at least a variant form of it) did manage to move out into the world, whereas up to now the world went to Zurich to visit the restaurant on Sihlstrasse which, despite all the changes, remains unique. Today it is called the House of Hiltl, and the next few pages will show what that involves.

Aspects of the House of Hiltl

If Ambrosius Hiltl, the founder of the restaurant, could walk into Sihl-strasse 28 today he would almost certainly be taken aback for a moment. But once he found his bearings he would probably relax, lean back comfortably, and nod his approval. The times are long past when guests, shamefaced, entered the restaurant by the back entrance to avoid the derision of the great mass of meat eaters. Today, more than 100 years later, the people of Zurich are proud of "their" veggie restaurant which, with its recent additions, has undergone the most far-reaching refurbishment in its long history. The construction work took about twelve months, during which time the restaurant operated successfully out of Zurich's old stock exchange. The result is the new House of Hiltl. Since it reopened at its old address in the spring of 2007, it hosts some 1,500 guests daily. The House of Hiltl is an all-in, multi-faceted package which, from morning coffee to throbbing music at midnight, is geared to the needs of those living in a pulsating major city. There is much more room than there used to be to accommodate the press of people hoping for a table. Including the al fresco area, it can now seat 550 guests. With the help of the architects Oberholzer and Brüschweiler, and the set designer Ushi Tamborriello, Rolf and Marielle Hiltl brought to life their vision of a modern lifestyle venue, a place to relax and feel at home. The result is an inviting combination of old and new elements – modern yet comfortable. A glassed-in expansion of the buildings facing the inner courtyard has, among other things, made it possible to double seating capacity on the restaurant's two floors. Moreover, an ingenious glass construction allows guests glimpses of the kitchen on the lower ground floor. The top floor now houses Hilt's cooking studio with a generously proportioned kitchen. This is where groups of hobby cooks learn the art of vegetarian cooking on the basis of Hiltl recipes. After the course they sit down to eat the result of their efforts and, after evening courses, they can even invite their friends to join them there. The buffet, the centrepiece of the business, serves as a kind of bridge between the restaurant and the newly styled bar lounge. With its mixture of antiques and specially designed elements, it has acquired some of the characteristics of a chameleon; not that it changes according to its surroundings, it changes according to the time of day or night. At weekends it turns into a club, a trendy venue for party-goers. The bar boasts a range of more than 30 Vodka specials – an amazing feat for a business which, for almost one hundred years, offered its guests the questionable pleasure of quaffing a glass of non-alcoholic wine. As a counterpart there is a central self-service "water pump" for tap water – an idea that should catch on in other Zurich restaurants.

Of course a so-called ladies lounge, a special service in the early years of the Hiltl restaurant for women dining out unaccompanied, has not been reintroduced. However, just as women played a major part in the history of the business, they are now in the majority among the House of Hiltl's guests. There are many reasons for this, ranging from women's well-known penchant for a healthy diet to the fact that, as one of the most child-friendly restaurants in Zurich, the Hiltl is particularly popular among mothers. One thing is certain, in hardly any other venue in Zurich can one find such a mixed bunch of guests: the "local regulars" range from senior citizens who still remember the days of Ambrosius Hiltl, to a top model with pram and offspring and groups of students enjoying their drinks in the bar; numerous guests come regularly from neighbouring parts of Zurich; finally there are the international visitors: Muslims and Jews – who can count on being able to eat as their religions require; people from overseas spending time in Zurich on business; and of course Indian nationals who are delighted to find so many dishes based on their own cuisine. Hiltl really does play host to the world.

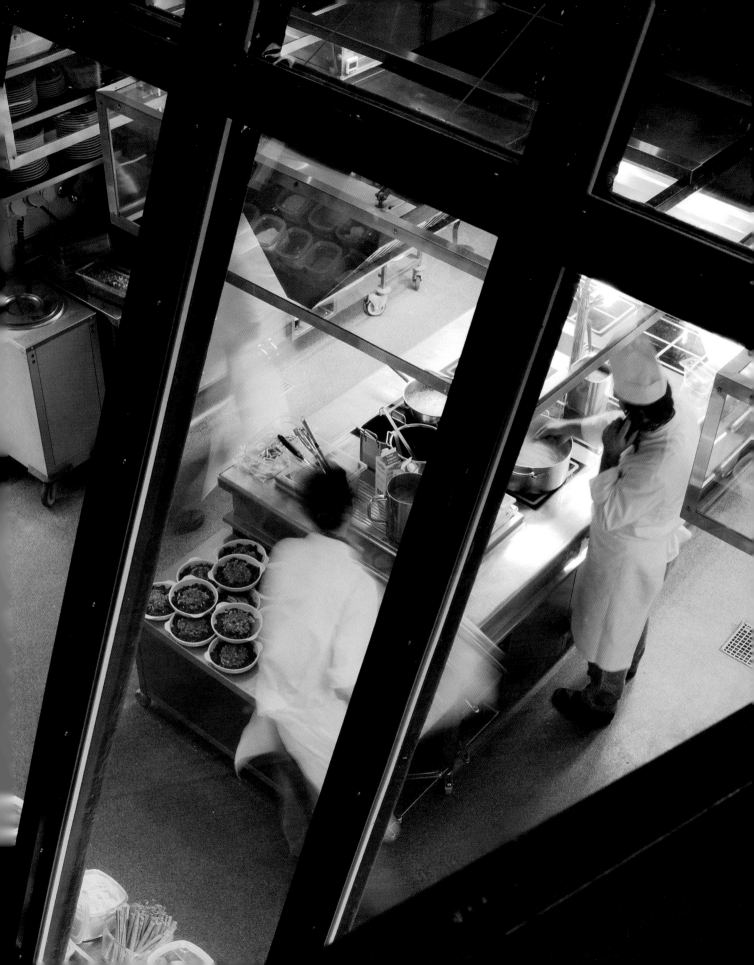

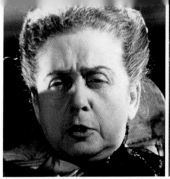
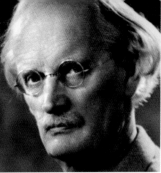
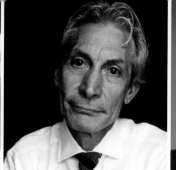
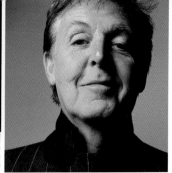

An international guestbook

Perhaps James Joyce ate at the Hiltl, or Elias Canetti, even Lenin or some of the other well-known people for whom, in the past century, Zurich was a domicile of choice, a refuge or merely a stopover. If they did, they remained anonymous – unlike the many personalities who have signed Hiltl's guestbook over the years.

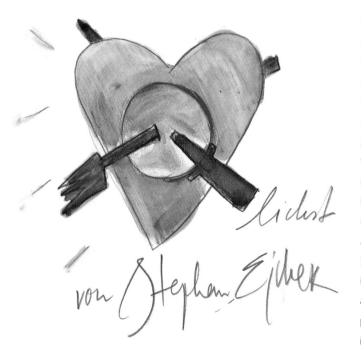

The 1950s – the decade in which Ambrosius Hiltl passed on management responsibility to his sons, when the most expensive dish on the menu (artichokes with mayonnaise) cost 2 francs and 80 cents, when the modest list of kitchen equipment was confined to such appliances as potato peelers, vegetable slicers, and rolling pins – brought a particularly rich crop of entries in the guestbook. In 1957 in particular, the restaurant seemed to draw prominent guest like a magnet. "I rarely come to Zurich now, but every time I do, I always manage to visit the Hiltl" Tadeus Reichstein wrote. Seven year earlier he had been awarded the Nobel Prize for Medicine for his work on the hormones of the adrenal cortex. He died at the age of 99, probably a record among Nobel laureates. In the same year the pioneer balloonist, Auguste Piccard, and his geologist friend, Arnold Heim (for whom Zurich's Heim Platz is named), recorded their visit to the restaurant at Sihlstrasse 28. And the legendary actress, Therese Giehse (who was to scribble another inscription five years later) together with her colleague Käthe Gold admitted that they were "two old Hiltl fans". Thirteen years later Maria Becker, another great actress, turned back the pages to their signatures and wrote just below: "Also an ardent Hiltl admirer". We are now in 1970, a fresh eight-minute, free-range egg "with choice of favourite sauce" cost 1 franc and 20 cents, a serving of salad 1 franc 30 cents. Turning the pages for the 1970s confirms the impression that over all those years Hiltl's vegetarian cuisine was especially popular among people active in the performing and visual arts. "For me, going to Hiltl's is an invitation to myself, to peace and common sense" is what the painter Alois Cargiet wrote. (He illustrated *Schellenursli*, a Swiss children's story first published in 1945 and still popular today). The German romantic pianist Elly Ney thanks Margrith Hiltl for "the only possible diet in the spirit of Bircher-Benner". In 1975 Paola, a Swiss singer, wrote an appreciative four-line verse that might almost be turned into a pop song. David Swift, the film director, praised the food lavishly and proposed establishing a Hiltl subsidiary in Beverly Hills. Then there are the sinatures of Rolling Stones drummer Charlie Watts, actors Karl-Heinz Böhm, Paul Hubschmid and Walter Roderer, Swiss mime Dimitri, and opera singer Noëmi Nadelmann – still a regular guest today.

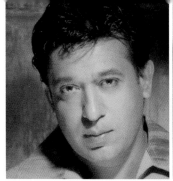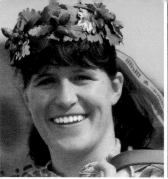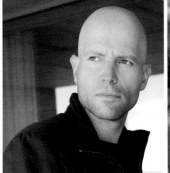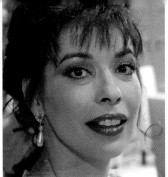

After the turn of the 21st century the stream of praise and proposals from public figures continued unabated. In 2004 the Swiss cabaret artist Emil asked for "vegetarian apple rösti" to be added to the menu. In 2005 the former Swiss Federal Councillor Ruth Dreifuss said that respecting animals was a major step on the road to civilisation. Bollywood star Mayur Verma praised one of the best veggie selections of all time and swore eternal love: "Will love to come again + again + again." Figure skating gold medallist Denise Biellmann merely left a mini message ("P.S. the drink was good"), whereas the video artist Pipilotti Rist did not leave a video message but simply a wish: "Please open a branch in Zurich's district 4 and district 5"; she added detailed proposals for possible locations. Several years before his cooperation with Secret Service agent 007, the film director Marc Forster left a card which shows considerable sensitivity: "Many thanks for a wonderful meal – one can feel the awareness in each dish." Just before this book went into print, Marc Forster, now with star status, was again sighted among the House of Hiltl's guests. In 2004 Paul McCartney said thank you for "a fabulous veggie meal, great service, food, and ambience" and hoped Hiltl would expand. This inscription carried two intertwined hearts and was co-signed by his then wife Heather – now his ex-wife. For singer Jimmy Somerville Hiltl is a "pesto heaven", and German singer Nena of '99 Red Balloons' fame took a whole page to write "All the best, Nena" in oversize letters. Swiss singer Stephan Eicher needed just as much space for his huge red heart pierced with two arrows. Internationally renowned chef Anton Mosimann and family expressed thanks "for a wonderful evening", and various Miss and Mister Switzerlands alone or in company announced that they had dined at Hiltl's. The former Krokus frontman Chris von Rohr inevitably expressed his appreciation in English: "Super Kitchen!" – "I will be back!" – "Keep on Vegi". As good a peroration as any! But not only VIPs leave messages, other guests also submit their suggestions, proposals, praise and criticism, often in the form of letters. A little boy, for example, sent drawings of samosas and other Hiltl favourites and then misspelt his best wishes. Or the lady who literally begged for Hiltl's taboulé recipe as served at the buffet. Her husband was obviously giving her a hard time with her efforts to produce some-

thing comparable: "Not a week passes without our having to try out yet another taboulé version." Or the couple who, since their marriage, had been regular guests until they moved to another part of Switzerland. They wanted to celebrate their wedding anniversary at Hiltl's – their diamond anniversary. That's sixty years!

Nowadays, of course, comments generally come via email: Suggestions, wishes and praise can be posted on Hiltl's website (www.hiltl.ch). The collection of emails goes back to 2000 and includes compliments and questions from guests around the world. It reflects the guests' dining pleasure but also some disappointments; and each of the mails, which can all be accessed on the Internet – sometimes very critical ones – is followed by a friendly reply from the Hiltl team. Even to the guest who considered an antique chair made of antlers in extremely poor taste for a vegetarian restaurant (it was installed after the last refurbishment as an ironic gesture to part-time vegetarians). And the electronic symbol for a twinkle in one's eye concludes the reply to the frequently asked question of whether dogs are allowed: Of course dogs are welcome – provided they are vegetarians.

Photos of guests:

Therese Giehse, Auguste Piccard, Charlie Watts, Paul McCartney, Mayur Verma, Jeanette Arnold, Marc Forster and Noëmi Nadelmann.

The House of Hiltl – faces and facets of a chameleon, that always reinvents itself

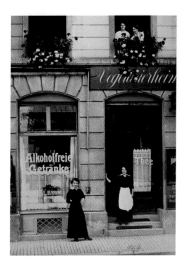

How everything began – the "Vegetarians' Home" at the end of the 19th century.

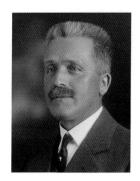

Ambrosius Hiltl, a man with an exceptional sense of purpose, launched the business 111 yeas ago.

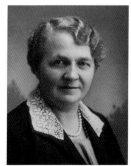

Martha Hiltl-Gneupel, the person active behind the scenes and the wife at Ambrosius' side.

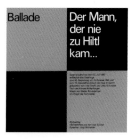

A special ballad was recorded for the 70th anniversary celebrations – sung by Ines Torelli and Jörg Schneider, with texts by Werner Wollenberger and music by Walter Baumgartner.

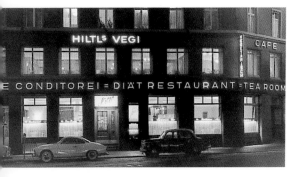

From 1931 to 1973 Hiltl Vegi was explicitly also a diet restaurant.

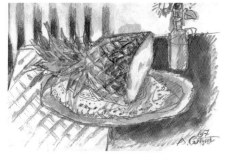

This appetising card reveals Alois Carigiet's characteristic style – especially designed for Hiltl.

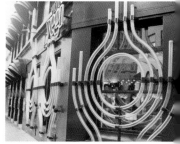

In 1973 the façade of the restaurant was livened up with bright, cheerful elements.

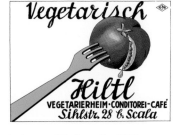

A cinema slide from the 1930s.

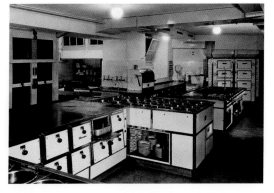

Often a step ahead of the times, even in technical matters: In 1931 Ambrosius' son Leonhard installed Zurich's first fully electric kitchen.

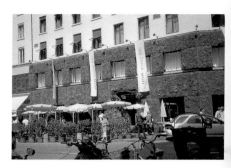

For its centenary in 1998, even the façade was a youthful green.

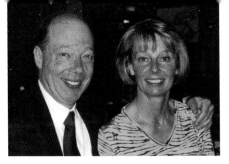

In the 1970s, the third generation took over with Heinz and Hanni Hiltl at the helm.

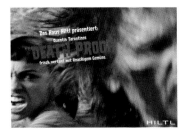

Hiltl advertising is sometimes provocative, like this cinema spot with its light-hearted allusion to a Hollywood film.

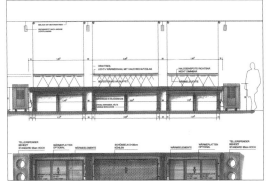

Guinness Buch der Rekorde Urkunde

Wir bestätigen hiermit Herrn Hiltl als Besitzer des ältesten vegetarischen Restaurants Europas Restaurant Hiltl (seit 1898).

Hamburg, im Oktober 1998

Redaktion Guinness Buch der Rekorde

The record has been certified. Hiltl is the oldest vegetarian restaurant in Europe.

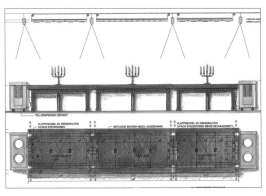

The House of Hiltl at Sihlstrasse 28 – an island in the heart of a pulsating city.

Looks good enough to eat. Not only Hiltl food but also its logo have become a symbol for quality.

As these plans show, the multifunctional buffet can be turned into a large table for club nights in next to no time.

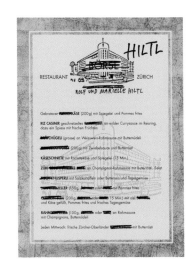

A stop-gap solution draws the public. The refurbishment phase in 2006/07 was bridged with an intermezzo in Zurich's Old Stock Exchange near Paradeplatz.

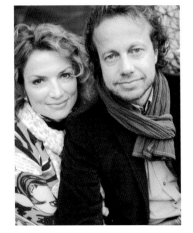

Marielle and Rolf Hiltl: As representatives of the fourth generation they have turned the House of Hiltl into an overall work of art.

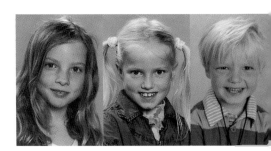

And the fifth generation is growing up – Céline, Léna and Téo.

From market to table – a feast for all the senses

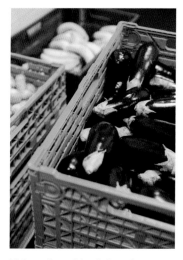

High quality cuisine is based on a long-term relationship with the very best suppliers.

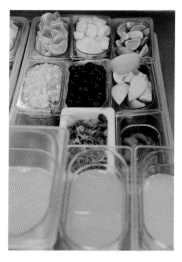

The ingredients alone are a feast for the eyes.

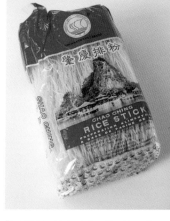

Readiness to incorporate aspects of other cooking cultures, particularly from the Asian area, has been a guiding principle for Hiltl for decades.

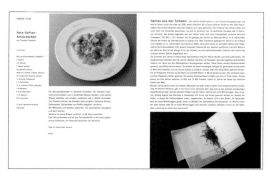

Passing on knowledge is a part of our credo – be this in the form of cookbooks or through courses in our cooking studio.

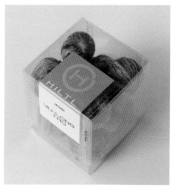

The House of Hiltl offers a whole range of products that make excellent gifts; or why not simply spoil yourself?

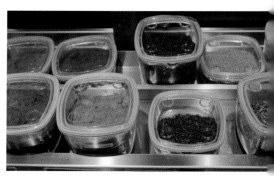

Hiltl's international focus is reflected in its wide range of spices from around the world.

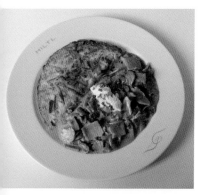

Hiltl's vegetarian cuisine can easily hold its own – how about Zurich's traditional *Geschnetzeltes* (veal fricassee) without meat?

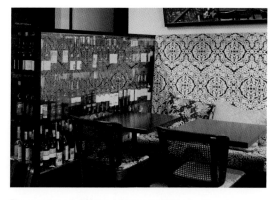

The number of different wines available by the glass is exceptional.

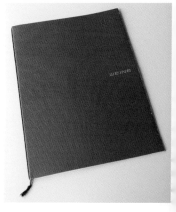

The House of Hiltl, once teetotal, now sees its wide choice of domestic and foreign wines as one of its strengths.

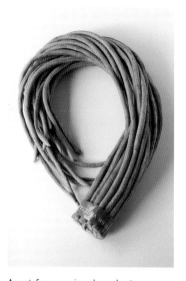

Apart from regional products, Hiltl's chefs use a number of more exotic vegetables, such as Indian yardlong beans.

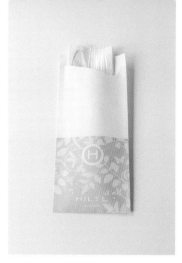

Eat here or elsewhere? Our takeaway ...

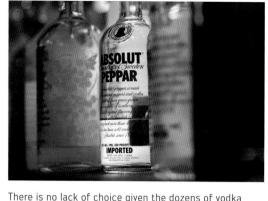

There is no lack of choice given the dozens of vodka specials available at the bar.

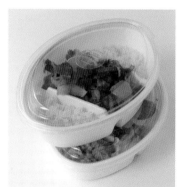

... is not only a welcome alternative for busy people.

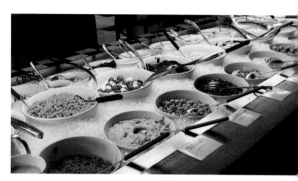

The buffet on the ground floor is the focal point and the pièce de résistance of the House of Hiltl – and a veritable feast for all the senses.

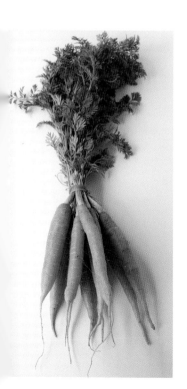

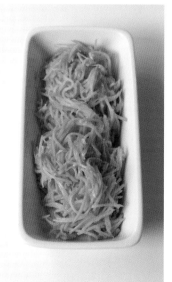

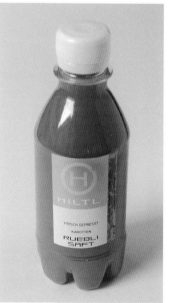

You get what you choose, you take the exact amount you want, and you only pay for what you took. That is another huge advantage of the Hiltl buffet.

A basic product for creative vegetarian cuisine – shown here as grated and as juice. The pure fruit and vegetable juices, also available in practical bottles from the takeaway, enjoy tremendous popularity.

The House of Hiltl hosts the world

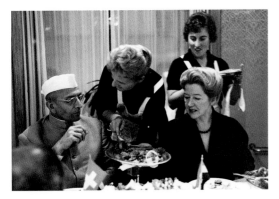

A very special guest from India in the 1960s –
prime minister Morarji Desai with Magrith Hiltl.

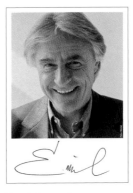

Top Swiss performers
as guests – from cabaret
star Emil...

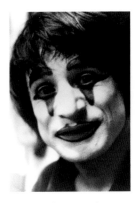

... to the famous mime
Dimitri.

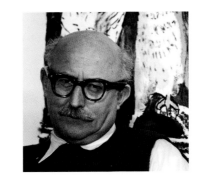

Alois Carigiet, artist and illustrator of
Schellenursli, was once a regular Hiltl guest.

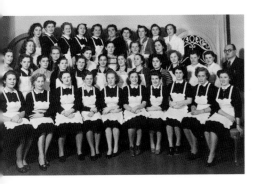

Very feminine and very Swiss – a glance at
the personnel before the Second World War
shows that Hiltl at that time was
by no means as multicultural as it is today.

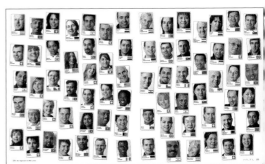

Cosmopolitan but with local roots – the House of Hiltl
and its faces.

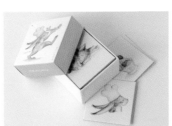

Not everything is as unforgettable as some
visits to Hiltl are – and so it can't do
any harm to train your memory with Hiltl's
own memory game.

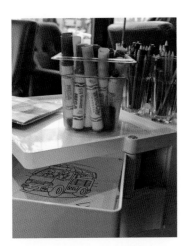

It's not for nothing that Hiltl has
a reputation for being one of
the most child-friendly restaurants
far and wide...

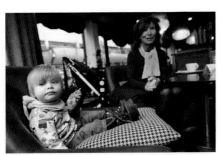

... which has made it especially popular among
mothers, fathers and families.

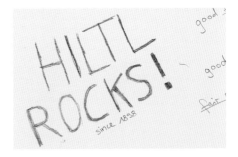

Hiltl's guests love inventiveness and originality –
it can even happen that on their table mat
they supply the inspiration for the motto of
the year (see inside back cover photo).

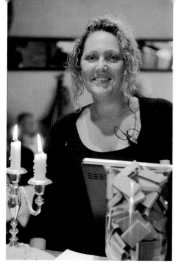

Every guest is made welcome here.

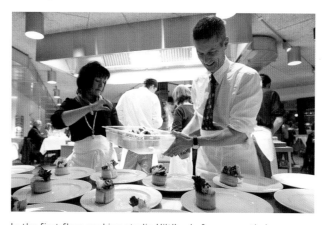

In the first floor cooking studio Hiltl's chefs pass on their know-how – as they do here to a group from the Orell Füssli publishing house.

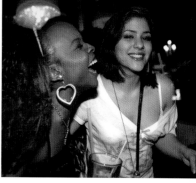

Sparkling, animated mood during a party night in the Hiltl Club.

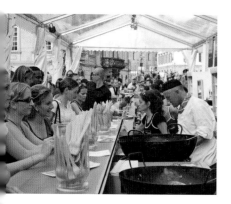

Hiltl is the right catering partner for that special celebration or get-together.

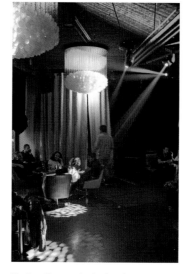

During the week the bar lounge offers a chill-out atmosphere late into the evening.

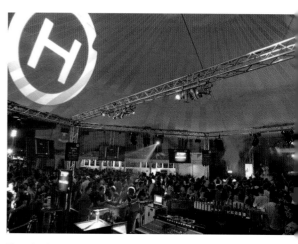

There's always a good reason for celebrating: The Hiltl tent on Zurich's Münsterhof was a very popular venue during the Euro 2008.

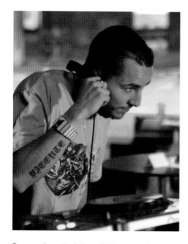

On weekend nights DJs turn the lounge into a pulsating club.

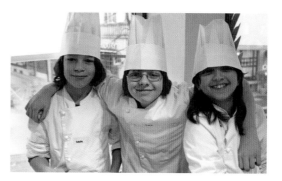

It's never too early to start... some offspring of Hiltl's guests in Hiltl's cooking studio.

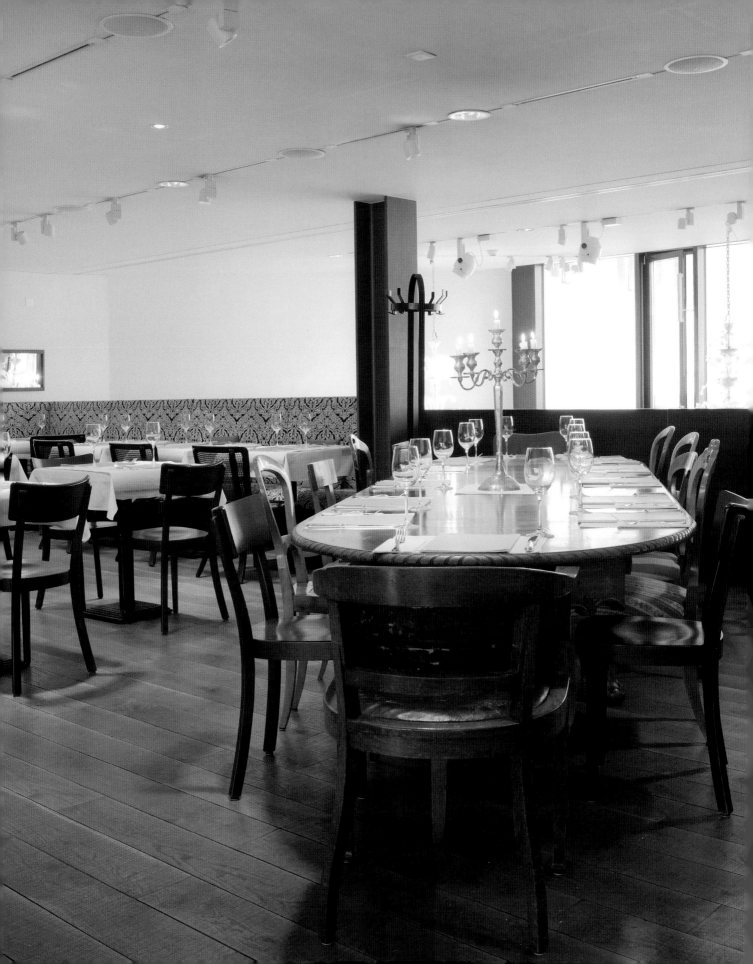

Hiltl advertising

Take a hearty dash of humour, sometimes a pinch of provocation, wrap it all in strong pictures and season with fitting texts: The originality of Hiltl advertising deftly served up by well known Zurich agencies regularly brings in awards and, in the form of posters or cinema spots, invariably attracts public attention.

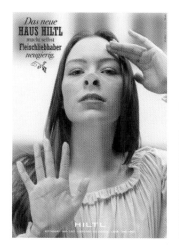
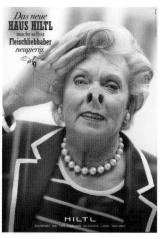
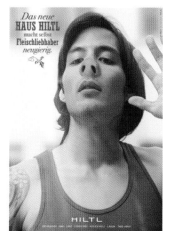
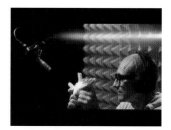
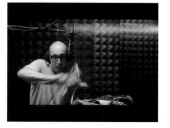
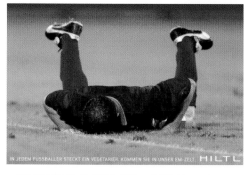
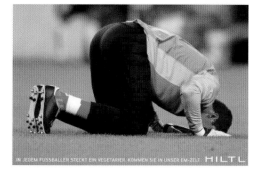
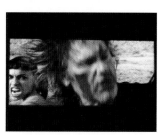
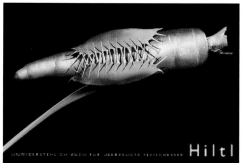
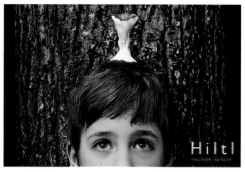
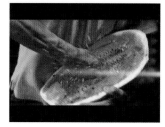
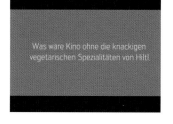

A vegetarian diet clears your head and stimulates your brain.
If you don't believe it, just look around on Hiltl's website (www.hiltl.ch) and take a fresh look at our advertising.

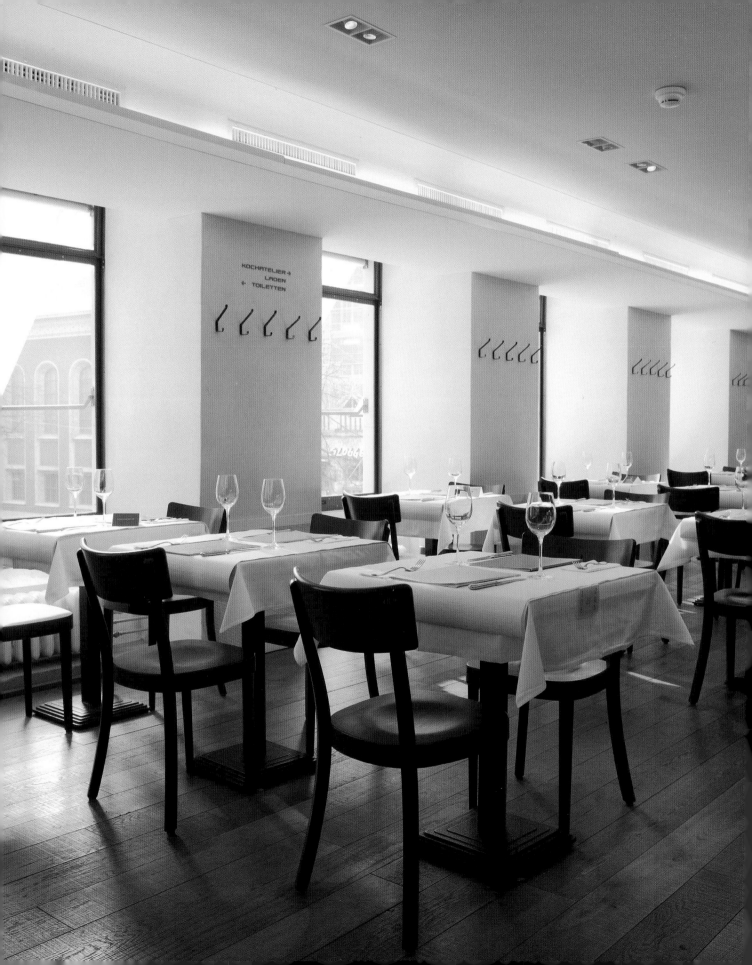

tibits – yet another success story

A recipe for success since the turn of the 21st century: With market-fresh vegetarian cuisine based on Hiltl recipes, tibits is now the trendsetter for vegetarian top-quality, mouth-watering fast food. Tibits restaurant – bar – takeaway with its richly filled buffet and relaxed atmosphere attracts guests in droves. This success story, which began in 2000 in Zurich's Seefeld as a partnership between the brothers Reto, Christian, and Daniel Frei and the Hiltl family now has its sequel in Berne, Basle and Winterthur – and recently also on the Thames: The first restaurant abroad was opened in London in the autumn of 2008. www.tibits.ch

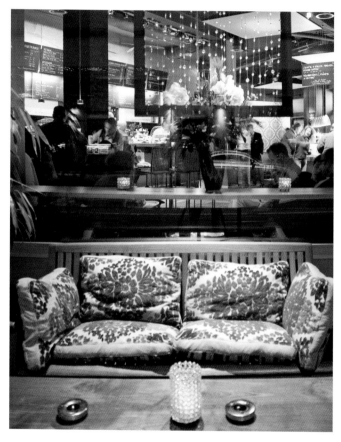

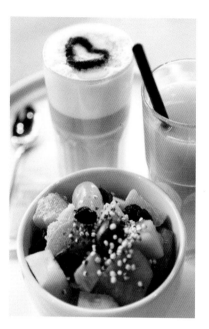

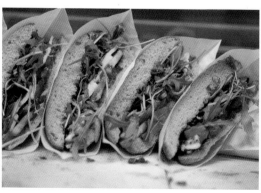

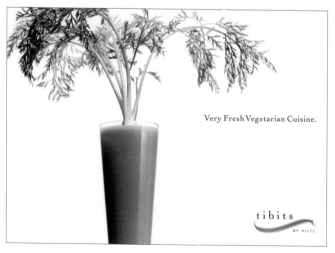

Very Fresh Vegetarian Cuisine.

tibits
BY HILTL

Hiltl books

You're interested in other delicious recipes from the House of Hiltl, you'd like further information on its cuisine and on its development over the past 111 years? Then you might want to buy "Hiltl. Virtuoso Vegetarian", our first volume of recipes. It was first published in 1998, and a new, revised and updated edition came out in 2006. With more than one hundred thousand copies sold, this cookbook was not only a great success, but has become a classic for vegetarian cuisine.

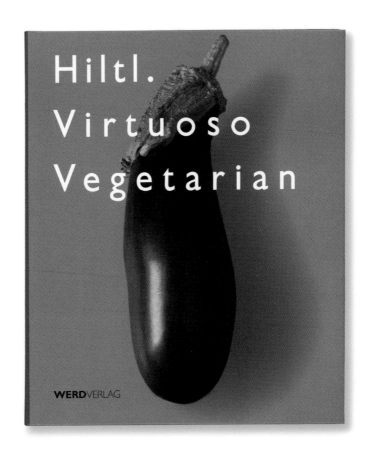

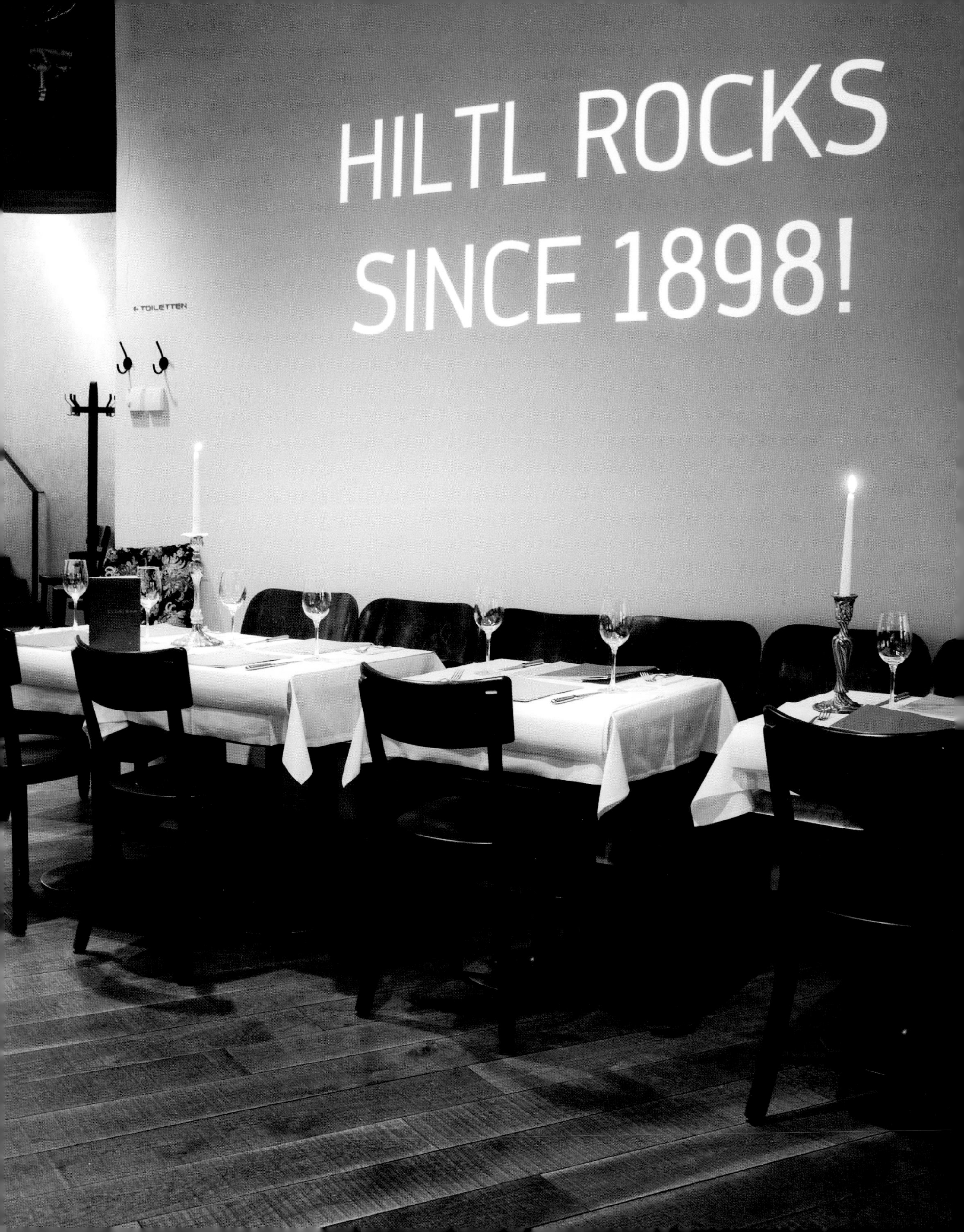
HILTL ROCKS
SINCE 1898!
← TOILETTEN